Professors Andrew Strathern and Pamela J Stewart (Strathern) are a husband and wife research team with a long history of joint publication and research. Presently based at the Anthropology Department, University of Pittsburgh, they have lived and worked in Asia, Australia, New Zealand, Europe and the Pacific, and presented lectures and published in many countries of the Pacific region, Europe and Asia. Their research interests are wide-ranging and include anthropology, philosophy and religious studies. They are co-editors of three book series and, for many years, of the *Journal of Ritual Studies*, and authors of more than 45 books and 175 articles. They have been jointly awarded the 2012 De Carle Lectureship (University of Otago, Dunedin, New Zealand) to present a series of public lectures.

Other titles in UQP's New Approaches to Peace and Conflict series
When Blood and Bones Cry Out: Journeys through the soundscape of healing and reconciliation by John Paul Lederach & Angela Jill Lederach

Reporting Conflict: New directions in peace journalism by Jake Lynch & Johan Galtung

Also by Andrew Strathern and Pamela J Stewart
Kinship in Action: Self and group Ritual (eds)
Landscape, Heritage, and Conservation: Farming issues in the European Union (eds)
Curing and Healing: Medical anthropology in global perspective (2nd edn)
Religious and Ritual Change: Cosmologies and histories (eds)
Exchange and Sacrifice (eds)
Asian Ritual Systems: Syncretisms and ruptures (eds)
Expressive Genres and Historical Change: Indonesia, Papua New Guinea and Taiwan (eds)
Contesting Rituals: Islam and practices of identity-making (eds)
Anthropology and Consultancy: Issues and debates (eds)
Empowering the Past, Confronting the Future: The Duna people of Papua New Guinea
Witchcraft, Sorcery, Rumors, and Gossip
Landscape, Memory, and History: Anthropological perspectives (eds)
Violence: Theory and ethnography
Remaking the World: Myth, mining and ritual change among the Duna of Papua New Guinea
Gender, Song, and Sensibility: Folktales and folksongs in the Highlands of New Guinea
Minorities and Memories: Survivals and extinctions in Scotland and Western Europe
Arrow Talk: Transaction, transition, and contradiction in New Guinea Highlands History
Identity Work: Constructing Pacific lives (eds)
The Python's Back: Pathways of comparison between Indonesia and Melanesia

NEW APPROACHES TO PEACE AND CONFLICT

PEACE-MAKING AND THE IMAGINATION:
Papua New Guinea perspectives

Andrew Strathern and Pamela J Stewart

UQP

First published 2011 by University of Queensland Press
PO Box 6042, St Lucia, Queensland 4067 Australia

www.uqp.com.au
uqp@uqp.uq.edu.au

© Andrew Strathern and Pamela J Stewart 2011

This book is copyright. Except for private study, research,
criticism or reviews, as permitted under the Copyright Act,
no part of this book may be reproduced, stored in a retrieval system,
or transmitted in any form or by any means without prior
written permission. Enquiries should be made to the publisher.

Cover design by i2i design
Typeset in Minion 11.5/16pt by Post Pre-press Group, Brisbane
Printed in Australia by McPherson's Printing Group

National Library of Australia Cataloguing-in-Publication Data
http://catalogue.nla.gov.au

ISBN (pbk) 9780702239083
ISBN (pdf) 9780702247552
ISBN (epub) 9780702247569
ISBN (kindle) 9780702247576

University of Queensland Press uses papers that are natural, renewable
and recyclable products made from wood grown in sustainable forests.
The logging and manufacturing processes conform to the environmental
regulations of the country of origin.

To those who are mindful of peaceful balance.

Note from Series Editor

UQP's New Approaches to Peace and Conflict series builds on the wisdom of the first wave of peace researchers while addressing important 21st century challenges to peace, human rights and sustainable development. The series publishes new theory, new research and new strategies for effective peacebuilding and the transformation of violent conflict. It challenges orthodox perspectives on development, conflict transformation and peacebuilding within an ethical framework of doing no harm while doing good.

Professor Kevin P Clements
Chair in Peace and Conflict Studies
Director of The National Centre for Peace and Conflict Studies
University of Otago, New Zealand

Contents

Preface		ix
CHAPTER 1	Terror and violence in imagination and practice	1
CHAPTER 2	Dimensions of violence: revenge and sorcery (Mount Hagen, PNG)	24
CHAPTER 3	Warfare and peace-making: comparative histories	49
CHAPTER 4	Escalations and complexities: early elections	75
CHAPTER 5	Escalations and complexities: turns of history	105
CHAPTER 6	The problems of peace-makers: intermediate sovereigns	138
CHAPTER 7	Transcending violence: the place of ritual	165
CHAPTER 8	Conclusions and comparisons	190
CHAPTER 9	Envoi: three themes beyond the local	212
Appendix	How do cases – instances of 'poisoning' accusations – fit in with the ideal picture of relations among groups?	225
Acknowledgements		231
Endnotes		233
References		247
Index		258

Preface

There are two opposite views of violence in human affairs. One is that it is an ingrained propensity and therefore there are inherent problems in peace-making. The other is that people are inclined to cooperative and peaceful behaviour, and violence represents an abnormal breakdown of this state of relationships. These two extreme views appear quite inadequate whenever we examine, in its full context, any sequence of behaviour or events. There is plenty of evidence of capacities for peace-making in the interests of political equilibrium; there is also plenty of evidence that such an equilibrium may become fragile and be replaced over time by episodes of violence that can even reach, or border on, genocide. If we take a processual or in longer diachronic terms a historical viewpoint, we are likely to see that there is an alternation or undulating swing between these extremes, or that the extremes are never met in practical terms: neither fully peaceful nor entirely violent outcomes are actually the norm, in the sense of the most usual outcomes. We need to study the forces that tip the patterns in one direction or another at different junctures of time. The forces in play include perceptions of self-interest, ideological syndromes and schemata, emotional dispositions, the structural encoding of values such as honour and revenge or religious notions of peace/war, and relative perceptions of power, including those involved in gendered fields of conduct. Whatever the underlying predispositions may be, then, the practical outcomes in any sequence of interactions will be the result of multiple interplays of factors of the sort we have just listed and will therefore be difficult to analyse and still more difficult to predict.

There can also be a tension between factors. Perceptions of self-interest are themselves influenced by cultural values, and these values may generate conflicts, for example between individuals and various levels of group interests. Self-interest, further, may collide with religious concerns or be ideologically welded together with these, as in cases where either violent or peaceful actions appear to be enjoined by religious notions and supplied with schemata of merit derived ultimately from cosmology. Senses of transcendence may be needed in order to pull outcomes in a particular direction. By transcendence here we mean influences that override others. The idea of 'enlightened self-interest' is an example of such influences, because it implies that the enlightenment at work may encompass many considerations and a balancing out among these with reference to some overall aims. We do not invoke the idea of 'rationality' here, because this term itself is often given an ideological loading and needs to be broken down into its various components. Even if we distinguish, as Max Weber did, between the rationality of means and the rationality of ends, ideologies may be involved at any point in the definitions used.

The Papua New Guinea Highlands provide an important arena in which a nuanced examination of such issues can be conducted, with an array of cross-cultural synchronic and diachronic materials. Using these materials it is possible to discuss and compare pre-colonial, colonial and post-colonial circumstances. One basic axis of comparison has to do with expansion in the scale of social relations. In the colonial state policies, the aim was to incorporate local societies into the state structure. 'Pacification' was the first plank of this policy, economic and political 'development' the second. (Development included expatriate business enterprises, which required a manageable social context for their profitable success. It also included over time the need to promote local cash-making activities, in order to acquire cooperation from the people and to create a category of tax-paying consumers. Plantations and small holdings were the initial instruments of this approach to inducing change.) The state power wished to claim a monopoly over the control of physical force, or violence, in the canonical Weberian mode. Local societies, however, were premised on the relative autonomy of local groups. Pacification was therefore a prerequisite of state control. With limited resources, the colonial government officers soon realised that they had to harness the indigenous people's own peace-making rituals in order to achieve 'pacification' itself, although this by no means precluded the use of governmental force on occasion, especially in initial periods of demonstrating governmental power.

Not long before the advent of political Independence for Papua New Guinea in September 1975, this colonially induced 'peace' suffered inroads of violent outbreaks of conflict which have continued ever since, escalating and waning from time to time, fuelled by issues surrounding periodic elections to the national Parliament as well as the awkward contingencies of contemporary life: uneven development, vehicle accidents leading to deaths, killings resulting from alcohol consumption, arguments over land and marriages, suicides, robberies, ambushes, sexual offences, the whole roster of events that can elicit either revenge actions or payments of compensation. Overall, with the uneasy integration of groups into the national political and economic structure, the possibilities for serious conflict have arguably increased rather than decreased since colonial times. The forms of integration via marriage alliances and exchanges of wealth that constituted the predominant pre-colonial ways of mediating conflict are no longer able to contain all of the pressures placed upon them.

The theme of 'terror', as it impinges on such a situation, represents a further added layer of complexity. Terror grows out of uncertainty, of not knowing where the next hostilities are coming from; and this in turn grows from the potential vulnerability of groups and individuals to surprise attacks or to attacks that cannot easily be warded off or guarded against. Compensation payments and peace-making can reduce this feature of terror in social life. We argue that successful peace-making needs to incorporate as many as possible of these 'horizontal' forms of inter-group negotiation that enabled groups in pre-colonial times to coexist. Vertical and involuntary integration into a hierarchical external structure cannot replicate the conditions of horizontal accommodations between groups.

Our ethnographic focus is on Papua New Guinea, particularly the Highlands region. But we begin our discussion on the wider front of considering terror and imagination in the broader global sphere. We use the term imagination here to mean how people perceive events and through these perceptions experience actions, but in addition how they think of the possibilities of creating their own futures by altering actions and events in their social fields.

These observations regarding terror and imagination can be taken in parallel with the consideration of violence and the imagination of peace-making. Our argument is that where a basic institution, such as an institution of exchange, has built into it a model of cyclical action that encompasses the possibility of making peace out of the act of violence itself, then peace-making is already imagined, or at least is imaginable, even in the moment of violence. Specifically, if each killing is balanced or measured against a potentiality for a compensation to be paid, this is a very different syndrome from one in which killings are not accounted for or reckoned in this way, allowing the numbers of deaths to multiply indefinitely. Just as terror lives in the imagination of violence, so peace lives in the imagination of compensation payments (or whatever other cultural scripts may operate in the same way). Indeed, a part of terror is that it is the exact opposite of compensation systems. Terror is not accountable to peace-making. It is, however, commensurable with ideologies of revenge, which can be seen as the negative counterparts of the positive force of compensation payments. So terror becomes the vehicle of imagining more terror as retribution; while peace-making depends on imagining compensation (or equivalent institutional practices) as reconciliation.

At the heart of this topic there is also the question of the ritualisation of conflict. Through ritual actions people can gain and communicate the ability to reframe events and experiences and transform them. Ritual, therefore, can be the switching agent between violence and peace-making. It is in ritual processes that imaginative constructions are most potently given shape and energised. Hence again we can discern the importance of compensation as a concept, because compensation is framed in ritual actions that express, affirm and, in effect, realise its value. In the growing difficulties of such ritualisations of action and the reasons for these difficulties we see why and how peace-making becomes more rather than less difficult over time. We will discuss this issue as the book proceeds with its narratives through different historical phases, including how the clock might be 'turned back' and ritual brought again into effective play.

Here we give a synopsis of the chapters of the book in which we seek to pursue our argument.

1. Terror and violence in imagination and practice
Drawing materials from global events and contexts we discuss the concept of terror in imagination and practice, and lead into a discussion of recent contemporary election-related reports of violence in Papua New Guinea.

2. Dimensions of violence: revenge and sorcery (Mount Hagen, PNG)

This chapter takes us back in time to one aspect of social life in the Mount Hagen area of the Western Highlands of Papua New Guinea, where we have the longest run of information from literature, oral sources and fieldwork over a number of decades. The twin themes of revenge-taking and what are said to be sorcery attacks provide some of the underworld of motivations for violence and feelings of hostility between groups. These motivations, legacies from the past, and motivational complexes have continued from pre-colonial into contemporary post-colonial times.

3. Warfare and peace-making: comparative histories

Highlands societies varied in terms of their patterns of warfare/inter-group conflict and patterns of compensation for killings or peace-making. In this chapter we compare the patterns from three Highlands areas where we have carried out long-term fieldwork – Hagen, Pangia and Lake Kopiago – with further reference to surrounding areas such as the Enga Province, and examine how peace-making capacities were shaped by the general configurations of ceremonial exchange relationships. These patterns were in turn deeply modified by colonial and post-colonial circumstances. The chapter provides an essential background to further chapters on how problems of achieving peaceful settlements have increased over time.

4. Escalations and complexities: early elections

After initial pacification, the colonial government in Papua New Guinea pursued policies of integrating areas together in Local Government Councils and electorates, from the 1960s onwards. At the same time the government introduced coffee and tea as cash crops on plantations and individual, local-owned garden areas.

Urbanisation also proceeded apace. People of different language groups were brought together in towns, and conflicts ensued. Christian missions entered the Highlands already from the 1930s onwards, hard on the heels of explorers and government officers. While the churches preached peace, their presence also brought new divisions and confusions. (Christian churches nevertheless represent a creative resource for the production of peace-making rituals.) These varying complexities all played into changing patterns of conflict and attempts at cooperation. Early forays into elections and electioneering were complicated by killings or attacks that occurred between groups now thrown together in new political structures. In this chapter we look in detail at an election process in Mount Hagen in 1968, before all these complexities had shown their effects. The amalgamation of two electorates, Mul and Dei, later reversed, showed in potentiality many of the dangers in the ideologies of political development pursued by the Australian colonial Administration at the time.

5. Escalations and complexities: turns of history
This chapter is a general overview of colonial and post-colonial history in Mount Hagen. The discussion centres on changes in exchange practices over time in the Hagen area. It explains how in the 1960s compensation payments for killings that had occurred earlier in pre-colonial times had effloresced into competitive *moka* exchanges between groups. Initial peace-making had been imaginatively transformed into an enhanced way of linking groups together through ongoing exchanges. The scale of these exchanges, however, itself became a possible source of instability; and when new conflicts emerged in the 1970s over land, vehicle accidents, and parliamentary political competition, the local institutions of exchange were less able to cope with the new situations that arose. In the 1980s this situation was compounded by the increasing introduction of

guns into inter-group fighting, which meant more casualties and more difficulties in arranging compensation payments. The presence of state money in these payments also led to higher demands for the monetary parts of compensation payments, in addition to the traditional item of pigs, and therefore to greater difficulties in meeting these demands. The imagination of peace thus became more problematic.

6. The problems of peace-makers: intermediate sovereigns

This chapter explains the problems that peace-makers in the segmentary acephalous societies of the Papua New Guinea Highlands faced prior to colonial times and in colonial times from the 1930s onwards. It goes on to consider further the uneven incorporation of the Highlanders into the colonial and post-colonial state structures, and the growing problems of violence that beset the local societies in the 1990s. The case studies adduced will illustrate how 'vertical integration' came about in the political sphere and how practices at elections, particularly paying for votes, exacerbated the situation. Separating conflicts that emerged at the national level from those that engaged people at the local level became progressively more difficult; but it is this kind of separation that is needed for the imagination of peace-making to become effective again. We consider here some of the limited ways in which Christian churches have been able to provide a different basis for such an imagination of peace. We also consider the role of government agents in processes of peace-making or the control of violence.

7. Transcending violence: the place of ritual

This chapter reconsiders questions of violence and its transformations into peace-making through the perspective of ritual theory and the 'performativity' of ritual. The term 'performativity' we use here has to do with what the actual effects of ritual practices are and with the mechanisms that are involved in making ritual practices more or less effective. Compensation ceremonies will be analysed and placed into the context of advances in the theory of embodied practice in ritual contexts to suggest ways in which peace-making potentialities can be better realised.

8. Conclusions and comparisons

This chapter will review Chapters 1 to 7 and bring these together in relation to an assessment of the futures of local societies in Highlands Papua New Guinea. Our main argument is that the best chances for peace-making lie in those local contexts where compensation practices, or other modes of the ritualisation of conflict, can flourish, be creatively modified, and act as symbolic markers of local identities and cultural patterns. Comparative references to other parts of the world are introduced as ancillary to, and supportive of, the main argument, and a final chapter (9) reviews urban contexts, the nation-state level, and terror and the imagination of peace, returning the study to its beginnings in Chapter 1.

9. Envoi: three themes beyond the local

In this final chapter, which functions as an envoi to the book, we take up three themes that take our topic beyond its local contexts. We look at urban contexts and how these are bound up with people's rural lives. The urban and rural contexts are closely interrelated and influence each other continuously, as case histories show, while urban–rural contrasts remain. We look further to national-level contexts, explicitly considering what kinds of social contracts, if any, are at work between national politicians and their local supporters, and how leaders are involved in both the escalation and the resolution of conflicts.

Finally, we advert to the general question of terror and the imagination, mentioned at the outset of the book, and argue for the importance of rumour and gossip in framing the popular imagination of violence but also for the imagination of peace, referring to the work of the imagination via a Melpa language image of the *pol*, or bridge.

CHAPTER 1

Terror and violence in imagination and practice

Terror and its manifold representations have taken hold of the global imagination in the decades since the collapse of the Soviet Union and the emergence of radical political movements opposed to the 'West', not simply in terms of political ideologies but also under the banner of religious differences. The events of 9/11 (2001) and the ongoing and intractable conflicts in the Middle East and Afghanistan have undoubtedly been central in this reconstruction of the global imagination as well as in the recognition of a new era of practices in relation to violence, at least from the perspective of the US, and mutatis mutandis in the expanding spheres of the European Union and other countries historically linked to the UK. Terror in the abstract and practical terrors in concrete reality have become very much a part of everyday media representations, making issues to do with terror palpably present in many people's lives. Present terrors surround people both in their imaginations and in the processes and practices of violence that feed into the imagination. Imagination and practice are closely linked (Strathern & Stewart

2006a). While we, as authors, have been at pains to stress in our Preface to this book how important the imagination is in relation to peace-making, it is equally important to note that violent practices also constantly lend themselves to the intensification of imaginative concerns, and that representations of these practices as events in the news constantly stimulate further imaginations and further practices, fusing together actions and images of actions in repetitive cycles. Images, constructed in a creative or fictional mode (such as newspaper cartoons), may have as their intended, half-intended or wholly unintended consequence the provocation of violent episodes of actions. Images and messages also stimulate and facilitate the mobilisation of masses of people in crowds, protesting against government actions and eliciting forceful, if not violent, actions from police or military authorities.

Our intellectual pathway into the heart of these global contemporary processes began in what may perhaps seem an unlikely way. For many years we have been interested in the study of small-scale processes of conflict, including violent conflict and the methods of mediating and settling conflict, in the local contexts of Papua New Guinea (see Stewart & Strathern 2000a, 2002a; Strathern 1993a, 1993b; Strathern & Stewart 1997b, 2000a), a nation-state, independent from Australia since 1975, in which the Highlands populations first encountered the 'outside world' in the early 1930s (see Strathern & Stewart 2003). These were populations long used to fighting one another, as a result of disputes over thefts of pigs, encroachments on land, marital abductions and infidelities, broken alliances, and suspicions of sorcery and witchcraft. All of these concerns are still ones that can and do lead to violence nowadays, including sorcery and witchcraft accusations, which we have discussed extensively in our book *Witchcraft, Sorcery, Rumors, and Gossip* (Stewart & Strathern 2004). These Highlands populations were equally adept at making peace with one another through the mediating influences of oratory, positive exchanges of wealth goods, and the intertwining of networks of kin relations resulting from marital alliances. Looked at from one viewpoint, these were societies built around the settlement of conflicts; from another viewpoint, they could appear societies in which violent practices were endemic. Of course, these processes varied historically and were greatly impacted by colonial pacification. Still, one salient impression of them was that they showed an enduring oscillation between periods of violence and periods of peace, and that recurrent processes of peace-making followed periods of conflict and violence in fairly predictable ways. In the global sphere today such patterns are hardly discernable, and in contemporary warfare the technology of terror is much more developed. The clashing of bows and arrows, the prodding of spears, the war cries and songs, the elaborate body adornments of the New Guinea Highlanders (prior to the introduction of guns in warfare in the 1980s) were all minor instruments of terror in their own way. And there were secret methods of killing, by physical ambush or putatively by sleight of hand, the introduction of supposedly fatal substances into food by acts of betrayal or by mysterious powers of assault sorcery or witchcraft. Terror there certainly was, then, and not all of it easily coped with or evanescent in people's lives. Songs and gossip carried rumours around, increasing fears much as the nightly news channels do on the television sets of the world. But the scale of these events was relatively small, and their duration was relatively short, although the memories of them and their aftermaths in cycles of revenge, including killings, were often long. The scale and reach of terror, its cycles of amplifications, were relatively restricted; in the wider world today, by contrast, it is as though a stone cast in the global pool may reach out in all directions, breaking against multiple shores, in both political and economic terms.

It is significant to note here that it is the existential aspects of witchcraft and sorcery notions that form the basis of a comparison between, for example, the witch and the 'terrorist'. 'Witchcraft' and 'sorcery' are terms in the English language, and their historical contexts do show clearly their existential comparability with notions of terror. But in other languages, the terms that we translate as witchcraft or sorcery may take on more explicit connotations of violence, as well as ambiguity, mystery, secrecy, surprise, conspiracy, hidden hostilities, greed and envy. Such explicit connotations point us to some parallelisms between witchcraft and terror, because the fear of witchcraft causes terror in the minds of people, and they may react violently in turn by persecuting or destroying those suspected of being witches. The witch, like the 'terrorist', also depends on being *within* the community and yet not normatively *of* it: an anomaly, a gash in the seams of the cosmos through which harm is thought to flow to people (see Whitehead 2002, 2006, for parallel reflections on the practice of kanaimà sorcery in Guayana; and Stewart & Strathern 1999).

We were led by reflections of this kind to conclude that small-scale and large-scale processes of conflict, and the terror that accompanies phases of violence, share many fundamental features. Scale itself, however, makes a crucial difference. The global village and the Papua New Guinea village are in many ways alike (and, certainly, villages in Papua New Guinea are themselves greatly affected by the world at large). Differences between these contexts lie in terms of the types of conflicts they experience and their relative intractability. The world, for example, does not have many very effective rituals of reconciliation such as the Papua New Guinea pig festivals and marriage exchanges.

Our studies in Papua New Guinea have over time merged with the general sphere of anthropological discussions of violence. As discussed in some of our earlier publications (for example, Stewart & Strathern 2002a; Strathern & Stewart 2006a), we began our entry into this sphere by referring to a transactional theory of interactions pioneered by David Riches (1986). Violent acts can be seen as belonging to 'the triangle of violence' between performers, victims and witnesses (p. 8; Stewart & Strathern 2002a, pp. 3, 9, 35). In the context of inter-group fighting, both sides are both performers and victims and include also witnesses. And casualties in fighting seen as 'warfare' may be considered by their kinsfolk as 'heroes' who have sacrificed their lives to the cause of their group rather than as 'victims'. Similarly, the killers of others may be lauded as heroes. Lethal acts in warfare are given fundamentally different *meanings* from their meanings in other contexts, as the anthropologist Reo Fortune (1939, p. 28) remarked on warfare among the Arapesh people of New Guinea. The assignment of labels and meanings is always context-dependent, depending on the side of the conflict parties align themselves with. The difference in meaning stems from the supposed significance of acts for group survival: defending the nation or group is seen as different from attacking one's neighbours or fellow group members.

Riches's (1986) transactional model is useful, especially when combined with two other observations he makes. He points out (1) that acts of physical violence have their own peculiar effectiveness; but also (2) that their legitimacy is often contested and ambiguous (pp. 11, 25). These contests regarding the legitimacy of violence take place to a good extent in the milieu of its witnesses. Acts of violence may therefore be regarded not only in terms of their immediate instrumental effects as practices from the viewpoint of their performers, but also in terms of their intended or unintended auras of meanings, meanings that they gather within the space of the triangle of violence as we have defined it. Violence is about meanings and thus enters easily into the worlds of discourse, representations and imagination, including the imagination of how to halt violence. 'Terror' refers to these worlds, worlds both beyond and yet constrained by physical acts. In many ways, terror also belongs distinctively to boundaries and borders, such as have existed in the historical past between Scotland and England (Strathern & Stewart 2001), in the more recent past between Northern Ireland and the Republic of Ireland (Strathern & Stewart 2006b), or historically also within Taiwan (for example, Katz 2005): all contexts in which we have been carrying out field and archival research for some years.

Furthermore, in terms of how meanings are created and communicated, rumour and gossip, whether spoken or in printed form, are often tremendously important, especially in the context of violence, threats of violence and fears of violence. We have previously argued for this viewpoint, particularly in relation to accusations of witchcraft and sorcery, but also more generally in terms of issues and feelings that conduce towards conflict (Stewart & Strathern 2004). Rumour and gossip, like violence itself, are transactional acts, passed from person to person, often demanding reciprocity, and subject to disparate evaluations by 'witnesses' who then enter into the communicational network in which rumour flourishes. Rumour and gossip trade on fear, uncertainty and ambiguity, and they deal with the boundaries of legitimate action and speculations about those boundaries. They operate at different levels of societal complexity, from the interpersonal to the international. Intelligence agencies of governments essentially trade on hearsay as much as on direct observations and so may be regarded as purveyors (as well as evaluators) of rumours. Deliberate misinformation is often mixed with sheer inaccuracies as well as kernels of truth in these contexts of international life. Such acts of rumour-making and receiving are not neutral; they are often political tools, and in any case they have consequences, leading to the mobilisation of people in favour of certain causes.

The study of events and physical acts inevitably, then, leads us back into the worlds of fluctuating, negotiated, constructed meanings, and thus in turn into representations of the events that form people's memories and link to their desires and frustrations.

Following these reflections, we offer here some further points, which can be regarded as both methodological and theoretical in character.

1. First, a major concern must be to situate violence (here including both physical acts of violence, for example, injuries, killings, torture, and psychological or mental correlates such as intimidation, often used in deliberate or political ways) and terror in relation to each other. All violent acts may induce terror to some extent; but terror is more specifically situated at the extreme margins of experience, challenging rationality and people's abilities to manage their lives. Today's 'war on terror' must itself inevitably contribute in some ways to the genesis of terror as well as being explicitly aimed at eradicating it.

2. Second, if terror is at the margins of experience, these margins are mediated through the imagination. Imagination therefore becomes a crucial tool for understanding and explaining acts of terror and responses to terror. Imagination here is the way that people perceive contexts in their worlds, as informed by language usages, experience, the media, religion, politics and desires such as the desire for 'security'. Imagination leads to actions, which change the world further.

Case histories relating to this point appear regularly and repetitively in the news media, and experiences relating to the themes involved can occur anywhere in the world. Following the invasion of Iraq by US and allied troops, especially troops from the UK, Britain repeatedly became the scene of rumours and actualities of terrorist attacks associated with controversies over the invasion itself and its aftermaths. We ourselves were on fieldwork (carried out on other topics to do with farming, conservation and heritage; see Stewart & Strathern 2010a) three times in Scotland and Ireland when issues of this sort struck home in the popular imagination. The first time was in 2005, when the London Underground bombings took place. (We draw here both on our own field experience and British newspaper reports in general: *The Guardian, The Scotsman, The Times, The Herald*, and so on.) The second was in 2006, when there was a report that there was a plot to blow up American aircraft travelling between the UK and the US. New rules about hand luggage and the inclusion of liquids in it were imposed at this time, along with heightened security at airports. Also, in late June to early July 2007 we were travelling between field areas in Scotland and Ireland when a Jeep Cherokee vehicle was reported to have crashed into the front entrance to Glasgow airport and burst into flames, causing chaos and consternation, the day after Gordon Brown took over from Tony Blair as Prime Minister of the UK. We had to travel back into Glasgow from the City of Derry Airport (Eglinton Airport) in Northern Ireland and then out of Glasgow shortly thereafter to the US. We experienced all these contexts, keenly, with practical difficulties, and inevitably with some anxiety, as did many others around us on these occasions. In particular, the incident of the car crashing into Glasgow Airport and the subsequent police reports of tracking down numbers of 'doctors' in hospital contexts nearby in Paisley led to a wave of public comment and reaction. First, people with whom we spoke speculated that the attack was timed deliberately to coincide with the political succession to the Prime Ministership. Gordon Brown is Scottish, and it was rumoured/speculated that this, the first attack of this kind on Scottish soil, was timed as a protest against Brown's inheritance of Blair's policies and the responsibility for the invasion of Iraq. Second, regardless of this point, people suddenly felt that the terror was much closer to them than it had been before. This reaction shows the inverse process to the first speculation. The first speculation raised the interpretation to the national level. The second response brought it firmly back to the local level. These two responses, however, were seamless, feeding into each other. Third, there was embarrassment and anger about the local provenance of the driver of the car and the passenger in it, for they were resident in a housing complex in the environs of Glasgow itself. Alex Salmond, the recently elected First Minister and leader of the Scottish National Party that had made considerable gains in a recent election to the Scottish Assembly, was reported to have commented that those involved did not seem to have been in Scotland very long. The implication here is that the home-grown terrorist is a disturbing concept: the sorcerer/witch/betrayer within (see Stewart & Strathern 2004, p. 44). The First Minister was suggesting that in this case the would-be attackers were not very much 'within'. The comment shows the importance of this symbolic theme. As an example of the 'real insider', a baggage handler who tackled one of the occupants of the car that burst into flames as he was running away from it appeared on television with a modest demeanour explaining, in his way, how he felt he could not let the fellow get away with having threatened people in this fashion.

Gordon Brown himself, while taking a 'hard line' on terror, shifted the discourse on it, in some ways, from the model of a 'war on terror' to treating terror as a crime, to be dealt with by police methods. We note here that police methods are continually altering, especially in relation to terrorism as a continuously evolving concept of criminality that also has repercussions on concepts of civil society and personal privacy. In this respect, the British Prime Minister aligned himself with European policies. Treating terrorism as crime takes any aura of glory away from it and brings it down to a mundane sphere of action that police policy and action can deal with, thus promoting a sense of public security rather than insecurity. As the baggage handler captured the runaway attacker, so terrorists under these policies are sought out to be discovered and punished. Such a formulation also implicitly negates the narrative of 'God's plan' or 'God's will' that is so much a part of the wider international rhetoric of violence and its 'justification'. On the other hand, it is consonant enough with a drive to uncover plots and conspiracies, to seek out the 'sorcerers' or 'witches' and lock them up or eradicate them; and with an increased emphasis on public surveillance of people by means of closed circuit digital television, or trawling through secretly intercepted telephone calls and emails for clues of possible conspiracies. At each turn the imagination of 'what terrorism is' and how to deal with 'it' is appealed to or invoked in different discursive formations. In late December 2009, a further wave of discussion and debate was generated by an attempt to set off a bomb on an aircraft about to land at Detroit on a flight from Amsterdam, triggering a further step-up in security procedures at airports, with full body scans, and a rash of international news media commentaries wondering about the effectiveness in the longer run of such reactive procedures. Once again, people's imaginative horizons were stretched beyond what might have been thought to be reasonable or likely to happen. The basic work of terror was accomplished, then, regardless of the fact that the bomb was not effectively detonated.

Numerous television programs have been based on these kinds of scenarios with potential twists and turns of plot lines, revealing the limitless imaginative potential to instil and project fear.

3. These considerations all feed into issues regarding terrorism, however terrorism is itself defined (see Strathern & Stewart 2006a, p. 9). Acts of terror take place within the 'triangle of violence' and are evaluated differently according to people's places in the triangle. Emotive matters influence the viewpoints of performers, victims and witnesses. The category of the witness is complex and manifold. And ongoing processes of violence and terror are regularly fuelled by the impulse, or the obligation, to take revenge. Politically orchestrated funeral rituals mobilise people's feelings and actions. Such rituals also define we/they kinds of identities, in which 'they'

are often seen in terms similar to how witches and sorcerers are seen in small-scale community contexts in Papua New Guinea and elsewhere. Leading figures in shadowy political movements dedicated to the violent overthrow of their opponents can be compared to master sorcerers or rulers of witches' covens. Such imaginative colourings of actions and events are themselves an intrinsic part of the aura of terror that is generated out of physical attacks or threats of attacks.

4. An important feature here is the element of secrecy, which is classically exhibited in the contexts of witchcraft and sorcery suspicions. Witchcraft and sorcery have to do with ideas about violence, and retribution against violence, committed in secrecy. There is often uncertainty, intrinsic lack of proof. Conspiracy theories flourish in such contexts, which are saturated both by fear and by attempts to cope with fear by producing explanatory, exculpatory and salvationist narratives around the issue of fear. Accusations of witchcraft and sorcery take place within established or evolving power structures, but they can also be efforts to change such structures, and so they insert themselves into history. Prehistories of events over time precede such explicit accusations. In contexts that have long been troubled and ambiguous and on the margins of power structures, distrust and conspiracy theories flourish particularly intensely. We have found that this observation applies decidedly to the historical context of Northern Ireland and the wider context of Ulster, where we have been carrying out research since 2001 (see Strathern & Stewart 2006b). Conspiracy theories, and the dissemination of rumours, often are promulgated through the news media and cycle endlessly through both oral and written forms of communication. One theme is very salient: that of internal betrayal or hidden hostility within a political state or an organisation. The sorcerer/betrayer within appears as a common figure analogous to scenarios of espionage and counterespionage, double agents, secret payments

and ambiguous loyalties. Examples can again be found in the fractured histories of conflict in Ireland between the British government and the supporters of Union with Britain, and the Irish Republican Army. Imagination, rhetoric and deep emotions cluster around the figure of the spy. Both the 'spy' and the 'terrorist' are in some ways seen as like the witch or sorcerer. Following the re-establishment of devolved government in Northern Ireland in 2007, and the sharing of power between the previously opposed Democratic Unionist Party and Sinn Fein there, these concerns and tensions seemed to have considerably eased, although a renewal of violent attacks on police and soldiers in 2009, and early in 2010 a set of issues in which the First Minister was unexpectedly enmeshed, threatened to disrupt the fragile terms of the ruling alliance between the two parties.

5. Conspiracies, like the other figures of thought we have mentioned, are conceptualised in terms of particular cosmological imaginations. Performers, victims and witnesses alike live within these cosmological frameworks of thought, which may be shared or markedly contradictory. It is necessary, then, to identify wherever possible what these frameworks are. Political élites attempt both to capitalise on and to shape such frameworks, often but not always from within some specific set of religious ideas involving teleologies or eschatologies as well as ideas of what is right and wrong or legitimate and illegitimate. Ideas about 'God's plan' or 'God's will' may be invoked by actors in these contexts, sometimes again in quite contradictory ways.

6. While it is obvious that the idea of terror depends on certain psychological propositions and inferences, our own theorising is at the level of process and communication, and the data we are interested in are accessible in phenomenological terms in the surfaces of social life. A processual model of terror indicates that terror may reach

heights and then decrease, either in cyclical or in linear ways. An undulating process of this kind may in turn be affected very greatly by rumour and its appeal to the imagination, as well as its usefulness for governmental propaganda, as is shown in the phenomenon of 'leaks', whether authorised or not. Leaks cannot easily be verified. But they appeal to the imagination precisely because of their covert provenance as the 'inside story'. Our point is not to stress either the fictional or the factual basis of such leaks, but rather to stress the real intentions behind them and their real effects in networks of communication. Real-world events that cause death become interlocked with their interpretations, causing a cycle of rumour, imagination, interpretation and further, potentially escalating, effects. (Byrne (2007) and Modell (2006) both discuss the importance of the imagination in general, including within the sphere of 'rational thought'.) This is an important point. The modes of thinking that lead to violence can equally lead in other, more peaceful, directions. Imagination should not be thought of as simply allied to fantasy or a sphere of the putatively irrational. It can be, indeed arguably always is, an important ingredient in the production of positive changes, such as the making of peace.

7. 'Suicide bombers' illustrate many of the points we have made above. They cause real deaths, injuries and terror. They are motivated by their own cosmologies. Their actions are judged very differently by different witnesses. They have further effects, often stimulating revenge or reprisals in kind. They are prime examples of the workings of imagination in the broadest sense. They also act historically as 'shock troops', pushing at the horizons of the imagination into the previously unimaginable (as argued in Strathern & Stewart 2006a). They bring the physical and the symbolic worlds together, in sharp focus, as front-page pictures of newspapers and prime-time news programs show. They are also personal, biographical figures with

their own narratives and concerns that feed into the wider picture of their representational status as icons of violence.

Studies on issues such as those outlined above need, therefore, to address first, the interrelation of the social and political sciences and historical ways of approaching terror; second, the analytical linkages between local, national and transnational forms of violence and terror, especially processes of escalation over time; third, the importance of ideas of revenge as a part of instituted complexes of violence (revenge links memory, history, anticipation and fear together, and is crucial to understanding the construction of ideologies and images of terror); fourth, the parallel between ideas of the occult, such as sorcery and witchcraft, and the figure of the terrorist or 'enemy within' the society; fifth, and finally, issues of representation and discourse over time, the ways in which processes of terror enter into the development of 'legends' forming a core of circulating rumours that feed into people's imaginations and back into the material world.

From a theoretical viewpoint we see imagination as a crucial concept around which ideas derived from different disciplines could cluster. From an applied viewpoint we also see this concept as crucial, because policy-makers appeal to, and play upon, people's imaginations and their fears in constructing world affairs around their own interests and agendas.

We return now to the context of Papua New Guinea, the main ethnographic focus of this book, where some of our studies on both violence and peace-making have been carried out (Stewart & Strathern 2002a; Strathern 1993a, 1993b; Strathern & Stewart 1997b, 2003), and in which our interest has always been in popular experience. We begin with a re-contextualised discussion on scales of violence and then move to an examination of themes arising out of the national election process in June to August 2007.

For many years we have followed and written about certain pervasive patterns of violence in Papua New Guinea (for example, Stewart & Strathern 2002a). These patterns can be productively compared with patterns of violent activity elsewhere. To do so here, we will make some distinctions between types, scales and contexts of violence. We recognise that the term violence has many meanings and is hard to reduce to a single essence. In fact, in the realm of discourse it is important to recognise the pluripotentality of the term, while also recognising its primordial or visceral connections with experiences of fear and danger. In particular, we recognise that while physical actions are the prototypical form of violence, the discursive and interpretive frameworks that people create around physical actions are also very significant, especially when we link our discussions to issues of terror and intimidation. Nevertheless, the threat or reality of physical action causing harm to others remains for us, and for many other analysts, a core element of definition.

There is plenty of evidence of the place of violent physical action in the historical and contemporary records of societies in Papua New Guinea. There is also plenty of evidence, as we have earlier noted, of harmonious activities and peace-making. Exchanges of wealth are the main vehicle for such peace-making. Competition or conflict over such exchanges can also lead to violence. There is, to repeat, a cyclicity of activities, an oscillation between peaceful and violent relations among people.

These observations provide an initial setting for considering the distinctions mentioned above between types, scales and contexts of violent forms of behaviour and the processes that flow from these forms. At local levels, the patterns of violence typically involved can be described as instrumental, episodic and fluctuating in scale between individual acts and massed collective combats or incursions by one group against others. It is in this sense that we can speak, in somewhat 'traditionalist' anthropological terms, of violence as a normal/expected/recurrent feature of ongoing social relations. Such a characterisation, however, is made by the outside observer. It does not correspond to the phenomenological view of the insider, for whom acts of violence are indeed experienced as a disruption of peace, even when warriorhood is an expected part of the lives of men. The important point to note is that in these contexts violence tends to be self-limiting. The chief reason why this is so lies in the requirement to pay compensation for certain deaths: either, in the case of Mount Hagen society in the Western Highlands of Papua New Guinea, reparations paid to allies who have lost a man in fighting to help one's own group, or compensation paid to minor enemies for deaths inflicted on them. Such minor enemies might, in pre-colonial times, be allies in other bouts of conflict with major enemy groups; hence, the need to pay them was similar in essence to the need to pay reparations to allies. Political self-interest ruled and was buttressed by the ideas regarding vengeful ghosts. Deaths not paid for could lead to hostile reprisals, it was thought, on the part of the spirits of those who had been killed. The reprisals would take the form of inflicting sickness or misfortune on their surviving relatives; hence, the kin of those killed would assiduously demand compensation from the side of the killers, in order to appease their dead. Another way of appeasing such spirits was to take revenge: here the spirits were appealed to directly, asking them to go before (that is, in front of) the nose and sit at the weapon-wielding elbows of their kin as they sought to inflict a killing in return for the initial killing. With major enemies this was the pattern. Terror and intimidation in particular belonged to conflicts between major enemies. For example, people might desecrate the bodies of enemies they had killed in combat by burning them on pyres at the borders between the groups in conflict. Ambushes and assassinations were also parts of patterns of revenge-taking and might be undertaken outside of an open context of combat or an active sequence of fighting. When one set of fighters invaded the territory of those they were fighting they would try to drive their enemies into places from which it was difficult to escape. They also would, so narratives declare, deliberately violate and sometimes capture womenfolk of the enemy group. Frightened male fighters and women would try to take refuge in out-of-the-way spots and avoid discovery. If the men were discovered, they would likely be killed. Maternal kinsfolk, related because of intermarriage, however, would not kill their individual relatives in this way. Minor enemies and allies were closely intermarried, thus restricting the scale of killing overall. With major enemies, this was not the case.

From these examples we can see that terror was a tactic between groups, especially major enemies. Its results, however, were temporary and constrained. Displays of intimidation, clearly evident, were also temporary. The purposes of terror were short-term. A group might be driven out. Later, with exchanges of wealth, it would be allowed to return (Strathern & Stewart 2003). There were no ideological aspects of terror other than the specificities of revenge-taking, with its spiritual or cosmological imperatives. Such patterns are different from the ideological warfare employed in national-level conflicts, wars of conquest and imperialism and wars between conflicting social ideologies, and the ideological substratum in today's global contexts of terror, terrorism and the 'war on terror'. In the small-scale, instrumental and episodically self-limiting patterns we have described, terror was an occasional concomitant of 'combat'; whereas in contemporary ideologically based conflicts, terror becomes a major instrument and component of combat and is directed mainly at 'non-combatants', the 'civilians' of societies with specialised, state-paid armies supported by state revenues.

Contemporary contexts in Papua New Guinea have also changed markedly from this picture of 'stable' patterns in the pre-colonial and early colonial past. 'Pacification' originally came from the 1930s onwards in Mount Hagen, with the advent of Australian patrol officers, gun-wielding police and missionary workers. Exchanges of wealth in pigs and shells effloresced through the 1960s, with an increase in the supply of shell valuables and an expansion of pig production (Strathern & Stewart 1999a). It is important to note that the fault line in peace-making that ran between major enemies of different named tribes was never substantially transformed in the efflorescence of exchanges that followed the pacification process. Exchanges linked together former allies and minor enemies at the inter-clan level rather than changing the patterns between major enemies, although some inroads into the older patterns were made by ambitious leaders seeking to extend the scope of their influence beyond existing ambits of social relations.

The pattern of colonially induced peace began to break down in the 1970s with a resurgence of large-scale conflicts along these fault lines between major enemies, occasioned by deaths in car accidents, deaths from fighting among inebriated men, disputes over land boundaries and tensions over wealth gained in the cash-cropping of coffee trees (see also Strathern & Stewart 2000a). Since then, patterns of episodic violence have come increasingly to centre around the periodic times when national elections are held. To a fair extent, these episodes are connected to the ways in which groups are lumped together in constituencies for the purposes of the elections. They are also, however, the products of vertical integration in the state structure whereby Members of the Parliament gain very considerable advantages for themselves and their supporters in terms of money and development projects.

Political competition in Papua New Guinea is intense and volatile. Over the years since Independence from Australia in 1975, very large numbers of political parties (39 in the 2007 elections, as reported in media outlets such as the *Post-Courier* and *The National*), mostly with very small numbers of MPs and intensely local bases, have sprung up. The rewards of office are perceived as great both by politicians and by their supporters (see also Gordon & Meggitt 1985, pp. 145–89). In a very real sense electoral races have taken on the aura of inter-group hostilities and alliances that have an enduring, if shifting, basis in historical patterns of societal formations. National politics are influenced by clan politics. Clan politics also become imbued with national-level meanings and issues. This context provides the basis for the ever-present possibility of violence, intimidation, reprisals and an increased sense of 'terror' during electoral periods (compare Ketan 1998; Standish 1992).

Learning from events in the 2002 elections, especially in the Southern Highlands Province, the government made special arrangements in 2007 for large reinforcements of police and special contingents of soldiers (Papua New Guinea Defence Force personnel) to be on hand at electoral booths and to protect roads and so on. These arrangements generally worked quite well. During the processes of nominating, voting and counting, and in the aftermath of the announcement of results, numbers of incidents nevertheless occurred, according to newspaper reports. We give a small selection here, in order to provide an idea of the kinds of contexts in which occasions of violence can arise. We have briefly categorised the kinds of processes involved, from the viewpoint of our general analyses of violence, in each example. The headings in quotes are those that appeared in the newspaper articles from which we have drawn our summaries.

1. 'Angry candidate, followers go on rampage in WHP [Western Highlands Province]'
The candidate was too late in putting in his nomination. His supporters threatened the electoral officer and crowded into the office to protest. (Intimidation, pre-electoral violence.)
<www.thenational.com.pg/051407/nation26.htm>, original reference, no longer accessible.

2. 'Voters' demands irk intending candidates'
Four candidates in WHP said people had approached them and demanded money and other goods in return for voting for them. (Intimidation, complaints by candidates.)
<www.thenational.com.pg/041007/nation18.htm>, original reference, no longer accessible.

3. 'Candidate threatened by rival supporters'
A candidate for a regional seat in the Southern Highlands Province reported that he and some of his supporters were stopped on a bridge and verbally abused, with advice that he should not stand for election. (Intimidation, complaints by candidates, pre-electoral violence.)
<www.thenational.com.pg/052007/nation10.htm>, original reference, no longer accessible.

4. An attack on the leader of the opposition
The leader and a political ally of his were approaching a landing strip in a helicopter when a group of men stoned the helicopter to prevent them from landing and to discourage the ally from nominating. (Physical violence, intimidation, pre-electoral violence.)
<www.thenational.com.pg/052307/nation1.htm >, original reference, no longer accessible.

5. 'Wewak runs amok'
Supporters of Prime Minister Sir Michael Somare caused a disturbance in Wewak town in celebration of his electoral victory, wanting to shop at the Member's expense in all the leading outlets in town. The shops had to be closed and armed police later regained control. (Violent celebration of a victory.)
<www.thenational.com.pg/073007/nation3.htm>, original reference, no longer accessible.

6. 'Ex-MP and Pastor nabbed in raid'
Security forces raided a local village near to Mount Hagen town and seized a cache of weapons from the pastor's house, arresting the pastor and the former MP. (Pre-emptive strike.)
<www.thenational.com.pg/080307/nation6.htm>, original reference, no longer accessible.

7. 'Two die, 10 houses burnt in rampage'
Supporters of a losing candidate in Simbu Province burnt down more than ten houses and killed two people in a conflict between tribes over an election loss. (Post-electoral violence, revenge.)
<www.thenational.com.pg/080307/nation9.htm>, original reference, no longer accessible.

8. 'Poll crimes rife in WHP'
Four girls were raped as they tried to avoid a roadblock set up by supporters of a losing candidate near to Mount Hagen in WHP. The rapists were implicitly taking revenge for their candidate's electoral loss. [The girls were presumably from the clan of the winning candidate. This kind of reprisal, motivated by *popokl* – anger or frustration – is highly reminiscent of actions that are narrated in Hagen oral narratives as being taken between major enemy groups in pre-colonial warfare.] Contemporary rumours and narratives about rape also circulated in peri-urban contexts as warnings to young women.
  Other crimes of hold-ups, theft and killings were also reported in the area. (Post-electoral violence, revenge.)
<www.postcourier.com.pg/20070806/news11.htm>, accessed 27 June 2011.

9. 'Armed men issue threats'
Alleged supporters of a losing candidate in a Western Highlands Open (not Regional) seat were armed with M16 military guns and

terrorised people living in a compound on the outskirts of Mount Hagen town. People were afraid and were moving their families out of town back to their own provincial areas because of threats made against them. It was alleged (rumoured) that one politician had paid six million kina [the Papua New Guinea currency] in bribes to get people's votes. [The Open seats comprise smaller areas within the larger regional constituencies. The candidate elected to a regional seat becomes the Governor of the Province corresponding to the Regional electorate.] (Post-electoral violence, revenge, intimidation, inter-ethnic conflict.)
<www.postcourier.com.pg/20070807/news09.htm>, accessed 27 June 2011.

Looking at this selection of cases, first, we see that they are intensely local in terms of the application of violence; yet the reason for their existing at all lies in the national electoral process. Second, we see that intimidation and revenge play striking roles in the 'meanings of violence' involved (Aijmer & Abbink 2000). Third, the episodes do not escalate, although they had the potential to multiply. The type of violence involved remains instrumental; although its contextualisation is wider than inter-clan relations, it is recognisably like such relations, down to the incidents of rape and other forms of physical violence, house burnings and discoveries of weaponry stashes. Such incidents can cumulatively provide serious problems for political order in Papua New Guinea; but they seem to be confined to the periodicities of elections themselves and have become recurrent and persistent without otherwise disrupting the overall political process in between elections. Also, they are not fuelled by, or geared into, transnational ideological concerns. In Highlands Papua New Guinea terror is pervasive at certain times but it does not exponentially expand. This is because of its local, non-ideological and narrowly self-interested character. Electoral violence is instigated for national-level reasons of perceived political advantage, but it rarely goes beyond local levels and does not lead to ideological revolutions; or at least it has not done so by 2011. The contrast with globalised ideological forms of conflict is clear. While local and global forms of terror are ultimately the same, or similar, then, in their existential impact and significance, their wider implications and potentialities are very different. Elections in Papua New Guinea do not give rise to suicide bombings, and electoral violence is episodic and circumstantial.

We wish to stress here, however, that the themes of intimidation as a conscious political tool of conflict, and of revenge as a motivating factor of action, are ones that are intrinsically and strikingly shared between these examples from Papua New Guinea and other, wider contexts in which ideological factors are palpably present. From the standpoint of state authorities, such actions represent a challenge to the state's monopoly of control over force. At the experiential level, they represent conditioning processes whereby persons are pervasively blocked from exercising their autonomies of choice in political action by others who are over-exercising their own autonomy. One autonomy cancels out the other. Moreover, in the context of elections, practices of inter-clan compensation and reconciliation do not operate so clearly as they do in cases that do not involve national-level concerns. The return to earlier patterns of violence, coupled with highly novel circumstances of national political competition, produces great difficulties for peace-making. Parliamentary democracy is intended to increase freedom and accountability; but it can instead become a trap in which people are caught, because of the entrance of vote-buying and physical violence into the process. At local levels, however, and outside of the context of national politics, compensation practices can, and do, still flourish.

CHAPTER 2

Dimensions of violence: revenge and sorcery (Mount Hagen, PNG)

We have remarked at the end of the preceding chapter how patterns of violence derived from pre-colonial times can return in new contexts. It is our argument that this recursion of processes contributes to the difficulties of settling or resolving issues, because of the intrinsic complexity that this phenomenon of mixing times generates. A practice that suited, or at least was consistent with, other practices and presuppositions in an earlier time may produce very complicated problems when it is pursued within an introduced state structure of control. At the same time it may possess the same primordial effectiveness that acts of violence and acts of compensation generally tend to entail.

We have also briefly discussed some of the formal patterns of warfare within the particular part of the Melpa-speaking region of the Hagen area in the Western Highlands of Papua New Guinea where most of our fieldwork has been done. Much of the overt stimulus to warfare in pre-colonial times came from the requirements of revenge. Discussion of this is crucial to analysis of the exchange system, because many of the most important historical forms of exchange activity were based upon death-compensations, and compensation is the alternative to procedures of revenge. It is therefore necessary to describe and compare the two 'alternative procedures' more explicitly. Moreover, the deaths of important men were most likely to precipitate procedures of physical revenge in the past, so the chapter will give us some background on the position of such significant social personages both in precipitating conflict and in settling it (see, for example, Strathern & Stewart 1999b).

Causes of death

First, it is necessary to explain the broad traditional/indigenous notions of the Hageners on 'causes of death'. Many deaths were, and still are, attributed to 'poisoning', and 'counter-poisoning' is considered an appropriate alternative or supplementary means of obtaining revenge for a death whose cause has been so diagnosed. Counter-poisoning thus stands along with physical violence in contrast to the exaction of compensation. We have used the term 'poisoning' here because it conveys an important aspect of the people's own ideas: that is, that it takes place through the insertion of putatively lethal substances into a victim's food. The expression in the Melpa language is *konga* or *kopna*, which literally refers to the edible ginger plant that is used as a condiment in ceremonial cooking of pork in traditional earth ovens but here refers by an inversion of meaning to a powerful lethal substance. Edible ginger is masticated and blown publicly onto food prepared for the communal earth oven. Substances thought to be able to kill are by contrast introduced surreptitiously into individual portions of already cooked food after they are distributed from the oven. Because of the complicated magical ideas associated with the administering of such substances, their preparation and their provenance, it is appropriate to refer to 'poisoning' also as 'sorcery', thus bringing the term more into line with references to sorcery in the wider ethnography on New Guinea.

The Hageners recognise in general four main causes of death: old age, sickness, 'poisoning' sorcery and physical violence. Sickness was traditionally held either to have no further cause or to be sent by spirits of the dead or by other categories of spirits, or by *kum*, a kind of dangerous witchcraft substance which, it is said, may work by itself without the manipulation of an immediate human actor, or may enter into a person and impart to them the characteristics of a cannibal witch. If the death was seen as the result of attack by dead spirits, these might be seen either as domestic spirits, immediately ancestral to the victim or otherwise closely related to him; or they might potentially be thought to be ghosts of enemy groups, killed in warfare or killed in sorcery by men of one's own group. Revenge was not taken or compensation exacted for deaths which were either thought to be spirit-caused in this way or had no further perceived cause; countermeasures were taken by the living only if the death was held to have been brought about by a living human agency, that is, by overt physical violence or by clandestine poisoning/sorcery. Some instances of sickness were attributed to attacks by wild spirits (*tipu römi, kor rakra* in Melpa), said to inhabit forest areas and ravines in clan territories. Ritual experts held the knowledge of spells with which to counteract such attacks.

To die by sickness is *pömngi kukli, we kui roklnga kukli*, 'to die of illness, to be sick and die simply'. It is also recognised that old men (or women) may die when they reach the end of their span (*ui pora nilinga kukli*, 'to die when one's time is finished'), but if younger men die of sickness their close kin are likely (still today) to suspect poisoning/sorcery – while maintaining to outsiders that it was a case of 'sickness simply', since they do not wish to become suspected of making attempts at counter-poisoning/sorcery. There is a gendered element here, since these concerns mostly focus on males, in particular on males who are socially prominent, as we have already noted.

Death by ghostly attack was historically regarded either as punishment by an ancestor for a severe wrong – for example, incest or adultery with a clansman's wife, particularly the former[1] – or as caused by a ghost which was for some other reason *popokl* – angry – with its victim (see Strathern & Stewart 2010a). For example, an elder brother who died unmarried might be held to return as a ghost to kill his younger brother's children, since he would be jealous of the younger brother for reaching the status of fatherhood. The killer ghost might be a patrilateral or matrilateral kinsperson and of senior or junior generation to the victims or contemporary with them. The father's and the mother's ghost might regularly be held to kill a person. More often they and other ghosts would be said to send their living kin a sickness that was less than lethal, in order to remind them to make pig-sacrifices to them. One image that was employed by ritual specialists was that if a person had done wrong and displeased their dead kin, these kin would withdraw their protection of the living and would permit hostile wild spirits to attack them. When a person was sick, if a ghost-attack was suspected, a ghost-diviner would be consulted or a man (a household senior person able to make a pig-sacrifice) would make divination by himself. The diviner was called *el mong porom wuö*, 'the man who pushes in the arrow'. He had a strong stick, part of a spear or an arrow, which he pushed into his house-floor or through its wall in order to contact the ghosts. The consultant told him who was sick and a few other circumstances. (A father consulted on behalf of his unmarried children, and a husband for his wife.) The practitioner proceeded to call the names of the patient's dead kin, asking them if they had sent the sickness and if so why; meanwhile, he pushed the stick forward and pulled it back vigorously. Suddenly the responsible ghost, hearing its name called, was supposed to seize the stick so that it could not be pulled back. The practitioner asked whether a sow or a barrow (castrated male pig), or a red or a black pig was wanted, until the stick was gripped again. The appropriate sacrifice was then arranged, and the practitioner was paid with a leg of cooked meat from this or a pearl shell or two. Most often, it was either the dead father or mother of the sick person who was held responsible, or both jointly, because of their imputed annoyance with some aspect of the patient's actions, perhaps simply that sacrifices had not been offered to them.

Such a practitioner, called a *mön wuö*, often doubled as a remover of poison/sorcery substances, menstrual blood and wild spirits that might attack a person. He might also know spells and ritual actions designed to prevent the ghost of a man killed in warfare from successfully returning and taking revenge on its murderer.[2] Only the ghosts of murdered men, it was said, could normally kill persons other than their agnatic or close cognatic kin, so they were especially feared. The sense of danger, experienced in relation to the expectation of retributive revenge, emerges clearly here, showing how ideas about the dead and the living are intertwined. Spells against such ghosts are called *wamb mömb* in the Melpa language.

In Hagen, attacks by 'wild spirits' (*tipu römi*), which are thought to live in the forest and are conceptualised as distinct from the spirits of men who were once alive, are sometimes said to be made at the behest of ancestral spirits, but may be described as simply the result of the spirit's malice. The spirit, people say, shoots an 'arrow' into its victim and he or she dies after a short sickness. Ideas about such spirits have not disappeared, although with the establishment over many years of both Christianity and biomedical treatment of sicknesses the practices of the *mön wuö* have gradually disappeared and the knowledge of them has been lost to many communities.[3]

Commonly, the spirit was thought to enter the victim's body and 'eat' him from inside. The specialist would then in the past be called in to draw the attacker out with spells and ritual that banished it to the depths of the forest or the bushy parts within clan territories where it belonged.

Another source of malevolence is said to be *kum*. This too belongs to the forests, especially those in the Jimi Valley, and may be seen as an aerial light that deludes hunters at night-time. It is also spoken of as taking the form of stones, which fly up and lodge in the victim's throat or elsewhere, and cause swellings or a general dryness and yellowness of the skin coupled with feelings of unusual hunger, followed by death if treatment is not applied. *Kum* stones could be removed, for a fee, by the expert ritual specialists (see Stewart & Strathern 2004, pp. 114–19).

Sickness, which could be lethal, but was less likely to be so, also was said to come from two 'transcendent' spirits, called *Kor Wöp* and *Kor Nganap* (male and female spirit; see Strathern 1970a). The *Wöp* cult centred partly on springs of water, and when such a spring was found running loosely within a grove people said it was this, 'the eye of *Kor Wöp*', which was causing sickness in the place. It should be closed over properly and pigs be sacrificed to it, when it would confer benefits of health and fertility rather than sickness (see Stewart & Strathern 2001b, pp. 99–112; Strathern & Stewart 2004a, pp. 123–25).

People made a definite distinction between death in the form of physical violence inflicted between living humans in conflict and death brought about by clandestine poisoning/sorcery. At the same time, it might be felt that a man killed in warfare was weakened by sorcery beforehand, and that moreover his ancestors may have 'deserted him' – withdrawn their protection – so enabling his enemies to kill him. The same may still be said if a death occurs by accident or by snakebite. Conversely, a man who comes miraculously through an ambush laid for him or recovers from a snakebite is felt to be especially under ancestral protection.

Causes of fighting

Why did groups fight with each other? What were the pretexts they gave, and what were the underlying reasons?

Hagen men readily expatiate on the general incidents that led to fighting between clans in the past. These are all variations of one theme: covert or individual aggression by one group against another leads to group retaliation or a demand for settlement. Aggression, in these narratives, takes the form of rape of women, theft of pigs or other property, and plundering of gardens for bananas or plantains (a valued special crop that takes a long time to mature). If settlement is not made, or tempers are roused, or the group of the aggressors is a traditional major enemy, fighting breaks out, which can rapidly turn to conflict with lethal weapons if the two groups are not members of an allied clan-pair. A particular act of aggression or revenge is represented as only one of a series that marks the tone of relationships between groups, and this tone is guided by the prevailing structure of enmity and alliance relationships. The actual frequency of troubles between groups, both in past times and today, depends partly on whether they are neighbours or not and what kind of boundary, if any, separates them. But the event most calculated to bring on a bout of warfare between even minor enemies who were at times exchange partners and allies was an apparently 'natural' death, that is, not a death by overt physical violence, for it would usually be suspected that someone had actually poisoned/sorcerised the dead person. From the initial suspicion a number of possibilities would emerge: the blame could be thrown at once on a traditional enemy group and revenge be called for; or it could be placed on a minor enemy group with which there had been some disturbances recently; or, as a result of divination and detective procedures, the individual suspected party would be named and this would create a feeling of hostility and anger even though there had been none previously between the groups of the accuser and the accused.

Establishing sorcery guilt

To establish 'sorcery guilt' a postmortem autopsy was performed. According to narratives given by leading men in the group of the Kawelka tribe, with whom we have worked over many years, before the putative victim died, he would be questioned closely by his kin as to where he had eaten within the last few days. They would establish where he had eaten taro, greens, sweet potatoes, bananas, and so on. When he died he would not be buried in the usual manner, but laid on a platform in the hole and covered with just a layer of earth over him. His stomach was then cut open and a hollow bamboo pipe set upright in it, so that it protruded from the surface of the grave. The stench from the corpse escaped through the pipe and the stomach would dry up. Apparently it took longer for thin men to dry out than fatter ones. The dried food fragments were then examined for traces of black in them. If black was found in taro traces, the men would match this fact with their knowledge of the place where the victim claimed to have eaten taro, and who gave it to him. The giver was then suspected as the poisoner/sorcerer. It could well be a woman, and if it was the wife of a clansman of the victim she would be, apparently, seized and tortured and probably executed, after she had divulged the 'road' along which the poison came to her, and it may have come from her kin if these were hired to do the killing or were themselves traditional enemies. It does not seem as though her kin could demand compensation for this. The confession of the woman in these cases was probably immaterial. Similarly, a man called by the Hageners a *wuö korpa* (man of low status, unmarried, and probably taken in by a leading man as a helper in the household) who had come to live with the victim's clan from an outside group was considered to be open to bribery by the group's enemies and a likely suspect. Such a man could also be caught, tortured and done away with. Men categorised in this way were well aware of this possibility and tended to run for it when a big-man (leader) of their host clan died. In one case the suspect was a father's sister's son of his alleged victim, a big-man of the Kawelka clan of the Melpa-speaking people. He came from a group that lived with an *el parka* (major traditional enemy) group of the Kawelka, the Keme, who used to be with the small Minembi Komonkae clan, and at the time of his host's death was the survivor of a set of three brothers who had originally come to join the Kawelka when they saw all their agnates dying off through sickness in the oppressively hot Baiyer Valley. He was forced to flee from the Kawelka area and went to the place where his wife's daughter by a previous marriage was married, to a Palke group tribesman in the Jimi Valley to the north of the Kawelka territory. There, he was later again accused of a poisoning and hunted down in the woods and killed. In another case the suspect was the mother's brother of the dead man, but he was classified locally in the category of a man of low status, whereas the sister's son was a big-man. He got away as soon as the death became known, and the clansmen of the dead man took up their weapons to get revenge by killing a man of the mother's brother's own clan. Usually, the aim was to kill at least a man for a man, but there are cases in which a boy or a woman was killed, either instead of a man, or in addition to one. It is clear, then, that we have isolated so far two forms that revenge for a 'poisoning' case would take: (1) the individual suspected of being the poisoner is seized and put to death; and (2) action is taken against the clan of the poisoner – either he and/or a number of men may be killed off by physical retaliation. There were many variants of these two procedures, however.

In the first place, the individual sorcerer/person blamed for administering the harmful substance might not be ultimately responsible for planning the death. He or she might be considered to have been bribed by others to give the poison to the victim in return for pay. This is why low-status men who are thought of as grasping but incapable of organising their exchange relationships profitably were typically suspected. (The term *korpa* literally means 'searching'.) A text gathered in the 1960s from a collaborator old enough to have knowledge of these matters illustrates the process:

> If a good man of ours is killed we hold a meeting and ask each other what we should do. Who has a friend close to their place? Will he hold this thing which we can give him? We have cassowaries, young women, fat pigs, and pearl shells. If we can find a road we shall give them away. If the man chosen agrees we send the poison to him and he kills a big-man at the place of our enemies. When their big-man is dead they are at a loss. He showed the way to them and without him they are weak. Now, then, we close in on them, finish them off in fighting and take their ground – for nothing. We pay the poisoner in secret, and win over our enemies. This is called *el klöngi*.
>
> (PJ Stewart & A Strathern, field notes)

The group that initially asks for the death to be brought about may not know the whole 'road' along which the poison/sorcery material travels before it is finally delivered. It will pay the man to whom it gave the poison and he will pay his aides in turn, although exactly how all this was supposed to work out in practice is a little obscure.

Alternatively, there might be no need to offer a bribe. It might be possible to get the poison to the victim directly through a female contact or through two female links. A woman whose agnates have been killed by her husband's group may, it is held, be angry enough to try to poison her husband, or a clansman of his at any rate. It is expected that her feelings will lie on her brothers' side, not on her husband's. Women from enemy groups who are in-married to one's own are watched for thefts and attempts to poison men with their menstrual blood, in particular. The violence with which a woman poisoner was treated reflected the anxiety in some men's feelings about their wives, which perhaps resulted particularly from marriages being made outside of the ambit of friendly political relations. Yet sometimes the woman would be let off, as the following story seems to show:

> A Pölingga wife was married to a Penambe man (in Temboka, the Nebilyer Valley, south of Mount Hagen town). The Penambe and the Pölingga were enemies and she was sorry for her brothers (immediate brothers by the same father) who had been killed by her husband's people, so she poisoned her husband, Penambe R—. The Penambe refrained from killing her, as she had borne children for their group and they were sorry for these (sorry = *kaemb*, literally 'liver'). Instead, they hatched a plot against her agnates. They tried to tempt them into bringing a girl for a bridewealth transaction. But the Pölingga sent the girl alone and did not show up themselves. The girl was allowed to return. The wife of R— was remarried to another Penambe man, but not to the one who had killed her brothers; he would have been afraid of further poisoning and would have refused.
> (PJ Stewart & A Strathern, field notes)

Here, the victim's group spares the woman, even though she is regarded as fully responsible for planning and carrying out the poisoning, because she has borne them children who will contribute to the strength of the group. Nor is she driven out, but instead she is remarried to another Penambe man.

Besides the autopsy method there were true divinatory methods of 'establishing' the guilt of poisoning suspects. Like the autopsies and the retaliatory murders, these appeared by the 1960s to have been given up, as scarcely acceptable either to the colonial Administration or to the missions. The two methods of divination were the taro test and the fire-thong test. If a member of the community, perhaps a wife or a co-resident kinsman, were suspected of poisoning, the taro test might be held, according to narratives. Each person was given a taro and these were cooked in separate small ovens. The person whose taro remained uncooked when all the others were ready was convicted as the poisoner – the ancestors were supposed to point the guilty one out in this way – and he or she is said to have been set upon at once and killed. As with all such procedures, which might appear in fact to depend upon chance, the test leaves us with more questions than we can answer: How was it manipulated? What if it pointed to an important man of the group? What happened if more than one person's taro remained uncooked or a person in a close kinship category, such as the father or mother of the dead person, were convicted? In the only narrative-specific case obtained, collected in the 1960s (and belonging to some years earlier), the convicted were two Penambe tribesmen living with their pair-tribesmen (allied group), the Elti tribe. They were killed, but the Elti had to pay compensation in pigs and valuables to the Penambe for this, which shows that their haste in executing the two men was hardly regarded as justifiable afterwards and was probably regarded as potentially damaging to the alliance between the two groups.

The fire-thong test was a simple one. The accused had to attempt to make fire with the fire-thong, and if he failed he was accounted guilty, again on the supposition that the verdict of the ancestors (of the dead man's group) was being given. This is better known than the taro test. Cases recorded as narratives from the past occurred between groups already hostile. So, for instance, the Kawelka Kundmbo clan once invited their minor enemies of the time, the Kawelka Kurupmbo sub-clan, up to their ceremonial ground, saying they would give cooked pigs to them in a peace ceremony. For some reason, the Kurupmbo went, and they were surrounded by Kundmbo spearmen and told to try the fire-thong test to see whether they had poisoned a Kundmbo man married to a Kurupmbo wife who had recently died. While they were trying the fire-thong they were set upon and some of them were killed before they could escape. Bitter suspicion between Kundmbo and Kurupmbo dated from this incident. Treachery of this kind was expected from an *el parka wuö* (major enemy) and guarded against, but not from a minor enemy and potential ally within the tribe.

Even if the victim's group could not lay hands on a suspect, it would form its opinions of where the poison had come from. If one asks, 'How did you know who had sent the poison?', one is always told:

> Our man died and that night and the next we watched over him inside one of the men's houses. We did not put the news of his death about, but gradually it became known. Then we waited and we would hear if any of our enemies were putting on fine feather headdresses, rubbing their bodies with fat, courting girls, and singing and beating drums. Whichever group did so we knew it was because they were happy since their plans had been fulfilled, and we were angry and planned revenge.
> (PJ Stewart & A Strathern, field notes)

The alleged custom of dressing oneself in finery in jubilation at a desired death is called *rönggeip etimin*. It is possible that *el parka* (major) enemies might wish to claim credit for deaths in this way and would dance at the death of a big-man on the other side. They would know the bereaved men would turn their grief to aggression, and they would prepare themselves for a fight with the psychological advantage on their side. If revenge came by poisoning this was no more than was perpetually to be suspected, since there were always scores to be paid off. But it would not be expected that minor enemies would make *rönggeip* festivities because of a death. They might be suspected of having bribed others, however, and the expression for this was *wuö pokla titimin*, 'they take the cordyline for the man'. The poisoner is said to have sent a knotted cordyline leaf as a sign that his job had been done. There can still be undercurrent assertions in speeches between political notables of different neighbouring groups that this or that big-man took the *wuö pokla* (cordyline marker) for the death of another, and the assertions may continue for years as part of the tissue of suspicion between neighbouring clans.

Joint responsibility: warfare and feud

What makes the clan a crucial group in the political system is the doctrine of joint responsibility. All the men of a clan group were morally involved if one of them was killed, physically or allegedly by poison/sorcery, by a person of another clan group. The duty to take revenge was incumbent on them all and it was discharged by joint physical retaliation. Hence, killings involved clans as solidary units against each other, and it is this which makes it possible when giving a description of the use of violence in the past to speak of clans 'fighting' each other without distinguishing between warfare and the 'blood-feud'. Nevertheless, the distinction can be made and is worth making here.

Evans-Pritchard in his classic work *The Nuer* (1940) distinguished between 'feud' and the 'blood-feud'. The 'feud' in his terms is a general state of hostility between communities as a whole, involving all their members in a diffuse way and breaking out into actual fighting from time to time. The 'blood-feud' is a more specific state of hostility between segments of communities, in the Nuer case the close agnates of a murdered man and the close agnates of the killer. The former are those who are strictly bound to seek revenge for him by taking another life, especially by killing the killer if possible, or one of his close agnates. Yet Evans-Pritchard admits that the blood-feud tends to spread out into a state of feud between communities.

Glasse (1968) makes a slightly different distinction between feud and warfare. Warfare, he says, involves whole groups in conflict and refers to the periods when they are actually fighting each other, when lines of men are running towards each other, screaming wildly and hurling weapons. Feud is a state of minor fighting between individuals that breaks out from time to time but can be terminated when a specific wrong is put right, perhaps by the accomplishment of a killing or by a compensation payment.

In order to apply these distinctions to the material for Hagen, the difference between revenge by physical violence and revenge by sorcery has to be kept in mind.

In the case of revenge by physical violence, the dominant image the Hageners have of themselves is that such revenge was taken up automatically by clansmen and would involve them in at least a minor variety of warfare in Glasse's sense. Such warfare would be the more bitter if it was against a traditional enemy group. This is supposed to have been done whether the death inflicted was by a physical killing or a suspected poisoning. But there are cases of individual men or small bands of men taking on themselves a special duty to revenge their clansmen by retaliatory killings, and their actions can best be seen as blood-feud action in Evans-Pritchard's sense. Yet these retaliatory killings would not necessarily be met by similar retaliation, but by resort to warfare or to poisoning/sorcery. Nor were the killing experts always the close agnates of the deceased men – this in fact shows how the joint responsibility of the clan might be shouldered by one or two men, simply as the clan-mates of a killed man, but also because they had a talent and a liking for taking revenge in this way. A clan might go to war because the son of a clan-sister had been killed also; but if the maternal parallel cousin of a man were killed or poisoned he might take action but his clan would not become involved, unless the cousin were also a clansman. This shows dramatically the special position of the sister's son, as potentially a member of his mother's clan. But the individual loyalty of a man to his mother's sister's son might be considerable, as a narrative case from pre-pacification times will show:

> An old big-man of the Tipuka Kendike clan recounted in the 1960s how the Tipuka Kelmbo once took the *wuö pokla* for the death of his mother's eldest sister's son and made *rönggeip* over this. His own sister was married to a Kelmbo man, and the husband in fact lived with the Kendike. Yet for the occasion the husband went back to the Kelmbo and made *rönggeip* with them. The Kendike big-man was angry over this and so was his cousin, the dead man, whose ghost came back and killed the sister in revenge, although it could not kill her husband (who was not related to it). This was too much for the big-man and in sorrow both for his sister and his cousin he killed the Kelmbo husband. Subsequently death-compensation payments were exchanged between the Kelmbo and his lineage, on this and some other accounts. On the Kendike side, only he and his close lineage brothers were involved, since only he had been concerned with the death of his cousin and subsequent events.
>
> (PJ Stewart & A Strathern, field notes)

After bouts of open conflict, if the relationship between a set of groups was not patched up they would fall into a state of feud, which could be terminated by peace ceremonies and settlements that would correspond to Glasse's sense of feud also. This would apply only to minor enemy (*el öninga*) groups in the past, although after the Australian colonial Administration halted open warfare, in the 1930s to the 1960s, there were attempts to extend friendship to previous *el parka* groups as well.

In the case of revenge by poisoning, only blood-feud might be involved, in the sense that only the close agnates of the deceased might make arrangements for counter-poisoning; but more than these might easily become involved if there was a clan meeting to decide on retaliation and clansmen were asked if they knew a road along which poison could be sent to finish off either the killer or a big-man of his clan if he was not himself a big-man, or if a road to kill him could not be found. This would be diffuse blood-feud on the side of the avengers, but the revenge would be taken on a close set of the first killer's kinsmen in the first instance; in the second it would be 'diffuse' also in one sense but still aimed at a specific man on the enemy side. At any stage such retaliation might be met with open physical force, and warfare could spring up; and in fact, especially between traditional enemies, accusations and counter-accusations of poisoning went on side by side with open fighting. A fresh accusation of poisoning led to further bouts of warfare, as the victim's side would feel that their enemies were 'finishing' them with poison and would soon close in and cut them down openly.

An alternative to seeking revenge for poisoning by further poisoning or physical force was to ask for compensation.[4]

Compensation

For deaths by physical violence it was more usual to demand compensation, and this was one of the bases of the elaborate ceremonial exchange system, which was built into the structure of warfare relations by the distinction between the root-of-war group and their allies (*el pukl wuö/kui wuö*). In the past, ally-compensation was by far the most common form of death-payment made, since groups that were directly fighting each other might refuse to give compensation. Following the colonial stoppage of war in the 1930s and 1940s onwards, there was a gradual extension of direct payments to enemies that enlarged the sphere of relatively friendly social relations between groups. This process, however, was halted in the 1970s by the resurgence of hostile engagements between groups, which in large part resulted from the actual extension of social ties that preceded it, since this extension pushed groups and individuals into ambiguous arenas of sociality, leaving room for suspicions of sorcery/poisoning and increasing the likelihood of accidents or conflict over resources.

Only in the case of poisoning sorcery or overt physical violence is special revenge or compensation sought. An ordinary death-compensation may be paid to the maternal clan of a dead man by his agnates, whether he has died by violence or not. This is a different matter from compensation for a deliberate killing. Poisoning is hard to prove and hence compensation claims can be denied; but it is easier to pin at least group-blame on others for a death by physical violence, especially in open warfare. Strictly, the ghost of a man killed required in the past that revenge be taken on his behalf, but this is not allowed to prevent compensation being given instead. There are spells known to the ritual specialists that can keep away ghosts of enemies who have been killed, and the ghosts of husbands and wives, it is thought, can kill their living partners. But men do not seem to have been afraid that their own clansmen, once killed, would make a habit of coming back to kill them in anger (*popokl*) if they were not avenged. Yet it is true that dead big-men, if unavenged, were expected to send sickness to their clansmen, and, in a case already cited above, a ghost was said to have killed its female matrilateral parallel cousin in a revenge situation. More regularly, it was expected that the ghost would help the clansmen against their enemies, and there was a special ritual to enlist its aid if it seemed sluggish.

This ritual was called *el kwun koklamon*, 'let us make our arrows straight'. The men of a group all brought little pigs trussed up under their arms, ready for sacrifice. Sacrifice would sometimes be made in a clan cemetery, sometimes at a ceremonial place used for exchanges of wealth. The sacrifice appears to have been similar to the regular one that was made when warfare was going badly. An account given by a senior Tipuka big-man in the 1960s illustrates this:

> If we Tipuka went out to fight the Kombukla and lost a man but were unable to kill one in return we felt pain in our stomachs as we came home. We would collect pigs together and make a sacrifice. Men who had no pigs would supply yams, taro, and bananas. We killed the pigs and put the heads and tails into the little sacrificial houses which each one of us kept. Only we men went inside the little houses (*kor manga rapa* = spirit men's house). The other parts of the pig were cooked and distributed outside, to the women as well. We prayed to our ancestors not to desert us, and to the other dead, our brothers, sisters and dead children. We returned into the house and ate the heads and tails.[5] A big-man might make a prayer for all of us. Then we went out and killed the Kombukla. We said, 'Now we are equal. It is finished. We cannot kill another person now'.[6]
>
> (PJ Stewart & A Strathern, field notes)

Compensation for death is payable in live pigs, cooked pig-meat, pearl shells, and since the 1960s in state money. For poisoning it is rarely paid; just two cases have been instanced above. For death by physical violence in warfare in the past compensation was payable to allies and to *el öninga* enemies, although not to traditional major enemies. There is also the ordinary death-compensation, payable to matrilateral kin, mentioned above. This seemed to have been given up in the Kopon sub-area (Dei Council) in the 1960s, but it remained popular nearer to Hagen town and was carried out regularly in parts of the Nebilyer.

The structure of sorcery accusations

From the point of view of each clan, other social groups fell into a series of categories, each category representing an increasing degree of social distance from itself. The ideal picture of 'poisoning relationships' is that within the clan (between its putatively agnatically related members) and between pair-clans poisoning does not occur (we may call these categories 1 and 2). But it is admitted to occur between one's own clan and its minor enemies, as well as its traditional major enemies (categories 3 and 4). Category 3 groups would have more opportunity to poison one, because of the greater number of marriages with them and the increased number of 'roads' resulting; but category 4 groups were regarded hypothetically as more dedicated to the task of harming one's own clan. As implied in case history descriptions given earlier in this chapter, minor enemy groups could on occasion be allies in fighting against major enemies. Thus, relations with these groups were complex and marked by numerous cross-cutting ties, conducing to the settlement of disputes. This circumstance held most markedly between clans that were paired as allies, and correspondingly were closely intermarried. We can identify the pair-clan relationship as a kind of safety zone or security circle in a social world marked by considerable danger, especially from major enemies. Elements of this pre-colonial structure have endured and are regenerated in bouts of conflict and suspicion that arise between groups in contemporary circumstances, for example over election issues in which candidates of different groups are pitted against one another. As we argued in Chapter 1, the chief fault line in peace-making in the field of social relations ran between major enemies. In this chapter we have seen that it was between these categories also that major enduring suspicions of poisoning-sorcery flourished.

The Appendix shows in some detail that this somewhat idealised picture of social relations was not always realised in practice. Individual enmities intervened, and people had, or were suspected of having, multiple and ambiguous allegiances that made them open to bribery or vulnerable to accusations of bribery. The resulting scene for any given tribe was patchy and much influenced by historical vicissitudes. We give here a brief conspectus of materials on one tribe, the Tipuka, as things were in the 1960s, to give an idea of these practical complexities. More details appear in the Appendix.

1. Within the Tipuka tribe, between minor enemies there was an ideal clustering of poisoning relationships. Thus, both the Kitepi and Oklembo clans, which constitute a clan-pair, experienced poisoning-sorcery accusations, which we mark as P, with the Kengeke clan but not P with Kendike. This is consistent with Kengeke being regarded as the 'root of war' in conflicts with Kitepi and Oklembo, and Kendike as merely the allies of Kengeke (these two are also pair-clans). But in fact, while this seems to be true for the Oklembo it was not so for the Kitepi, who once accused the Kendike of a poisoning and hence had a separate *el pukl* with them.

2. Between Kengeke and Kendike, despite the fact that they are a pair, it is admitted that poisonings occurred. (This parallels cases between the Minembi Papeke and Yelipi clans, which were historically paired, but had outbreaks of hostility between them.) The ideal of the clan-pair as a 'brotherhood alliance' definitely broke down in some cases. This cannot be correlated simply with the size of the groups involved; it is not simply a sign that one of them is dividing internally into two separate clans and so loosening its ties with the previous pair-clan and becoming itself a pair-clan set. It is rather to be looked on as a historical circumstance or event. Where the fear of poisoning and the spirit of competition between groups were both strong it is easy enough to see how accusations could disrupt even close alliances. It is only within the smaller exogamous clans (below approximately 500 in numbers) that fighting and accusations were and still are met by quick attempts to smother them and arrange for compensation.

3. With the *el parka* (major enemy) groups Kombukla and Wölyi, the pattern is simple: no clan of Tipuka had any alliance with these,

and all had fighting relations, F, as well as P relations with them, although the data do not cover all the clans. With the Minembi clans living relatively near to Tipuka territory – Papeke, Mimke and Engambo – and with the pair-clan of Engambo – Kimbo – there was a modified and less certain pattern: there were certainly battles against them, but these groups were seen as only the *wör wuö kup* ('the helping group at the edge') of the Kombukla, and poisoning accusations against them were made much less frequently.

4. The Klamakae are a group with only limited contacts with the Tipuka. They are separated by the Kawelka and are not neighbours at any point other than at the back of the Jimi Divide. As such, they are somewhat outside of the most relevant range for poisoning to operate. But there was an alliance between the Klamakae Rokmbo and the Oklembo – *not* mentioned by the informants in this instance, for the Rokmbo killed some of the Kawelka from behind when they were running from an Oklembo attack. What they do mention is the existence of a history of serious fighting between a section of Kengeke and a section of Klamakae. The Kengeke settled in one part of the Jimi and the Klamakae drove them out, it seems. This was an isolated incident, not relevant to the general relationship between the two tribes and not correlated with poisoning accusations.

The data above show some of the poisoning relationships between the Tipuka and their pair-tribe and with other tribes as well. In the Nebilyer Valley the pairing of tribes is more persistent and the tribes are smaller than they are in the central and northern areas (Hagen and Dei councils). In fact, since some of these Nebilyer tribes are single exogamous units, it might be better to treat the relationship between these pair-'tribes' as closer to that between 'pair-clans' in the larger hierarchies. Poisoning relationships can provide one index for this. An example is provided by the Poyaka–Paklim pair, among whom it was asserted by one interlocutor in the 1960s that the subgroups intermarried but did not fight and also did not make poisoning accusations among themselves, partly because they had so many major enemies to face in warfare. This assertion makes a lot of sense, since it was always political relations that guided other patterns of activity, and politics was a matter of strength in numbers and wealth. It is clear, at any rate, that they were allies in a far more automatic and total way than were tribe-pairs in other parts of the Hagen area, and it is this which makes it useful to compare them to clan-pairs. Many of the Mendi clan-clusters described by Ryan (1959) are built up from what he calls clan-pairs, and the Nebilyer groups, especially those in the Kulir part, seem to be similarly organised. It seems possible that the Kulir groups are ones which have been in the past forced out by expanding and more successful groups in the central Nebilyer. Perhaps their population was further kept down by the tight pattern of warfare in the Kulir, in which the paired groups were staunch allies but could not rely on many others to help them. This, at least, is the way the Kulir groups spoke of their warfare relations when these were discussed with them in the 1960s (see also Merlan & Rumsey 1991, in which the Kulir groups are called Ku Waru).

Conclusion

In conclusion, throughout this chapter we have been examining the historical interplay between sorcery ('poisoning'), revenge, feuding, full-scale fighting (that is, 'warfare'), and settlements by compensation payments ('peace-making') in the Mount Hagen area. The materials are complex. However, some structuring elements can be found, applying primarily to a putative pre-colonial period prior to the 1930s, but with implications stretching forward in time up to contemporary or recent events. A major enduring distinction is that between major and minor categories of enemy groups relating to warfare in the past. With major enemies, an ongoing state of hostility was prevalent and expected, intermarriage was limited, and no, or few, cross-cutting alliances operated through compensation payments. Senses of hostility were expressed both in overt fighting and in covert acts, or suspicions of acts, of sorcery. Major enemies were always of different tribes, and tribes were paired together as allies and opposed to another pair notionally balanced against them. Thus, Tipuka+Kawelka were opposed to Kombukla+Minembi in the area that in colonial times post-1960 became Dei Council. Between pair-tribes there were minor, but not major, hostilities. The same pattern held within a tribe, between pair-clans. So, with minor enemies of one's clan, hostility was intermittent, and intermarriage was frequent and contributed to cross-cutting alliances along lines of exchange partnerships and consanguineal kinship.

All this did not mean that there were no problems or bouts of conflict among groups linked by exchange partnerships. Sorcery suspicions could potentially arise from any quarter, and personal enmities and dissatisfactions could easily flare up. Women had their own strong agency, which could be expressed either in promoting exchanges centred on the pigs that they reared or in trafficking in supposedly lethal substances. Overall, though, the possibility of compensation meant the possibility of peace-making, and there was no other effective way of making peace.

In the 1960s, this basic structure was parlayed into a situation in which compensation payments were progressively transformed into ongoing exchanges among allied groups and a wider form of integration began to be developed through the enchainment of exchange occasions between a series of neighbouring groups. Nevertheless, throughout all this expansion, the divides between major enemies remained strong. After the Administration halted warfare from the 1940s onwards, suspicions of sorcery, if anything, increased, and were further exacerbated by disparities in new forms of wealth obtained by cash-cropping. The ideology of revenge and competitive hostility flourished, in the temporary absence of overt concerted fighting between groups, through the notion of sorcery ('poisoning'). Moreover, sorcery accusations could always precipitate a threat of physical fighting, as they had done in the past. These circumstances persisted into the period of Councils and elections, which we will look at in more detail in Chapter 4. In the next chapter we will set the Hagen structures of enmity and peace-making into a wider regional comparative context.

CHAPTER 3

Warfare and peace-making: comparative histories

Highlands Papua New Guinea societies varied in terms of their patterns of warfare/inter-group conflict and compensation for killings or peace-making. In this chapter, we compare these patterns from three Highlands areas where we have carried out long-term fieldwork – Hagen (Melpa), Pangia (Wiru) and Lake Kopiago (Duna) – with further reference to surrounding areas such as Kompiam in the Enga Province and the Huli of Southern Highlands Province, and we examine how peace-making capacities were shaped by the general configurations of ceremonial exchange relationships. These patterns were in turn deeply modified by colonial and post-colonial circumstances. The chapter provides an essential background to further chapters on how problems of achieving peaceful settlements have increased over time.

In making our general argument so far regarding conflict, compensation and peace-making, we have taken as our model, explicit or implicit, historical arrangements that came to the fore in the Mount Hagen area of the Western Highlands Province, Papua New

Guinea. And in Chapter 2 we looked at some specific parameters and contexts in terms of which compensation payments operated in Hagen: overt violence, sorcery and major enmities placed limits on peace-making among clan and tribal groups. Nevertheless, at least in the colonial period of the 1960s, and arguably prior to direct contact with the outside world in the 1930s, a major characteristic of the Hagen system lay in its capacity for the expansion of peaceful relations. The key to this capacity was the ethic of *moka* exchange, by which compensation payments were potentially turned into political alliance through competitive giving. The supreme maker of *moka* was the leader who outdid others in what he gave away in displays of wealth (pigs and shell valuables). Since men displayed ambition to become known as such leaders, there was an inbuilt drive to achieve the expansion of exchange ties and, with these, relatively peaceful relations between the leaders' groups. The collateral importance of ability in speech-making went hand-in-hand with the ability to raise wealth, since leaders persuaded others to subsidise their wealth-raising efforts and also brought lustre and pride to their groups and networks of supporters when they made formal speeches at exchange occasions when goods were handed over to their partners. In short, as always, nothing succeeded like success, and supporters were both the means whereby leaders ('big-men') gained their positions and the beneficiaries of the prestige that the leaders brought to their groups. The relatively high population density in the Central Hagen area, facilitated by the fertility of the land and the level of yield obtained from the sweet potato staple crop, set further conditions for the development of *moka*. As groups expanded, they had to come increasingly to terms with one another, either by warfare or by exchange (and both factors swung into play). Polygamy enabled leaders to make multiple interpersonal ties with numbers of neighbouring groups and consequently to make pathways for *moka* exchange and thus periods of peace.

Exchange thus promoted peace and was disrupted by warfare. But exchange also grew out of the killings in warfare. If the fighting was with minor enemies (*el öninga wamb*), such killings would be followed by direct payments of compensation. Indeed, compensation could be paid also for woundings inflicted in stick-fights between minor enemies (Strathern & Stewart 1999b [Ongka's story], p. 41). This type of compensation was call *mongaemb*, Ongka notes (p. 41). If fighting was with major traditional enemies (*el parka wamb*, 'red bird of paradise war people', from the practice of wearing *Raggiana* plumes as headdresses in such fights), then no compensation would be offered between the enemies, but each side would pay reparations to its allies and supporters (their *kui wuö*, 'dead man'). In either case the main aim was to re-establish a status quo of peaceful relations between those for whom this was feasible. Since allies/minor enemies were also the source of major exchange partnerships in *moka* and, concomitantly, those with whom most intermarriages took place, it is evident that the segmentary sets of allies formed the cores of extended social solidarity.

The structural and demographic features that stand out here are:

1. Complexly segmented autonomous clan groups forming separate tribes.
2. A division between major and minor enemies/allies.
3. A system of compensation that strengthened ties of alliance via marriage.
4. Ambitious leaders who fostered competitive exchange.
5. Fairly high population density in fertile areas, leading to historical accommodations, as well as conflicts, between groups.

Conditions of these kinds were found to comparable degrees in the Wahgi and Chimbu (Simbu) area to the east of Hagen, and among Central Enga populations to the west. Exchange practices were highly developed in these areas also (for example, see Brookfield & Brown 1963; Feil 1984; Meggitt 1965; Reay 1959). They were also found among the Huli of the Southern Highlands (Glasse 1968). In the Wahgi and Chimbu areas *moka* exchange was not practised. Social integration took place through the periodic organisation of massive pig-killing festivals hosted by congeries of groups, involving the distribution of pork to many individual recipients. Such pig festivals created diffuse conditions of solidarity in wide areas and provided avenues for big-men to achieve prominence. They were not, however, immediately geared towards the settlement of conflicts.[1]

In the Enga areas, there was a form of complex social integration periodically achieved through long, concatenating sequences of gifts and counter-gifts of pigs and pork that snaked their way across the territories of numerous otherwise autonomous clan groups, temporarily halting hostilities while in places generating conflicts over the timing, staging and adequacy of the gifts involved (Feil 1984, 1987; Meggitt 1974). These exchange cycles were referred to as the Te (Meggitt 1974) or Tee (Wiessner & Tumu 1998) cycles.[2] They were like the smaller *moka* chains that from time to time developed in Mount Hagen in the 1960s (Strathern 1971 [2007]), only written much larger over the landscape and consequently being vulnerable to many vicissitudes of execution in practice. Among the Enga-speaking populations, the Mae Enga, studied by Meggitt (1977) in the 1950s and 1960s, were deeply involved in the Te but were also caught up in inter-clan conflicts centring on disputes over land, women and pigs, to use the shorthand stereotypes often applied by male Highlanders when explaining – and simplifying – the causes of their troubles to outsiders such as government officers or visiting anthropologists. The Tombema Enga of Kompiam, north-east of Wabag, where the Mae Enga live, also reported themselves to Feil as having been regularly involved in fighting, and in the payment of homicide compensations, prior to colonially induced pacification in the 1950s (Feil 1984, based on fieldwork in 1974 and his PhD thesis of 1978). Feil argued that, overall, the individual partnerships between men of different clans acted as an inhibiting force on the incidence of violence in the society at large: in other words, that the *tee* was a force for peace. At the same time, his study showed that fighting and killings did chronically take place. In broad terms, the same is true, of course, for Hagen. But there were some interesting differences between Hagen and the apparent situation among the Tombema Enga, which we can use as a comparative tool to stretch a kind of yardstick of potentialities for the peaceful settlement of conflicts among other Highlands societies as well. (We use 'societies' here in a general way to index areas in which relatively homogeneous institutions are found. We do not mean that these are bounded units that have an organised political structure.)

The crucial issues are: What were the characteristics and purposes of the main forms of exchange of wealth? And, in particular, at the political level, who were one's allies?

It was an important part of Feil's argument that the activities of big-men and others in the *tee* exchanges should be seen as individually based, not as expressions of group leadership or of the power of corporate groups. In this regard, Feil's analyses of the Tombema parallel closely the views of Paul Sillitoe on the Wola people of the Nipa (Was Valley) area in the Southern Highlands Province of Papua New Guinea (for example, Sillitoe 1978, 1979; Sillitoe & Sillitoe 2010; and many other publications). Feil also stressed that the *tee* was founded on an ideology of 'friendship' between partners of different clans, and that these friendships were combined with rivalry between men of the same clan. *Tee* exchanges and warfare were not, he argued, alternative ways of expressing competition or aggression between groups. The *tee*, in fact, might be argued to undermine clan solidarity by pitting rival big-men of the same clan against each other. Feil contrasted this argument with the situation Meggitt (1965) delineated for the Mae Enga, and also with the materials portrayed for the Melpa in *The Rope of Moka* (Strathern 1971 [2007]).

Allies, then, in Feil's model of the Tombema, were individuals linked by the *tee* nexus and motivated by an ideology of friendship. Certainly, in many ways, similarities appear here with the Melpa, but so do differences. *Moka* is also based on an ideology of friendship, *monge* (see Strathern & Stewart 2000a, pp. 21–41; 2000d). Partners were typically of different clans and were swayed by individual discussion and negotiation, even though they were also often related by marriage or kin ties. But in *moka* there was an explicit rule, making it *moka* as opposed to a simple friendly act, of giving more than one had received in a previous round. Repaying debts was not enough to gain prestige. What gave some stability to the process was that most *moka* exchanges took place between allies, either within the wider tribe or with clans in a paired tribe. Alliances, while not permanent, were relatively stable over time. The *moka* chains that emerged in 1964–65 were based on this framework (Strathern 1971 [2007]). The same groups might fight as minor enemies but combined against major enemies. With the Tombema Enga this was not so. While enemies were fixed, allies were not, it seems, and individuals recruited helpers ad hoc in circumstances of warfare, doing so mostly via *tee* partnerships. The clan was the basic fighting unit, as in Hagen, but the frameworks of alliance and exchange were different, if not diametrically opposite. These differences can be expressed as follows:

	Alliances	**Warfare**
Melpa	maintained on a group basis	minor enemies might also be allies against major enemies
Tombema Enga	maintained on an individual basis	no stable alliances, only stable enemies

If Tombema Enga *tee* transactions lacked the systematic Melpa element of increment in the *moka*, this would make another fundamental difference between the two systems, in spite of obvious and great similarities in the processes that constituted *tee* and *moka* transactions as cultural forms of practice.[3]

Similarly, if Tombema allies were recruited on a shifting and individual basis, this makes their system very different from the Melpa, although in both cases the deaths of allies had to be paid for by those who recruited them. In effect, the Tombema pattern shows similarities with the cases of the Huli and the Duna in the matter of alliances and responsibilities for deaths in warfare; while it also shows a pattern of emphasis on elaborate exchanges linking affines as partners across clan boundaries that we find with the Melpa (but apparently without the group significance these exchanges acquired among the Melpa).

We have previously discussed Huli and Duna patterns of warfare (Stewart & Strathern 2000b, pp. 6–20), and we give here some extended excerpts from that discussion, which mainly relates to pre-colonial times as reconstructed from informants' accounts at various times of remove from initial pacification.

Huli warfare

Glasse (1968) bases his account of Huli social structure in general on the parish, which he defines as the largest local political group that could act together against an attack. Parish members, he says, are described as *hamigini*, 'children of brothers', and sections within the parish are called by the same term. These 'children' or 'descendants' of brothers are seen in cognatic terms, but within them agnates may have particular status, as among the Duna (pp. 23–24). Because descent and potential parish membership are traced cognatically and because parishes intermarry, people have claims to membership in more than one parish and can move around. This gives individuals flexibility of choice of residence and the possibility to maintain an interest in several places. It also, as Glasse points out, modifies the solidarity and exclusiveness of any given political grouping. This is a basic point, and one that applies equally to the Duna. Also, when parish members do not fulfil their duties, they may be asked to, or decide to, leave. Glasse also notes a statistical bias towards agnatic membership of the parish, finding that one in five members are agnates, something that in a pure cognatic system would not be expected (p. 35). By the same token, it is obvious that the majority of members are non-agnatic cognates. Glasse found that wide genealogical knowledge tended to correlate with high social status among men, and that such knowledge was used to activate social links (pp. 79–80). Cognatic ties are therefore significant in the overall picture of how social status is generated and maintained, a conclusion that again applies also to the Duna whom we know. This point is further relevant to the discussion of conflict. Cognatic ties give people flexible choices as well as multiple and potentially competing loyalties, obligations and interests which come into play in circumstances of conflict between people. From one point of view, this fact tends to reduce the escalation of conflict since group hostilities are extensively cross-cut by networks of kinship and friendship. In the absence of systematic exchange alliances such as are found among the Melpa of Mount Hagen in the Western Highlands Province, these cognatic networks operate to mitigate enmities and to open pathways to the negotiation of settlements. From another point of view, however, the network of cognatic ties may encourage or precipitate the development of enmities and hostile actions, owing to dissatisfactions and resentments among kin and the possibility of provoking conflict and then fleeing from it in one direction or another by using a ramifying set of kin ties.

Glasse argues that Huli men expected to be warriors and admired most those who were brave and daring, placing a premium on physical action rather than negotiation (p. 87). Further, he argues that men tried to inflict injuries greater than those they suffered, and that chains of counter-vengeance were unending. Allies in fighting also quarrelled about indemnities for deaths. In sum, 'each conflict, however it may be resolved, breeds new problems' (p. 87). These observations fit with the underlying tendencies of the cognatic structures of kinship that we have identified above. Glasse further observes that 'most Huli wars originate not from traditional hostilities between groups but from personal disputes between individuals' (p. 87). This also is a fundamental point. Although parish sections or whole parishes were on occasion drawn into battles, this did not lead to permanent overriding inter-group hostilities. Instead, the individuals recognised as the fight initiators remained responsible for casualties and indemnity payments flowing from these, and they were responsible to the factions and coalitions that gave them support, which included men of groups other than their own. Glasse notes that 'nearly every man nurses a grievance that can precipitate war' (p. 88); such grievances ranged from the murder of a close relative, through failure to meet debts or to pay indemnities (a kind of debt), pig theft, rape and breach of brideprice rules, to the least common category, land encroachment. Huli wars were thus mostly about grievances over wrongs in the interpersonal domain, not about the land of corporate groups. Brideprice distribution disputes mostly occurred *within* the sections of the parish, while failure to indemnify for deaths sparked disputes mostly *between* the sections of the parish. Notable here is the potential for physical conflict within the same parish, but injuries, even killings, within the parish did not necessarily result in retaliatory violence. Glasse records eight cases in which men killed their own wives for adultery or other putative wrongdoing, and none of these killings led to war, although the killer paid damages to his affines in five cases (pp. 89–90). Glasse also records the incidence of warfare. Here, he makes a distinction between minor war (*wai emene*) and major war (*wai timbuni*), but notes that a minor war can easily escalate into a major one. Of 43 cases of warfare, he classifies ten as major and 33 as minor (p. 91). Eight major and 18 minor wars took place between different parish groups (26 out of 43); one major and nine minor wars involved different sections of the same parish (ten out of 43); and one major and six minor wars embroiled members of a single parish section (seven out of 43). While there is less fighting within the section, then, and most wars take place between parishes, it is evident that the parish is by no means a simple unitary group. Its complex internal structure precludes this.

Glasse observes also that kin and affines might often fight on opposed sides in a battle, and if so they tried to protect each other and ask that their relative not be shot, a request that might be respected for the time being but later contravened. The ghosts of those killed were expected to seek vengeance and to exact it if their killer should speak their name (p. 93). This probably acted as a sanction against killing close kin, since their ghosts might in any case be active in sending sickness to the living. However, intra-parish disputes could lead to killing, and a defeated section might flee elsewhere without settling the compensation payments later.

Men of the same parish section as a fight initiator were obliged to assist him, but if he belonged to more than one parish (as was possible under cognatic rules of affiliation) only those co-resident with him were obligated in this way. All others who helped became 'allies on a personal, rather than a regional or group basis' (p. 96). This again is a significant point, indicating how long-term stable enmities between groups as such did not emerge. Initiators were responsible for offering indemnities for deaths and so to bring a war to an end. Here, Glasse notes that 'men of high status often undertake the delicate task of mediation' (p. 97). This observation shows that leadership was not based simply on warriorhood, even though Glasse says that those known for bravery in war were 'most admired'. He also notes that 'important men of the parish are often called on to settle internal disputes in which they are not personally involved' (p. 98). Both observations would appear to relate to men of coordinate status among the Huli to the *kango* among the Duna. Finally, Glasse notes that most wars ended inconclusively (p. 98). This means that there would be a great emphasis on the mediation skills of leaders after a bout of warfare ended. In cases in which mediation was unsuccessful the memories of hostilities would linger and perhaps vengeance would be commuted into sorcery actions (pp. 100–106).

Glasse classifies all payments of compensation as indemnities and divides these into private payments for damages, reparations paid by fight initiators to allies, and payments to enemies (called *wergild* by Glasse). By accepting *wergild* the enemy relinquished the right to take revenge and risked supernatural danger if this rule was not adhered to. We see here the great symbolic significance of wealth payments (p. 114). Wounds had to be compensated for as well as deaths. The initiator and his kin paid pigs to a wounded man, who sacrificed them in hopes of recovering. If his wound healed, his claim was acquitted; if not, he could claim a further payment of up to 15 pigs, which could also be collected by his near kin if he died (see also Glasse 1959).

At payments the donors orated regarding their generosity, while the recipients deprecated the amounts of wealth given and bemoaned 'their inconsolable loss' (p. 119). *Wergild* payments were made to stop a fight escalating or to compensate for killing a kinsperson. It appears that most payments were reparations and *wergild* payments were less frequently made and were smaller in size (p. 124). The major emphasis was therefore on reparations. This fits with the fact that allies might be relied on again, and next time the enemies might be a different set of people. As Glasse points out in his summing up, 'the interplay of vengeance and compensation mobilizes new but temporary combinations of allies and enemies' (p. 132).

Glasse does not say much about the position of women or about women's agency in warfare. His focus is on men. However, he does note that wars could develop from sexual affairs that could be initiated by either men or women or by the theft of pigs by women as well as by men. More male deaths, proportionately, were attributed to warfare than female deaths (p. 98). Glasse reports that a virgin's menstrual blood could be used as an especially potent poison (*tomia*) to kill someone by mixing it into their food. Also, he notes that a woman could use 'blood sorcery' to avenge her brother's death. She could take blood from his wound and mix it with charcoal on her forehead. The killer might inadvertently attempt to court this woman and look into her eyes, in which case the blood was said to kill him. She could also put a drop of the dead man's blood into spring water. If the killer drank the water he would become sick. Or she could dissect the liver and lungs of a pig killed at the brother's funeral feast, causing the killer to suffer internal pains and possibly die (p. 104). Finally, female diviners played an important role in determining whether vengeance should be sought for a killing. The woman sat alone with the corpse at night and sang a spell over it. She then inspected the dead man's penis and determined whether vengeance would be successful; if she felt it would not, she advised acceptance of *wergild* if offered (p. 114).

The Duna case

Almost all of Glasse's major observations regarding warfare among the Huli apply also to the Duna. In particular, Duna wars, or battle sequences, as we may perhaps call them, were precipitated by personal grievances of men who became fight initiators and were responsible subsequently for indemnities. Consequently, major corporate groupings of an enduring kind at the parish level were not organised primarily around warfare or around the payment of compensation over time between the same groups. Each instance of fighting and each compensation case had its specific rationale and constellation of people who were involved (Strathern & Stewart 2000e). Compensation, however, was of prime importance because it was the only way either to make peace or to settle with one's allies. Men who often began fights did not become *kango* on that basis alone. Rather, if they managed to organise the indemnity payments that ensued from the fighting they might become recognised as *kango* over time.

Modjeska (1982, pp. 91–92) provides some related observations here. Fight initiators were called *wei tse* (fight origin/base) and they began fights 'in defence of their interests' or those of their 'lineage' (lineage here equals parish section). They were responsible for compensations, and so warfare was regulated by this consideration. Serious battles might be planned in advance and require the planting of 'war gardens' to support production of pigs that would be needed for indemnities. These required the collaboration and effort of the females in the community to carry out this work. *Damba*, 'blood compensation payments', required 30 or more pigs per death. Modjeska quotes an informant as saying that if a man 'is *wei tse* two or three times, then he is truly a man. That is strength!' (p. 91). Modjeska infers that the war/compensation nexus thus constitutes a focus comparable to the elaborate exchange practices of the Western Highlands societies such as the Melpa. However, he also recognises that people could shift residence easily, so a *wei tse* could not rely on a stable support group. Nor could he, we can add, work within a framework of stable enmities and alliances, as Western Highlands leaders did. Informants also simply stress that the *kango* (*gango* in Modjeska's transcription based on usage in the parish of Horaile) was and is defined by his access to resources or 'wealth', however this was deployed. And although by no means all *kango* were men of speaking ability, nevertheless Modjeska notes that 'there is a strong tendency for wealth, influence in speaking and participation in exchanges and distributions to be associated together' (p. 99). This observation, derived from a statistical analysis of data, coincides with the 'folk models' of people in the Aluni Valley also. The *kango* we know all tend to be prominent in both exchanges and in speaking, and their influence does not appear to have declined because of the cessation of warfare. In the past, their ritual roles were also just as significant as their activities in the arena of warfare, and the expressions they used in their speeches on occasions of compensation payments deeply reflected the ritual structuring of their cultural universe (Strathern 1998). The same conclusion can be drawn from inspection of Goldman's (1983) detailed analyses of speech-making and verbal discourse generally among the Huli of Koroba.

As Glasse's (1968) account of Huli warfare also suggests in a number of places, warfare itself was attended by a considerable number of ritual practices and observances among the Duna. These involved collaboration between *kango* men and others, including ritual bachelors and the practitioners of *ndekao* sorcery; between agnates and non-agnatic cognates of the parish or parish section; and also between the sexes. These forms of collaboration and division of labour reveal a sense of the overall cosmic framework that surrounded warfare and other activities. For example, rituals directed to a forest shrine of the *Timako* spirit were used to build up confidence before going to fight and involved pork sacrifices to sacred stones, presided over by an expert. *Halaka* divination was also employed in the pursuit of victory in battle. It was presided over by unmarried men only, directed by senior bachelors, *uruwali*, who instructed younger men in the art also. A senior *uruwali* would segregate youths in a forest hut away from the houses of women and away from married men. Cutting the leaves of a particular tree (*kuke*) with his teeth, he would test the boys on their ability to say whether someone had travelled out of the group territory or was still there, or on their capacity to find pearl shells or cowries that he had hidden. Youths who succeeded in these tests would be further taught *ndekao* sorcery, in which they would plant their toes firmly pointing towards an enemy area, place a stone between the toes and chant a spell. *Halaka* divination was also supposed to enable the expert to predict who would die and who would survive in a battle. He held the *kuke* leaves in his hand while making his predictions. Clearly, the fight leaders and warriors were beholden to the ritual experts for these services of prediction. *Halaka* men were expected to remain permanently unmarried, and their powers were associated with the forest *Timako* and another spirit being, the *Tsinali*, also belonging to the high forest.

When men went out to fight, the men and women staying at home had to observe certain taboos on what they could eat or touch. While men took their spears, painted their faces and rubbed ashes on themselves, the community women were supportive of the men's activities. The women avoided tying knots with the rope used for making netbags. The sisters and mothers of men involved in fighting were especially vigilant in following a set of taboos that assisted the men in their actions while engaged in combat. During these times they did not cut down trees or break the vines of sweet potato plants by pulling at the tubers attached to the vines. They avoided stepping over or moving about pieces of wood to clear spaces for putting in new gardens. Likewise, they did not remove stones from or dig up the ground to make gardens. If the women at home did not support their men in these ways various unfortunate consequences could occur, for example, the arrow that hit one of their kinsfolk while fighting would break off inside him and cause his death. If, on the other hand, the taboos were followed carefully, it was said that the curers would find the arrow and it would be easy to remove it from any wound that the fighter sustained. If the women decided not to support their men and to break the taboo against tying rope when the men were fighting then the fighters trying to flee from the enemy would find that their legs were 'fastened' or 'tied' and the enemy would catch them and kill them. Likewise, if the women at home broke sweet potato vines, then the arrow lodged in a man's wounded body would break when the curers tried to remove it. And if stones or pieces of wood were turned over, then when a man was shot he too would turn over as he fell and then he would die.

These examples reveal clearly the sense of importance of solidarity and loyalty between men and women during times of fighting. Women could determine if a man were going to live or die through their actions. Female kinsfolk refrained from the usual gardening practices and craft actions that they would normally be involved in when the men were at home. This demonstrated their day-to-day concern for the welfare of the men since their thoughts could be concentrated on the return of the men. Newborn children are carried in netbags, as are many other items. Women often spend time over several months making new netbags for an expected birth. By refraining from this activity they demonstrated the imbalance that the society had been placed in through warfare, without the normal balance of male and female components of activity. The usual activities of production and reproduction were suspended.

The warriors were identified with the trees and stones of their own local territories, on which the women worked to make gardens. For the sick and wounded warrior there was an emphasis on care to be given by his local male kin. He was not to drink water or eat sweet potato for 14 days, a ritually enjoined period of time. His own blood was taken by an expert and rubbed further on the arrow that had caused the injury as a kind of 'food' for it. He could, however, eat sugarcane, ripe *suku* bananas and pork. On the 15th day the taboo on sweet potato consumption was lifted, but the warrior should convalesce further before moving around much because his joints would otherwise crack as he moved over logs and stones in his area.

These taboos that women followed do not seem to be reported from the Huli area, although this does not mean they were necessarily absent there. Regardless of this question, they do reveal a sense of the complementary axis of obligations tying men and women together in warfare as in other aspects of life. Perhaps something of this same sense is conveyed by the Duna folkloric motif that in the past women were the first to possess bows and arrows and later passed these over to men, who thus became the warriors.

Like the Huli, the Duna paid both reparations to allies and direct payments of *wergild* to enemies; but they were probably more concerned with the former than with the latter. Compensatory payments of *wergild* were spoken of as making the fight 'sleep' (*wei wiya*) with the understanding that it might 'wake' again on renewed grounds and allies or helpers would again be needed. Interim payments of pigs were offered to allies (*wei panda*, 'battle fences'), partly for use in sacrifices at funerals, and these were called *heke rowa ita*, 'heavy pole pigs', a phrase describing how such pigs were slung upside down and tied to poles for carrying over to the allies' place. Serious disputes could arise within a parish, resulting in one parish section moving out and affiliating itself elsewhere, leaving its ground unoccupied or else for others to use; but, at least from the accounts we have, these disputes seem to have been less frequent in the Aluni Valley than among the Huli as described by Glasse (1968; see also above). It is not hard to suggest why, since population density among the Huli with whom Glasse worked in the Tari Basin was considerably greater than the density in the Aluni Valley. Hence, disputes over land, for example, would have been less likely to erupt among the Aluni Valley Duna and more easy to settle through relocation or cutting into fresh stands of forest. Given this, less effort was perhaps needed to hold the parishes together internally as solidary groups.

In addition, inter-parish cooperative rituals classified under the headings of *Kira Pulu* or *rindi kiniya* ('straightening the ground') emphasised the necessity for parishes to be at peace internally and with one another in order to renew the earth's fertility, threatened by periods of drought and poor crop yields (Stewart 1998). The *Kira Pulu* cult also brought together male cult members of adjoining parishes in forms of graded cult membership (see Modjeska 1977, 1991; Stewart & Strathern 2002b; Strathern 1995). For example, the parishes of Haiyuwi and Aluni had a joint site for the *Kira* cult at a place on their border called *Kiranda* (*Kira*-house). Inter-parish links of these sorts inhibited the proliferation of hostilities between the parishes and provided an overall ideological framework within which a positive value could be given to peace. While considerations of these kinds do not directly contradict the observations made by Sinclair (1966, p. 135, for example) regarding the readiness of Duna men to enter into fights, they do suggest that the Duna cosmos was not one in which warfare was simply regarded as an activity of the highest value. Rather, we may suggest that competence in fighting was seen as a normal prerequisite for adult males, and prowess in it was certainly esteemed; but the ritual system overall was geared as much to inter-parish peace and the promotion of environmental fertility as to the values of fighting in battle. Sinclair himself notes that compensation payments could be made to avert revenge actions between groups, while applying the term *moga* to these payments (a term that belongs to Hagen, not Duna) (p. 135).

Nevertheless, there is one context today in which some of the 'heroic' qualities of men and women are preserved and extolled: the performance of sung ballads or epics that typically recount the adventures of a *pikono nane*, 'ballad boy', who is involved in fighting battles against *auwape*, cannibal giants who inhabited the Duna area before humans moved into the area. Humans had to defeat the *auwape* in battle or trick them into entering a ceremonial house and then burn them alive inside it, in order to rid the land of the giants and make it safe for humans to live in. The *pikono nane* are assisted in their actions by both human women and spirit women who provide knowledge of how to defeat enemies. *Pikono* are eloquent expositions of bravery and adventure that have an extensive vocabulary of their own. They are sung by specialists, who are supposed to receive their inspiration for storytelling and song from the *Payame Ima* female spirit. As with all repertoires of expression that depend on an intimate and intensive knowledge of local language and history, by no means everyone can be considered an 'expert' on *pikono* merely because he or she happens to have been brought up in the area where such repertoires have developed and are performed. Already by the 1990s it was apparent in one part of the Duna area, Aluni, that younger men, who were just trying to begin to exercise their skills at *pikono*, were lacking in some of the knowledge that had underpinned the performances of established experts. In each case, to assess a person's knowledge, one would have to find out something of their biography and experience, whether they had heard *pikono*, how often, where, sung by whom, and whether they had asked questions. Certainly, not every young man in Aluni was an expert in this genre. Indeed, only a very small minority held this knowledge, largely in cases in which they themselves were performers. The singers narrate them in men's houses at night, and they are highly popular, preserving a mixture of values from the past relating to warriorhood, the process of finding a bride, travels through high forest areas and advice or assistance from the *Payame Ima* herself. The *pikono nane* is himself a creature of the forest, not yet married, representing fledgling manhood in the making. *Pikono* ballads are therefore repositories of the values that informed pre-colonial life, as well as acquiring a recent modern value in terms of the people's renewed interests in environmental themes that link them to the *Payame Ima*. This spirit is, for example, seen as a custodian of the

Strickland River, into which tailings from the Porgera gold mine have been introduced, putatively causing environmental effects and disturbing the spirit woman (see further Stewart & Strathern 2002c, 2005a). Compensation speeches are also rich repositories of cultural themes. The same is eminently true of the ceremonial speeches called *el ik*, 'arrow-talk', made on exchange occasions among the Melpa people of the Western Highlands Province, and no compensation event can be effective without these elaborate, skilful speeches.

The Pangia Case

If we now turn to the Wiru speakers of Pangia in the Southern Highlands Province, we find some further transformations of pattern. Wiru social structure bears witness both to processes of warfare and the consequent scattering of parts of groups over the landscape and to principles of locality that were used to identify 'big places' (*tumbea ta*) with large named categories of persons that claimed a predominant position within these places. These named categories have origin stories that tell a narrative of migrations and fighting, leading to their establishment in a 'big place' of their own. For one part of the Wiru-speaking area, centred on the colonially named 'village' of Tunda, the relevant category name is Peri (see, for example, Stewart & Strathern 2001c; Strathern 1984, pp. 9–15; Strathern & Stewart 1999d, 2000g); for another, with a somewhat different history, centred on the place Takuru, it is Koliri (see, for example, Clark 2000, pp. 18–22). Peri and Koliri, in turn, are two category names among many others that are recognised widely in the Wiru area as the 'place-root-men', *tapinango*, associated with specific localities. Implicitly, such categories are conceived of as agnatic in character, stressing continuity through males. But they are also recognised as having pockets of members dispersed in numbers of places other than those where they are *tapinango*. Such dispersals have resulted from internal quarrels, misfortunes, sorcery suspicions, fighting, disputes over adultery or thefts of pigs, within the 'large places' where the group's men have consolidated themselves over time. Origin stories also already explain the splitting off of group splinters to different places along their migration tracks. Indeed, one classic origin place is north of the Wiru area, around Lake Mbuna in Ialibu, and a stereotypical reason given for the initial migration itself is that it began over the 'stomach of a cassowary'. A cassowary was sacrificed and cooked and some 'brothers' refused to share its meat with other brothers, and so the disgruntled ones split off and headed south to the Wiru area, according to the narrative. Failure to share meat is tantamount to moral treachery or political disavowal of solidarity, with schismatic results. These narratives reflect the volatile and fissile character of micro-political relations within parts of the large named categories located in the same place. For convenience, and in accord with usages already established, we may call the 'large places' districts and the large named categories 'phratries'. (See Clark 2000, pp. 19–22 on cassowary meat in origin stories; Strathern 1984, p. 13 on phratry as a term. Districts is a term borrowed from Eastern Highlands ethnography and refers to the fact that a 'large place' contains a number of 'small places', *dendea ta*, settlement places in which particular clusters of people traditionally lived.)

Districts were composed of clusters of groups variously related to the dominant phratry name within them. Unlike the Melpa clan, the district in Pangia was not an exogamous group as such. In this regard it was similar to the Duna *rindi* or parish, as we have called it (Strathern & Stewart 2004b, pp. 10, 26–29). Intermarriage took place among the subgroups within the parish, including those who regarded themselves as linked by descent to the origins of the dominant phratry. With intermarriage went some strengthening of inter-family ties, but also the possibility of dissension and disputes, bringing centrifugal tendencies to the local groups. These tendencies were in part checked by ritual institutions centred on the places of spirit propitiation and celebration of ritual power that took place in the *tumbea ta* cult areas. Male ancestral spirits were approached with sacrifices at the *tapa yapu*, a conical-roofed house where bones of ancestors were kept. In the same general area pigs were regularly killed for the *timbu* spirit and their bones hung on a central pole in the *timbu* house. A special cordyline was planted in the middle of the ritual arena, called a *kendo*. When enemies attacked this area, they would burn houses around it and cut down the *kendo*, as a mark of their temporary dominance. Ritual practices maintained the solidarity and centripetal forces in the small places around the big place. Concomitantly, these practices were targeted by enemies bent on humbling and enfeebling their foes. In the big place Tunda, what solidarity the community could muster was done in the name of the Peri, rhetorically conceived of as an agnatic group of males.

Intermarriage patterns in Pangia, at least in two areas originally studied intensively, Tunda and Takuru, showed a greater fluidity than among the Kawelka studied in the Hagen area in the 1960s. Marriage patterns in Pangia were more diffuse, with a greater spread of marriages contracted with groups that were enemies. There was no systematic tying in of marriage patterns with exchanges or with political blocs. At pig festivals, when large numbers of pigs were killed and their meat distributed to guests, many individual gifts were made to in-laws and maternal kin coming from a wide array of groups in the Wiru area. Andrew Strathern (1978) first identified this pattern for the Tunda area during fieldwork in 1967 and subsequently. Jeffrey Clark (1985), however, who studied Takuru in 1980–82, interpreted his data on Koliri intermarriage patterns rather differently, arguing that there was considerable marriage within a small set of allies on one hand and, by contrast, a bigger set of diverse 'neutrals', whether from nearby or further away. He was inclined to equate neutrals with allies, because neutrals were seen as 'friendly'. He also stressed that marriages with allies were concentrated on three groups, and a majority on a single group, at the place Poloko (p. 68). However, it was also the case that a large number of marriages were with enemies (about a quarter of the total), distributed among some 15 groups. The greatest number of marriages with any one place was indeed with an ally, Poloko; but there was a great fan of marriages spreading widely around covering neutrals and enemies. In constructing his table, Clark followed a format adopted by Strathern (1978), and his first observation was how closely the Takuru statistics followed those for Tunda, at least in broad terms.

Looking at those data again, the similarities in pattern are indeed striking, as are also the different interpretive spins put on the data. It seems that the discrepancies in interpretation can be resolved as follows: in comparison with the Melpa patterns, there is indeed no clear overall correlation between marriage patterns, gift exchange and alliance. The Pangia pattern of warfare was less segmentary than among the Melpa. It was, instead, radial (a term that Clark (1985) adopted from Strathern (1968)).

At a cost of some simplification of the practical complexities and vicissitudes of historical processes, we can set up a model contrast between radial and segmentary patterns of warfare and intermarriage. In a radial pattern, fight initiators from a particular group or subgroup would call upon assistance along certain lines from a wide number of places, both nearby and distant. The lines involved would be, on one hand, affinal ties and, on the other, named category ties. Thus, for example, if the fight initiators were of the Koliri category, they might be able to recruit help from other Koliri men living in different places where they had settled or dispersed to in their historical tracks or pathways of settlement. They could also call on some help on individual bases from a diverse set of groups based on their own marriages or those of their sisters. The temporary coalition or network assembled in this way would have no long-term stability, but it would pull together people from a whole set of areas around the initiators of the fight. After the conclusion of a period of fighting, it would dissolve. In this sense, the build-up of powerful coalitions would be inhibited; but conflicts based on demands for compensation over deaths would potentially cause dissension and violence within the erstwhile coalitions themselves (as happened also among the Huli, according to Glasse (1968)).

In a segmentary model, the pattern is quite different. In this, there would be in principle an ordered form of escalation, as well as limitation, of conflict along segmentary lines. The segments would be defined by a combination of descent and locality, and typically marriages between segments would be concentrated and would lead to intensive exchanges, including compensation payments following deaths in fighting.

As we have noted, the Pangia data point in the direction of the radial model, while the Melpa (or Hagen) data point in the direction of the segmentary model. The implications for peace-making are clear. Both an ordered escalation of conflict and an ordered making of peace are facilitated by the segmentary model. In the radial model a more volatile and 'chaotic' set of possibilities emerges, leading to a more fragmented and endemic form of fighting and group dispersals, as well as inherent limitations on the build-up of power.

These possibilities would be realised most clearly in pre-pacification contexts. After colonial pacification and post-colonial changes further perturbatory patterns could emerge. With the segmentary structures greater escalations or levels of conflict could emerge, making settlements of conflict harder. With the radial pattern, initial pacification would be easier, but the continued chances of small-scale conflicts would be high and might be fuelled by exacerbating circumstances, such as disputes over land or over new resources, or disputes arising out of sexual predations or marital breakdowns. In either case both positive and negative possibilities are thus apparent for the maintenance or establishment of peace. In the periods of enforced colonial pacification we find, in either case, the most propitious elements came into play for the establishment of peace through exchanges. Thus, in the 1960s in both Pangia and Mount Hagen, in spite of their different historical circumstances, there were the most obvious manifestations of peace-making through exchanges based initially on an ideology of compensation. At the same time it is true that in the Pangia area, where social change was less rapid than in Hagen, there was a period of minor efflorescence in festivals of exchange that took place after the departure of the 'kiaps', or expatriate government officers, and a revival of practices of self-decoration and ambitious activities by big-men in exchanges of pearl shells (Strathern 1984, pp. 98–99). But this expansion was in turn overtaken later by renewed problems of conflict and the incursions of criminal gangs of youths.

It is important to note here, as with all of our examples, that peace-making is an outcome of multiple factors. Colonial pacification in the Highlands provided leaders with a historical opportunity to pursue their pre-existing aims in a new context. With the halting of overt hostilities and killings between groups, leaders could expand marital alliances and networks of exchange. The synergistic outcome of enforced change and free improvisation was the efflorescence of exchange occasions. Colonial force was transmuted into self-managed ritual competition. But this period of self-management was itself a hostage to further historical forces. In particular, it depended on the idea of governmental force as its backstop, and expatriate field officers, through their patrols, gave the impression to local people that the government was powerful and in control. The removal of these colonial outsiders, the diminution in field patrols, and the whole ideology of self-government that replaced what we might call the colonial mirage, led in effect to a weakening of people's fears of government power. This, coupled with numerous other factors of change, including urban movements, cash-cropping, youthful alienation and the growth of crime and 'raskol' activity, led quickly enough to a host of new problems and cumulative deaths and conflicts on a greater scale than heretofore. Local-level rituals were now less able to cope with these new circumstances, although the Highlanders struggled hard to do so. Further complicating their efforts were all the introductions of the apparatus of 'democratic' elections that were enjoined on the Australian Administration by its international overseers the United Nations, requiring a raft of new institutions leading up to political independence from Australia.

In the next chapter we consider the relatively benign early context in which these elections began, and how problems later emerged precisely because of changes in scale and changes in the movements of people in vehicles between areas that became a part of the new, 'modern' ways of living. 'Modernity', projected as a horizon of benefit, also became a burden.

CHAPTER 4

Escalations and complexities: early elections

Elections were something entirely new for the Mount Hagen people. They were introduced by the Australian Administration as a part of a general program of political development intended to move Papua New Guinea towards Self-Government and later Independence. Highlands areas were pushed fast into this whole process, because colonial control came late to them by comparison with coastal regions, and international pressure was placed on Australia to hasten the process of self-determination. Clan politics in Hagen were based on consensus and agreed patterns of activity, with leadership exercised through oratory and eminence in exchanges by big-men rather than through any form of chiefship and hierarchical control. Inter-tribal relations were governed by the enmities and alliances that we examined in detail in Chapters 2 and 3, including the significance of sorcery suspicions. The new political processes did not replace or obliterate these earlier established patterns. They merely overlaid them with a wider scale of decision-making and with a more hierarchical form of leadership. Local Government Council elections preceded the national-level elections and were intended to provide the training ground for the understanding and use of voting, debating, majority decision, budgets, road-building, and senses of unity not encompassed in the clan-tribal complex of affairs. While Hageners showed only a relatively lukewarm response to Council elections, the Council areas became more politically relevant when national electorates were established and Councils became components of electorates that combined many clan and tribal groups together. Individual Councillors generally represented groups that were clans or small combinations of clans, but Councils as a whole comprised an inter-tribal mix of former enemies and allies in warfare. When two Councils were combined into a single electorate, the problems that emerged from this amalgamation of distinct groups were further compounded. In this chapter we look in some detail at an early phase of this pre-Independence Administration-engineered political experimentation, seeing within it some seeds of later problems of peace-making between groups, and reasons for modifying the make-up of the artificial units that were initially set up. The electorate involved was the amalgamated electorate of Dei Council (the subsequent focus of long-term fieldwork) and the neighbouring Mul Council, and the election was the 1968 election for the national-level House of Assembly that was set up as a forerunner to a fully independent Parliament that emerged in 1975 after Self-Government in 1973.[1]

We begin the account with some background information.

The area

The electorate combined two Council areas, Dei and Mul, founded in 1963 and 1964 respectively. These two areas, dominated by mountain ridges and slopes, along which most of their people live, lie to the north and west of Hagen town. The two populations meet in a stretch of plain that opens in the east to the Wahgi and in the west to the Baiyer Valley. The two Mul Council candidates, Pu— and M—, both came from this intermediate plains area. The four Dei candidates, P—, W—, E— and Pi—, were from places along the Wahgi–Sepik divide that runs through their Council. Dei is much larger than Mul and had a lower population density at this time: 211.2 square miles with a gross density of 67.81 per square mile, compared with 52.3 square miles and a density of 268.31. Moreover, Dei splits into a larger number of tribes, and its dominant tribes are smaller than the two largest ones in Mul. It is not surprising, then, that Dei produced more candidates and showed less political unity than Mul in the election. The total populations of the areas were similar: in 1964 Mul had 14,033 people, Dei 14,323. Dei was later augmented by the admission of some small tribes from the Jimmi Valley, whose members share the language (Melpa) of all the Dei speakers and those of Mul who live nearest to them. The other Mul groups speak Temboka, a related dialect of the Hagen language; but Melpa is widely understood, even by those who do not speak it as their first dialect. Melpa is also spoken by many of the tribes near to Hagen town; Temboka is prevalent in the Nebilyer Valley to the south-east of Mul.

The Councils were composed from a number of colonial census divisions: the bulk of Mul from the Western division, with a few groups of the Nebilyer, Baiyer, North-West Wahgi and Central divisions, and most of Dei from the North-West Wahgi with several groups from the Baiyer division. The aim of the Administration was to produce units based on the groups themselves and not simply on rough geographical areas. For example, in Dei, the Kawelka, from the Baiyer division, were included, as their closest alliance is with the Tipuka to their east in the North-West Wahgi. One clan of the Remndi tribe decided, after an internal struggle, to join Dei Council: perhaps 20 years previously one of their men had been killed by a neighbouring Remndi clan, and they had migrated away from the main bloc of their tribe in protest at this. The Mul candidates were actually both from this same section of the Remndi, divided between the two Councils. This is a significant point for political analysis. While the Dei candidates all belonged to a central bloc of the Dei area, the Mul candidates were interstitial, with some claims to affiliation with Dei based on historical vicissitudes within their own tribe. One of them (M—) was able to capitalise on this seeming marginality of affiliation and turn it into political success. As a candidate with dual or mediating status, he was also in a position that corresponded to intermediaries in peace-making processes.

When the Councils were proclaimed, expatriate missions and plantation owners were already established there. In Dei, 4,177 acres had been alienated to eight Australian planters and to the Lutheran Mission; in Mul only 211.7 acres to a single planter and both the Lutheran and the Catholic missions. Mul had 14 trade stores, two native-owned, and Dei eight, all owned by expatriates. Later, a tea plantation was started in Mul; in Dei, indigenous-owned trade stores proliferated and Highlanders from Chimbu and Wabag (neighbouring Provinces) settled on blocks intended for tea at the far eastern end of the Council area. Plantations and missions all employed a handful of expatriates and indigenous craftsmen, together with batches of labourers, often from outside the Hagen language area. The Administration estimated that from all sources the indigenous people had a total income of Australian £16,694 per annum in Mul, £21,803 in Dei.[2] The highest single source of income in Dei was casual day labour on the numerous plantations; in Mul, the sale of coffee to the Hagen Kofi factory. Mul had a better network of secondary roads than Dei. Buyers of coffee, vegetables and passionfruit in Dei multiplied after roads were improved.

The social structure of the two areas is broadly the same. Briefly, to recapitulate here, it is based on named tribes, segmented into territorial, exogamous clans. Tribes are regularly paired or loosely linked by origin myths, as are their constituent clans. Paired clans, and sometimes tribes, are close allies. All the formal units have some variety of patrilineal ideology, applied more strongly to dogmas of group unity than to processes of group affiliation. Warfare was frequent in the past. Enemies were either major traditional enemies, or minor ones, who against major enemies became allies. Intermarriage and ceremonial exchange of valuables tends still today to be maximal among minor enemies and allies. There is a strong ethic of compensating these for deaths. Internally, groups were, and are, led by big-men, self-made orators, polygynists, financiers, adjudicaters and planners, whose influence can increase or accentuate either opposition or friendly ties between groups. Both groups and individuals compete for status, and the results show in the range of status variations within clans. In four clans of Dei Council in 1964–65, the big-men comprised 13 per cent of the adult males; 59 per cent were 'ordinary men', and 28 per cent men of lower status (men without a wife or who did not participate in exchange activities). Groups also varied in size. In Dei, the range of population sizes of tribes in the mid-1960s was 73 to 2,813, with an average of 903; for Mul, it is harder to give comparable figures, since there were more groups there that are attached as refugees to the larger groups, or are associated closely with these. Omitting the two smallest of these refugee groups, we obtain a range of 264 to 5,414 and an average of 1,386.

The traditional political system, then, is competitive and segmentary at all levels, and leadership depends on achievement. The situation creates problems for candidates seeking election to the House of Assembly (since 1975, the national Parliament): they must prove themselves by their own efforts and try to overcome potential segmentary opposition. One solution tried in 1968 was to depend on the Councillors, who represent particular clans.

The two major developments in the areas had been the stopping of warfare, accompanied by the beginnings of Administration censussing, from 1944 onwards, and the foundation of the Councils in 1963–64, with a resulting emphasis on local economic and political change. Both developments (according to the Administration) were welcomed by the people, who were anxious not to fall behind the Central Hagen groups living to their south, which had experienced changes earlier. The mid-1940s to 1960 were marked by the extension of censussing, the appointment of luluais and tultuls as local officials, major road-building works and the settlement of missionaries and planters. In Dei, the Kotna Lutheran Mission built a school and hospital as well as a mission centre. The year 1960 up to the foundation of Councils saw the introduction of Administration aid posts for health, plans for primary schools and the consolidation of coffee-planting that had begun earlier. All these processes continued, but their tempo increased: Council tax enabled the Councils to finance projects and required each adult person to find some means of obtaining cash. In Dei, the people wished to pay a high tax, which could be devoted to buying machines for public works, and so free them to see to their own 'business'. The House of Assembly Member should help them, they said, by bringing them more business and more bulldozers.

Councillors had rapidly in practice become important local figures, even if there was not much interest shown in the whole process of getting them elected. Their position differed from that of the traditional big-men in that the people could formally elect and depose them and they were linked to the 'new order' of things dating from the initial intrusion by outsiders into the Highlanders' world. Like the old-style luluais and tultuls (who, however, were appointed by the colonial Administration, not elected by the people), they partly represented government authority and plans to their clans, but unlike them they depended on the people for their office. This dual source of authority made their position ambiguous. Only if a Councillor was also a big-man or could show the qualities of one was he likely to succeed in the new office. In other words, the new system at this time worked only by incorporating the processes of the old system into itself via the personnel inducted into it.

Clans thus had more formally established heads than before. Moreover, they were expected to cooperate in larger units than before – to accept, for example, planning for the whole of their Council area. In practice, group competitiveness survived, and Council unity showed most strongly only in segmentary situations. The election was precisely such a situation, with its division between Mul and Dei. Indeed, the implications of this crucial point were shown even more clearly in the aftermath of the 1968 events. The segmentary principle proved durable and applicable even outside of the realm of kinship and descent within which it had been historically forged.

Political change

There was little knowledge of, or interest in, the details of the House of Assembly's functions in 1968, or even the fact that it was composed of representatives from all over Papua and New Guinea. Only one of the candidates, P—, was able to compare it to the Canberra Parliament, which he had seen on an educational visit in 1967; and he was eager to compare this with his own work as a Councillor and make this a reason for feeling that he should stand for election. The more common view, promulgated in candidates' speeches and proffered as a description by others, had a more mythological ring: 'the House of Assembly is a strong place, made of bricks and cement, and only a strong man, made like a pickaxe and a crowbar, can break into it and bring back money and business to us.' The implication is that the House of Assembly is an arcane place, from which advantages can be gained only with difficulty – they are 'buried' deep. Moreover, one candidate, W—, emphasised that the House was filled with strong (= old or powerful) 'Masters' (expatriates) with bald heads, ties and spectacles, and only a very brave man, who was unashamed, would speak up to them. This candidate's policy was also identical to that of the others, but stated more bluntly in his speeches:

> The Member must get up and say: 'I am the Member for Mul–Dei in the Western Highlands, and I have come to speak to you, the white man's government [this reveals W—'s view of who held the power]. You, Government, must give a great deal of money to my area, I have many people and we haven't enough money. Also you, the Government, must give plenty of bulldozers so that my people no longer have hard work and injure themselves on the roads, but can work at their own business instead. We want to give up government work [unpaid community work on road maintenance] and see to our business only.

This emphasis on what the Member of the House of Assembly, or MHA, could obtain for his area by negotiating with 'the white men' was agreed to take precedence over other criteria. Thus, the Member, it was thought, would have to be both strong and knowledgeable about the white man's world. Hence, only youngish candidates, with years of experience in some sector of this world, would be fit for the job. The MHA's leadership qualities were not formally stressed; it was his forcefulness as a negotiator that was considered important. It seems, then, that the people, including the Councillors, saw him as someone who would bypass the Kiap, or locally based expatriate government officer, who to date had held a crucial position in relation to the allocation of government money, and obtain things directly for them. His potential role as a 'boss' was hardly mentioned (whereas in 1964 it was prominent). Indeed, the candidates were at pains to declare that they would be like the servants (*kintmant*) of the people, like low-status men who fetch greens when big-men are cooking pigs, that they would 'carry the talk' of the people to the capital city, Port Moresby, and bring back work for them, and so on.

There remained some doubts in the electors' minds. An alternative model for the Member was that he should be like a 'good big-man', that is, one who was generous and who adjudicated fairly in disputes; or at least that he should be free of despotic tendencies, since clearly he would be like a Kiap as well as like a Councillor. At an early stage (September–October 1967) there were fears among the Kawelka, paired allies of the Tipuka, that one of the candidates would be too overbearing if he became an MHA. Some professed to prefer the Lutheran Mission candidate, E—, either because he could write and understand English, or because he would behave with moderation.

Doubts of these kinds were suppressed by the time the election was imminent, from mid-January 1968. For example, P—'s potential supporters then realised more sharply what the opposition was, who the candidates from Mul were, and they were trying to persuade as many groups as possible to follow P—. P— himself had returned from Australia and impressed everyone with his lectures on what he had seen there. In particular, the conflict was now seen in terms of which Council area would 'win'. P—'s supporters thought he was the only Dei candidate with a chance of winning.

Constituents had clear ideas of both political and economic change since 1964. They felt they now had to work much harder than before, to find money for taxes. Each man must have a business. No-one could even walk up and down the road without having a financial purpose. Politically, the change came in realising what the MHA could do for them. More positive improvements in 'business' were now wanted. The issue of Self-Government or Independence was not very widely discussed, though it exercised the candidates themselves a good deal, and a 'hard line' against it being introduced for the time being was developed.

Internally, certain issues had been perpetually discussed since 1964, and others were becoming exacerbated. For example, Council rulings over the size of bridewealth payments for divorcées as well as young girls were constantly debated. Older Councillors tried to retain payments, while 'progressives' such as P— were regarded as trying to abolish them. There were rumours also that soon all land boundaries between groups were to be marked, and certain enclave or ex-refugee groups that had permissive residency with larger groups might have to move. The notion of rent for the use of land and of tradestores was introduced and complicated this issue; but no conflicts on a group scale were begun. These internal problems were not felt to be essentially the concern of the Member, and were temporarily in the background during the election. Only P— took an anti-bridewealth stand as part of his platform, and he implied that this was a logical concomitant of being pro-business, since Councillors should not have to waste time on courts over women, and if bridewealth were abolished there would be no courts. Arguments of this kind later simply lapsed, and bridewealth practices continued.

Political and electoral education

One of the candidates in the Regional electorate, J— C—, remarked at an election meeting in Dei how much more informed, interested and wary the people were than they had been in 1964. This was more because of their experience of what their Members had done or not done since then than because of specific education through local government. Local Councils were seen as one means of obtaining advantages for one's area and working to change it. Members were seen as another means.

Few people had difficulty in understanding the procedures of voting, even of listing a number of candidates in order of preference, although the precise purpose of this might elude them. There were stock jokes, of course: about the woman who gave the candidate's name to the name-clerk instead of her father's; or, when asked by the Kiap for the candidate's name with the words 'Who is your man?', gave her husband's name; or about the man who did not know that he had to drop his ballot paper into a box and walked away with it folded in his wallet. But these were jokes simply because they were exceptions, told to highlight the implied 'modernity' of those who told them.

In Dei, however, this knowledge was not due to practice at Council elections, which remained different from those for the House of Assembly. Council elections were still a matter for open demonstrations of group opinion to the Kiap. They were decided by a show of hands. In 1964, at least, most decisions were unanimous, and attempts were made to achieve consensus before the vote-taking in those cases in which there was some internal difference of opinion. The elections of the Council President and Vice-President were also taken by an open show of hands by Councillors (who were used to the formal process of majority decision-taking).

Consensus operated with less certainty and less formality in the House of Assembly elections. In many cases groups held meetings, led by Councillors and big-men, shortly before the elections, to decide whom they would vote for. But they specifically could not demonstrate their consensus in action; nor could they be sure it would succeed, that is, that their candidate would win. Moreover, leaders could not be sure that each person would vote as 'agreed'; and the whole decision was modified by the possibility of giving variant preferences. Formally, the electoral process was the very antithesis of the Council voting, and everyone knew that 'it was up to each person to decide for himself, that Councillors were not to tell people how to vote, and that voting was a secret matter'. In practice, however, group decisions were still made and probably acted on in many cases as far as the first and second preference votes were concerned; and Councillors briefly reminded their people of these decisions just before voting began.

At one place in Dei, Ambukla (Ambugga), for example, the Council Adviser made a long speech on 5 February 1968, and there were election speeches at two other places that same day. At his own place, P— repeated much of what the Kiap said at Ambukla.

The Adviser explained carefully the distinction between the Open and the Regional electorates, named the candidates, and said that preference votes should be given to all of them in order by each elector. Then in case their first choice did not win, perhaps their second or third choice would do so. In Wabag (west of Hagen), the Adviser said, there was no election, because the people agreed that Tei Abal was good, but here in Mul–Dei six men were standing in the Open and only one could win. The people must think who would be good at making the right kind of talk, who would work properly with Australia and would make good laws. He outlined his election patrol, and went on to emphasise that voting was not compulsory by law, but if they thought about their country they would vote. It did not matter where they voted, or whether they remembered all the candidates, but they could vote only once and only if they were 21 years old or older. He explained who could count the votes, where, and how preferences would be allotted. He suggested they should vote because otherwise a good man might be defeated by a bad one. Each man should think for himself. He, the Kiap, would write the votes, but would not notice how each individual voted. The election was to help Papua New Guinea, 'since there must be a man to "boss" this place, to look after work and law, to decide things, to apportion money, to divide out work to the men. The Member of the House of Assembly does this'. He stressed that all depended on the people themselves. In some countries, House of Assembly Members were appointed by the Government 'headmen' themselves, 'but here you people are the bosses, it is you who decide who will boss you. You people must look after government carefully'. He made a pyramid with two sticks, and explained that at the bottom were the people, in the middle above them were all the officers of the Government, and at the very top was the House of Assembly.[3] Australia, however, was still in control and debated things with the House of Assembly, because Self-Government and Independence had not come yet. But all progress for the future must come from the people: they must make use of their ground, work at business and ask their Member of the House of Assembly for things.

At a number of crucial points, the interpreter failed to put the Adviser's full message across, and at others he altered it slightly. For instance, the Adviser's sentence (spoken in Tok Pisin) 'Now I will tell you who is standing and how to vote' was rendered as 'Now as you do not know who will win in this election I will tell you, and if you are not clear you can ask me again'. His statement that only persons of 21 years of age or above could vote was given a more ambiguous translation. His explanation of preference voting and vote-counting was not translated. And his discussion of relations between the House of Assembly and the Australian Administration was largely curtailed. The Adviser's educational points here seem to be twofold. He is trying to explain the responsibilities of electors in a democratic system. The electors hold the power to put persons in office, and these then have power to direct the people's affairs. So elections are crucial occasions. What is obscure in his account is the relationship between the District Administration and the MHA. He places the House of Assembly above the 'workers for the Government' in his pyramid; and his account of the MHA's functions seems reminiscent of those of himself as Council Adviser. Neither of these two points seemed wholly realistic at the time. The House of Assembly at this time was not clearly above the Administration but contraposed to it; and the Member could not be in his constituency as often as, or act as an overseer as much as, the Council Adviser himself did.

Moreover, the Adviser's position was radically different from that of the Member for he was not elected from below but appointed from above.

Such a simplified account of political structure is indicative of the ambiguities created by the fostering of democratic government within the framework of paternalistic administration. Nevertheless, the Administration was committed to its own gradual abolition, and at the Local Council level much was done to make Councillors accustomed to running their affairs and taking decisions on area development: for example, whether to help mission schools with grants from Council tax money. Opposition to the increasing importance of Councils and to the potential political force of the House of Assembly came from expatriate planters, who depended on casual labour for their coffee-picking, and had to pay more as the people became more demanding. This embarrassed the Administration personnel, for socially and culturally they were linked with the settlers, but politically they were committed to pursuing their own line. One 'solution' was to make sure 'progress' was not too fast. Another was to diversify into the production of tea, which required much greater capital than coffee and seemed to make expatriate land-based companies indispensable. Yet another (available at this early stage of political change but not later when politicians had to be citizens of the new independent state) was for expatriates to stand for the House of Assembly, and at a lower level to participate in Council work. At either level, only if they had something to offer could they succeed, and the people saw this under the heading of business advice and guarantees.

Mul–Dei

The major important lines of cleavage within the electorate, as far as the Open election was concerned, were the division between the two Councils, and, within each Council, tribal divisions. The clan is the unit within which consensus decisions are usually taken, but unless there were two candidates from one tribe such decisions could readily be extrapolated to the tribal level. Tribes linked by alliances could not necessarily be expected to vote together, but the preference system would allow them to give 'second votes' to each other's candidates. In addition, Dei Council divides into wards, and one ward, at least, coincided with the likely sphere of a single candidate, W—: the 'Mala road' ward. This ward, dominated by W—'s tribe, the Kendipi, apparently voted for the expatriate planter Ian Parsons in 1964, whereas most of those in what became Tiki road ward voted for Kaibelt under P—'s persuasion. One of the Mala Councillors also stood for higher tax rates in 1968, in competition with the Tiki road groups, which probably had less access to cash income at this time.

In Dei Council, the Lutheran Mission predominated; in Mul, there was a more equal division between the Lutherans and the Catholics. However, it is doubtful whether mission affiliation was a basis for political action by the Mul candidates, since neither was baptised (and both were polygynists, a practice not permitted to those baptised as Christians). Moreover, even E—, the Dei mission candidate, although he was endorsed by the mission congregation, did not specifically take his mission status as part of his platform. However, his steady minority 'scoring' in each Dei ballot box up to the last two does suggest that Christians voted for him.

In Mul, since the two candidates came from a single lineage in a fringe tribe, it was by no means obvious how the two dominant tribes, Kumndi and Nengka, would vote. Only the Mundika and Mile tribes speak predominantly the Temboka dialect as contrasted with the Melpa spoken universally in Dei, and language affiliation did not appear to have been made a political issue.

The Mul–Dei opposition needs more treatment, particularly because of its later importance. A merger of the two Councils was envisaged by the Administration from the beginning, but not much welcomed in Dei. In April 1967, Kum, a Councillor of Dei, asked at a meeting whether the merger was to take place. The Assistant District Commissioner Mr Littler replied that this would be a decision for the people and the MHA. P— claimed Mul had already gone behind their backs in refusing to set up a joint aid post at Koipke (Koibuga, the place of the two Mul candidates, P— and M—).[4] In August, P— said that Dei and Mul should not join for two years, to allow them to complete existing works projects (including an elaborate permanent Council house at Dei). He was clearly opposed in principle to such a merger, which had no basis in existing social relations, perhaps also because it might reduce his own political opportunities.

Then, on 8 October, a Nengka tribesman driver from Mul was attacked near the Lutheran Mission station Kotna in Dei by clansmen of a Minembi Yelipi man whom he had hit through careless driving. The Nengka man afterwards died from head wounds in Hagen hospital. Election nominations were not clearly established at this time. P— was away in Australia.

At once, the whole Council was in a state of crisis. Three separate rumours circulated, to effect that Dei men (not just Minembi tribesmen) had been killed in revenge. The Nengka had put the body of the driver on a *paka*, or ceremonial platform, and were making emotional funeral speeches (traditional signs of intention to take revenge actions). The Dei 'Kiap' (Council Adviser) forbade cars from Dei to go either to Hagen town or to Mul. Labourers working outside of Dei at Banz returned home as a precaution against violence. On 13 October most of the Dei Councillors met and after a day of speeches found that all were agreed that the Council as a whole must raise a sum of money, and the clan of the killers should raise pigs and shells also, for a death-compensation payment. Councillors of small and fringe groups affirmed their allegiance, and all agreed that unless this were done the election would be ruined. Payments were raised hurriedly, and when P— returned they were handed over. The event had its results in the election. Despite many formal protestations that the old division between the Councils was to be ended, Dei candidates were still afraid to do individual canvassing in Mul. P—, in particular, professed fear, and would not go to Mul at all except after the main campaign was over, and in a private vehicle. After the initial period of shame at the Nengka man's death, the Dei Councillors returned to their hope that a Dei man would win the election and the Councils would not join. We see here all the seeds of later political disturbances and problems of peace-making in the area, induced by the intersection of new scales of political process with the movements of people in vehicles and entrenched ideas about revenge and compensation. Most remarkably, we see how a whole Council area mobilised itself to deal with a crisis emerging from an election situation.

This issue, although not often discussed during the election period, was really more significant than others, but many other issues were superficially more prominent and mentioned regularly as *wari* (worries – a word introduced in 1965). The potential future of the political system was shelved by all the candidates, whether in the Open or the Regional, although each probably held slightly varying ambitions with regard to it. Everyone agreed that Self-Government could come only when the people 'understood law and business' sufficiently, that is, when enough children had been put through school and the income from agriculture and forestry was greater. Of the Open candidates, only M— had a vision of what Self-Government would mean and he discussed this only in private with the fieldworker: the MHA, he thought, would eventually take over the chair of the District Commissioner (DC) and his office in Hagen, and the flag would fly in a village where both Europeans and expatriates lived together, with the MHA's personal house at the head. When asked if the expatriates would stay or go, he vacillated between the two possibilities.

His picture here reflects again the ambiguities of a transitional political situation. He models the eventual position of the MHA on the DC. Real government must be powerful, like the DC. But this would imply that the DC and perhaps all the other Europeans would leave. Yet he knows also the contrary ethic, that expatriates and indigenous people must work together, and this he includes in an image based not in Hagen town suburbia but a Lutheran mission 'house-line' village, of the kind that the mission had set up in many places as a mark of change and 'modernity'.

Other potential problems similarly appeared at this time but remained undiscussed. In the Adviser's address to the people at Ambukla in Dei the problem of the distribution of power between the rulers and the ruled was presented, and the Adviser stressed the ultimate power and importance of the 'people' as a whole. Yet in practice he was compelled to favour the élite and 'progressive' persons, such as younger politicians, who then tended to model themselves on him in their relations with their own people: a model not appropriate to the future 'democratic' political system.

Political parties also received short shrift. The trend here seems to have been set from mid-July 1967. On 14 July in a Council meeting P— announced that he had been to a meeting in the office of the District Commissioner (also attended by delegates from Wabag and Chimbu) and had heard that there were two parties, PANGU and the Christian Democratic Party. Some people in Papua New Guinea liked these and their promoters had come to discuss them. No more was said; and P— did not stress later in conversation that in Australia there are two main parties. Instead, he said that in Australia, 'everyone says "yessir" to the Government, and so work goes ahead quickly'. W— was sure, like others, that parties were appropriate only when all the people were ready for self-government and this was not yet. If he were elected, he said, he would speak out against them. Parties and educated Papuans from the capital city,

Port Moresby, were linked together, and Highlanders wanted to catch up with the Papuans before they joined their political forces with them.

The candidates

All the candidates had a long history of relations with expatriates, mostly in subordinate posts with a number of responsibilites, intermediate between an expatriate boss and workers or a local population. *Tanim tok, manki masta* and *bosboi* (interpreter, cook and labour overseer) were the standard jobs at which boys without education learnt about the white men's ways. E— had a long, moderately successful education. Only P— and Pu— had held any formal political office: Pu— as boss-boy, tultul and then luluai, before he was a Councillor, and since then a member of the Finance and Land Demarcation Committees in Mul; finally, in 1968, he was elected President.[5] 'An enthusiastic worker for the Administration', the Council survey called him. But he lacked either P—'s sophisticated knowledge or M—'s vision.

P— was too young to have been made a tultul or luluai but was already a dominating character when he was elected a Councillor. Through his impressive use of the lingua franca Tok Pisin (Pidgin English), strong demeanour and ability to understand white men's ideas, he was soon chosen to attend conferences, travel to other places to look at machinery and reply to visiting United Nations delegations.

By 1968 P— had learnt much. He was promoted from Vice-President to President when the Council became multiracial in September 1966, began to work more closely with the Council Adviser after that, and had learnt that self-government was a thing best delayed until the Highlanders were richer and better educated. His stay in Australia impressed him with a sense of the lack of development in his own country and committed him more seriously to the Administration's values. After a United Nations visit of 1968, which took place during the elections, he remarked that the country of the only coloured delegate, Mr Caine of Liberia, had received self-government too quickly and was in difficulties as a result: New Guinea would not make the same mistake. (Self-Government, as it happened, came as early as 1973.)

P— had already thought of standing in the first election of 1964. All the other candidates disclaimed this, although E— had been favoured by the Kotna missionary, who thought he could carry all the area from Kotna to Tiki (an optimistic view). M—, who actually won, seems to have had no dealing with the Department of District Administration at all. A priori, his association with the Public Works Department and roadwork, although likely to make him widely known, was scarcely likely to conduce to his popularity. He seems to have succeeded through personal character, not through his prior association with an expatriate organisation.

All the candidates (in common with those in the Regional electorate) took a hopeful view of their chances. P— thought he would have won if so many Dei candidates had not put in (which was probably true) but had little real hope for Mul votes. E— and W— felt (correctly) that they each had a secure niche of the electorate in their own tribal areas. Both Pu— and M— had done some solid auspice-taking and patrolling, especially in Mul itself, and while Pu— marshalled the names of Councillors whom he considered to be behind him, M— declared (in private) that only he, M—, was the people's choice, and that Pu—'s candidature was unwelcome and would be rewarded with only a few hundred votes.

P—'s confident non-campaign in Dei made people there suspect even more that he had Administration support. He himself emphasised the enigmatic character of his position by referring to dreams. In one, he caught a *Raggiana* bird of paradise in his hand and saw underneath it the tail of a Princess Stephanie bird (in Melpa called

M—, the same as one of the Mul candidates). This was interpreted as a sign that he would win, with M— second. In a second he saw a boar pig – another 'strong' thing, which meant success. And he maintained that as he went in to vote on the opening day he heard a *kot* bird cry and at the same time voted for a candidate different from the one he had intended to support – he broadcast this news, suggesting that it meant this candidate would lose. People suggested that all these dreams were *ik ek*, 'hidden talk', which really meant that the Kiap had told him both he and one of the expatriate Regional candidates would win.

P— did, however, participate in the Dei section of the whistlestop campaign, at least from Kendipi to Tiki, where he held his chances were best. And he also sent an agent into the Jimi Valley, a Komiti of the clan paired in alliance to his own, at the end of January. Whereas in their public speeches the candidates were very polite about each other at this stage, in private they allowed their agents to be more partial.

The results

The Dei Council reaction to the voting patterns was aired at a Council meeting on 22 March 1968. Since M— was ahead, it was assumed he had won. Some reports of the specific ballot-box patterns must have filtered through. There were minor recriminations against the other Dei candidates for standing in opposition to P—, and against Mul for not giving any votes to Dei, but most of the resentment of P— and his supporters was turned on the Gumants ward Councillors near to Keraldung and Muglamb (ballot box no. 14), since these were suspected of favouring M—. P— as Council President shouted down Kum, who was from this area, and dubbed him a rubbishman. Rumint of Keraldung urged that they wait until the 'no. 2 votes were counted', and M—, who came to the meeting, did the same. Kawelka Ongka, an established traditional-style leader (from P—'s area), excoriated those who had split Dei unity by putting up other candidates and assured them that now they would be the servants of Mul; they would even have to put themselves back inside their mothers' vaginas if the Mul men told them to! He blamed the Minembi tribesmen (old enemies of Kawelka); and Nore (of Kendipi, W—'s group) blamed both the Tipuka and the Minembi tribes, asserting that his own group had voted properly (that is, solidly for their own choice).

There was no gambling in Dei on the outcome of the election. Occasionally, candidates spoke rather too close to the voting enclosure. Persons were sometimes allowed through to vote even if their name was not found on the roll, and another name was crossed off instead. The Kiap allowed the second and did not appear to notice the first.

M— won, following his lead in the first preferences. The main reasons for his success were, first, the divisions between the Dei candidates, which prevented P— from reaching him on the first preferences; second, the lack of preference voting among W—'s supporters; and third, the overwhelming tendency of Mul voters to give their second preferences to M— if they gave their first to Pu—.

Conclusions

There are several notions involved in the modern elective process which had no counterpart in the traditional system: for example, the idea of secret, individual choice by formal voting, the idea of electing someone to be a representative of one's own area in a place far distant on the coast, and the expectation that such an election will be repeated at set intervals and the representatives perhaps changed.

Nevertheless, there are certain broad parallels. In the first place, Hagen (and Mul–Dei) leaders traditionally won and maintained their position by consensus, and it is still consensus that operates to endorse candidates and to decide part of the voting pattern of particular groups. Second, leaders had to be able to offer things to their supporters, for example, help with ceremonial exchanges or bridewealth. Such help was reciprocal, and a shrewd leader could ensure that he would benefit. Just so, the MHA (now the Member of Parliament) must bring returns to his electorate if he is to survive in office; if he does this, he secures for himself an income far above that of the bulk of his electors. Third, leaders always were representatives to the outside world, if only to the next clan, and concerned to inaugurate useful exchanges between their group and others. The MP can offer his electorate's products and labour force and hope that 'business' will be forthcoming. The notion that he can be formally put out of office is much more rigid than the traditional process of a man gradually losing or passing on his influence to someone else; however, it is in line with the process started when many of the old luluais lost their positions as the Councils were begun.

However, more careful definition was needed in these early times of the MHA's full role. If he was also President of a Council the problem could be partly solved; but if he was not, his relationship to the Local Councils, as well as to the European Council Advisers, became problematic. The ambiguity shows in the switch between notions that he was to be a 'boss' in his electorate area (that is, rather like a Kiap) or only a representative to the 'White man's government' (as W— put it in his conservative way). That a certain anxiety was felt on both sides is shown, on the one hand, by M—'s occasional diffidence in dealing with Europeans – he did not possess P—'s *hauteur* – and, on the other hand, by the Dei Council Adviser's hope that M— would not spend all his time in Mul but would visit him often at Dei.

The MHA had to act as liaison agent both between his two Council areas (and their Advisers) and between these and the House of Assembly. In the first case, his problem was to establish cooperation – and the opposition of Dei, at least, to a rapid marriage with

Mul suggested that this would be difficult – and in the second, it was to make realistic demands and to learn how the House of Assembly was run.

The problem between the two Council areas was how they could be of mutual advantage to each other. In the traditional system, political relations are segmentary and governed by competitive reciprocity. If there had been some way in which a Mul–Dei combination could be seen as putting the two areas together in competition with the joint Hagen–Kui council, then the opposition between them could have been, in certain contexts, overcome. It was felt, however, that Mul's gain was Dei's loss, and that Dei Council would now have to 'help Mul' only; but if it could have been shown that Mul could help Dei too, this feeling might conceivably have been dispelled.

The problem of the relationship between the MHA and the Administration was more difficult at this time. It was a part of the whole complex alternation between defined autonomy and broad dependency that characterised the Administration's relationship with the people as a whole. At this time, full political autonomy, with its implication of a dismantled Department of District Administration, was a prospect definitely kept remote. What enlarged functions Councils and MHAs would eventually have was unclear. M—'s picture of the 'office and the flag' needed clarifying. The authority of the Councillors to decide courts was also held rather cautiously in check, pending the supposed creation of specialist tribunals. It was only in the sphere of economic activity that the people were exhorted to show strong initiative, and even this was complicated by the necessity to make group capital investments such as improving secondary roads, which was still looked on as government work. For the time being, however, this suited the Dei people at least. Although the Council Adviser felt he had to drive them into activity, they themselves were keen to make as much from 'business' as possible. Since 1964, they had learnt to adjust to the idea of recurring elections and in principle welcomed these as an assurance that they need not suffer an inadequate representative to remain in office for long. They also hoped that their MHA could obtain 'money' for them from the House of Assembly, provided he was 'strong' enough.

For the Mul–Dei electors, and probably for all the Highlanders, the problem was one of specific returns, specific prestations. Their question was: what can their own Member, what can a European, what can the United Nations, what can the people of another Council area, *do* for them? The question, which reflected both the pragmatism and 'dependency syndrome' of the Highlanders, is really only one side of a fuller question which also makes sense in terms of traditional political ideas: what kinds of reciprocal relationships could be set up with these categories of persons? If the question had been put in that way, it might in Mul–Dei at any rate have eased inter-Council relations, if not the somewhat more complicated dependency syndrome.

Envoi: looking back and thinking about ritual

These events of the 1960s seem extraordinarily long ago in terms of political history. Two matters stand out. One is that in 1968 the whole area was much more obviously peaceful than it became by the 1980s. This was probably because of the colonial presence at the time, and conditions changed rapidly after Independence and the departure of the Kiaps at local levels from 1975 onwards. The other is that the whole idea that indigenous and foreign expatriate candidates could be involved together in elections disappeared soon after citizenship was introduced along with Independence.

It was not long before further events stemming from the death of the Mul driver irrevocably separated the two councils. P— was attacked and wounded while attending the opening of a new aid post on the border between the councils, and his attacker was from the clan of the driver killed in Dei: this happened in spite of the large compensation that had been paid to Mul. In the next election, the Councils became two separate electorates, and limits were placed thereby on the process envisaged by the Administration of consolidating units as the path to political change. As we will see in the next chapter, many further problems emerged from this point on. The limits were set on peace-making by the incursion into politics of ideologies of revenge and group competition.

Although the main narrative focus in this chapter has been on the narrative of an early pre-Independence election in Papua New Guinea, the underlying implications for the theme of peace-making are considerable. In 1968, the people's attentions were directed to 'development': roads, cash-cropping, vehicles, business, money-making. Elections were about political consolidation, but it was unclear to the people at large how this might benefit them, as we have seen. Both concerns – development and political consolidation – were urgently interrupted by the death of the Nengka driver in Dei Council territory. The driver came from a small and relatively peripheral clan within the large Nengka tribe; those who struck him after he had run into one of their clansmen, who was deaf and probably did not hear the vehicle coming, also came from a small clan, weakly integrated into the large Minembi group, whose further territories abut on those of Mul. If there had been no introduced Council structure, and particularly if there had not been an election impending that joined the two Councils, Mul and Dei, together, such an incident would probably never have provoked much widespread concern. But, given the new structures of historical consciousness, and given the cultural schema of segmentary opposition that remained deeply rooted in people's minds, an entirely new political field was created. The Council chambers in Dei became like a men's house of a clan; the whole Council accepted a kind of obligation to raise wealth as compensation, with a special role given to the responsible clan to find traditional items because of their imputed responsibility in the killing.

The political field of compensation across a Council (rather than a clan) boundary was fraught with perceived dangers and ambiguities. On the one hand, the ability of the Dei Councillors to mobilise and organise a compensation of this kind evinced an impressive capacity for peace-making: a capacity that depended clearly on the agency and initiative of those involved, realistic fears of escalating contexts of revenge, and the habitual cultural models of how disputes of these sorts could be settled. On the other hand, as events developed around this crisis, the situation worsened. P—, the Dei Council President, took part in the ceremonial handing over of wealth to the kinsfolk of the dead driver. Rumours, however, had spread that reprisal killings had already taken place, thus complicating matters. Another set of rumours suggested that the tribe of those involved in the killing, which is a traditional enemy of the President's tribe, were saying that it was really the President's own clan who had killed the driver and that this was being covered up. This kind of inter-clan and inter-tribe rumour is in general very characteristic of the Hagen area. Concerns over the upcoming election entered in, because the driver who had died came from a clan that was under the protection of the clan of one of the candidates from Mul Council, standing against P— in the election. This candidate was, in fact, M—, who was eventually to win the election. Moreover, within Dei Council, P—'s tribe, the Tipuka, were (and are) traditional major enemies of the Minembi tribe, and the Vice-President of Dei Council came from the Minembi group and was known or said to be annoyed that P—, a much younger man, had displaced him as the President. In other words, both structural and personal aspects of enmity were multiply at work as this case unfolded.

The further sequel was more serious, as we have already noted. In 1969, the year following the election and M—'s victory in it, threats were seemingly made against P—, and in the following year, 1970, he was actually attacked and seriously wounded by a blow to his face. He had agreed to attend an opening of a new police post right on the border between Mul and Dei and close to the territory of the Nengka man killed in 1967. (This was the place Koipke, precisely where P— had noted earlier the Administration had decided to open such a post, as a means of bringing Mul and Dei together.) In the event, the result was to definitively split them apart. His attacker was from the actual small lineage of the 1967 victim. P—'s life was saved by his being rushed to hospital in town, but rumours swiftly spread that he had been killed, and a reprisal attack was quickly mounted inside Dei, in which someone who happened to be of the same large tribe as the attackers was pulled out of his house and battered. He fortunately did not die, and compensation was quickly offered to him and paid over in 1971, although apparently in a lesser amount than was originally gathered.

It must be remembered that all these events were not taking place in any kind of pristine pre-colonial environment, but rather in what, looking back, was a part of the latter days of colonial control, when the rapid introduction of new political forms from within the colonial structures of administration was producing considerable strains in the social fabric at large. Combining paternalistic control with the encouragement of moves to democratic self-governing was bound to be a difficult balancing act for an administration under pressure from international sources to both move the country to independence and maintain an orderly process of doing so. In the longer, post-Independence, run of things the same kind of political act also proved fraught with difficulties for the elected parliamentary government as its ministers sought to promote 'development'.

In the meantime, government force was very much in evidence but made little difference to the concerns of the people or the outcomes of issues that divided them. The original attackers of the Mul Council driver were speedily arrested and placed in jail for riotous behaviour (rather than murder or manslaughter). This satisfied no-one, and in fact little attention was paid to this part of the 'justice system'. The focus was rather on rumours and their interpretation, on questions of revenge, and on strategies of compensation. After the subsequent attack on the Council President (which occurred in spite of a speedy compensation having been raised and handed over to the driver's kin), his attacker was also arrested and put on trial in Mount Hagen, receiving a ten-year sentence. Again, no-one was mollified by this display of judicial retribution. Group issues were in focus, as ever. The attacker's kin said they had lost both the dead driver and the revenge-taker (the latter for ten years at least). The President's kin and supporters declared that the attacker's whole group was implicated in an unprovoked attack on him, making nonsense of 'law and order', since it was precisely at a new police post, where the values of both law and order and inter-Council cooperation were expected to be strengthened, that the attack was planned and executed. The clan of the attacker was tardy in approaching the question of compensation to the President for the attack on him. Interestingly, in the absence of other neutral venues, the town itself became the venue for various abortive discussions between the parties. The Administration suggested that a joint Mul and Dei Council Committee be set up and meet to try to achieve a reconciliation of the parties. This kind of procedure was typical of Administration-instigated actions and in line with the ideology of gathering something called 'public opinion'. However, the concerns of the groups immediately involved were not addressed. These concerns centred on matters of a primordial and existential kind: how to get overt compensation or, if not, then covert revenge by sorcery or acts of assassination; and how to survive on their territories by maintaining their prestige relative to other political actors in their fields of agency. P—'s group demanded that the group of his attacker should be driven out from their border territory near to Dei Council. The attacker's group was small and politically weak in itself, but it belonged to a much larger and populous tribe in Mul Council, and its sponsors in Mul came from the Römndi tribe and indeed included politicians in the introduced electoral system.

The longer-term outcome of these events was predictable enough. Following the next round of review of electoral boundaries, Mul and Dei became separate electorates. This definitive split indicated two things: first, the colonial Administration's aim of producing wider levels of political unity by amalgamating introduced structural blocs (Councils) into single electorates had fallen foul of hostilities predicated on the revenge and compensation nexus; and second, the two Council areas became formally analogous to major enemies in the tribal system. Instead of being brought more together by 'modernisation', they were separated by a novel process of 'tribalisation' (see Ferguson & Whitehead 1992).

Compensation payments thus could not settle the political relations between Mul and Dei, even though the remarkable political and ritual innovations of 1967 had essayed to do exactly that. From the time of the attack on P—, Mul and Dei became separate, rather than joined together. On a minor scale, this case mirrors the wider-scale problems in Papua New Guinea today, where local enmities not only persist but are consistently regenerated and reconfigured precisely by the forces of so-called modernisation, such as drilling operations for oil and gas, gold, or other resources. It is these same forces that challenge the ritual improvisations of peace-making through compensation that local people constantly try to reinstantiate in their actions.[6]

CHAPTER 5

Escalations and complexities: turns of history

The narratives pursued by colonial powers that create empires often have to do with the supposed benefits of civilisation and the associated suppression of internecine conflicts, considered as a necessary precursor to the creation of a rule of law. These narratives amount to a rationale, from the point of view of the colonising power, for actions that may be seen as instances of hostile violence by those colonised. In addition, there may be a narrative of the intrinsic superiority of centralised state authority as a foundation for society by contrast with the supposed anarchy of societies without state institutions. The concept of 'pacification' encapsulates this kind of narrative. In Hagen, the narrative dates from the early 1930s, when outsiders arrived in the area and after a while proceeded to ban fighting between local groups.

These narrative themes also conceal great complexities. First, while the colonial power tends to see itself as possessing in advance a mandate to use physical force in pursuit of imperial aims, in practice a whole range of negotiations may be set in hand in order to establish a colonial presence. Ferguson and Whitehead (1992, p. 7) have neatly summarised this point in their distinction between coercion and seduction as colonial strategies. Seduction itself may be regarded from some analytical viewpoints as a kind of 'symbolic violence' in Pierre Bourdieu's terms (1977, p. 191). Bourdieu argues that there is a relationship between overt, physical violence and socially coercive mechanisms that conceal domination under bonds of kinship or patronage that he calls symbolic violence. However, for our purposes it is worthwhile to make an initial distinction between coercion and seduction as Ferguson and Whitehead (1992) do, in order to point out that seduction may sometimes be a more effective strategy than coercion for a colonial power to pursue, especially when it is operating in what Ferguson and Whitehead have aptly called 'the tribal zone', the zone at the edges of expanding states in which state powers engage with peoples outside their immediate territorial control but within their sphere of influence, though not exclusively so (p. 8). Coercion may be most effective when it can be unequivocally exercised; but seduction may work better when the state cannot or is not prepared to bring overwhelming force to bear. In such cases, state agents tend to operate in Bourdieu's (1977) modality of symbolic violence. To quote, 'they cannot appropriate the labour, services, goods, homage, and respect of others without "winning" them personally, "tying" them – in short, creating a bond between persons' (p. 190). This observation applies equally to the concept of seduction. It is clearly also related to the idea of hegemony; and at a certain point along the line between coercion and seduction, it becomes doubtful whether we can continue to speak of 'violence', at least in the commonly accepted sense of the term.

The context of colonialism in the Highlands of Papua New Guinea from the 1930s onwards provides an excellent illustration of this theme. Equally, this case shows that seduction tends not to work alone but in tandem with coercion as its guarantor. Elements of both continually appear. The two strategies do not appear separately but together, although one may predominate over the other at a particular phase of history. In the context we are looking at here, this interplay between seduction and coercion takes the form of an alternating stress on the lethal power of the gun vis-à-vis the 'life-giving' (from the viewpoint of the indigenous people) powers of shell valuables that the early colonial explorers brought with them. Pearl shell valuables encapsulate hegemony, in a sense close to that famously developed by Antonio Gramsci, who argued that hegemony involves an acceptance of social inequality grounded in practical processes or activities (see Crehan 2002, pp. 173–74). Our account is organised around the local systems of exchange and how these were affected by, and in turn affected, the colonial presence, tracing the narrative into post-colonial times when these systems of exchange have themselves been greatly transformed and severe problems of intergroup conflict and interpersonal violence have emerged. One reason for this is that the systems of exchange were themselves historically underpinned by threats of force: when exchange breaks down, there is a fundamental possibility of violence. Some analysts argue that these two, exchange and violence, are intrinsically linked. This argument depends on a number of considerations. One of these is that exchanges that encode inter-group competition also express hostility that may later break out into violence. Another is that exchanges that fail to reach a desired level of satisfaction between the parties can also lead to violence. At one stage in the history of post-pacification conflicts in the Highlands of Papua New Guinea, it appeared that the traditions of speech-making about past fighting and killings in the Mount Hagen area had become vehicles for a local sense of history that could express an ongoing sense of grievance against other groups and so could extend the possibilities of violence into the future. By comparison, in the Eastern Highlands, where such post-pacification exchanges and speech-making were less stressed, hostilities were also fewer. This was in the 1970s (Strathern 1977). Later, episodes of renewed fighting also broke out in the Eastern Highlands over a range of contemporary issues, indicating that fighting can have many causes that are independent of the effects of rhetorical traditions. In the Eastern Highlands case, renewed fears of sorcery between groups were instrumental in channelling conflicts and continued to be into the 21st century.

'Exchange' has been taken by many writers as a defining principle or characteristic of Highlands societies in Papua New Guinea, and more widely in the Pacific region (see, for example, Stewart & Strathern 2008). Whether this characteristic is especially true of the region or not, it is certainly pervasive. But as a characteristic it is both fluid and historically flexible. In this chapter, we look at the ways in which the European explorers, government officers and businessmen entered into a series of exchanges with Highlanders, how these exchanges were perceived on both sides, and how the local patterns of exchange were altered over time. We also look at a particular span of history in which changes took place – from the flowering of ceremonial exchange activities in the 1960s in Hagen to the decline and transformation of these ceremonial exchanges in the late 1990s (see Strathern & Stewart 2000a).

The history presented is largely 'internalist', in the sense that it depicts the ideas and actions of the Hageners themselves, but these ideas and actions have always been directed by perceptions of the outside world also. We look at the continuous interaction between government and mission pronouncements, and the local people's interpretations of these. For example, the shell valuables currency in Hagen was replaced with introduced money during the 1970s, largely because the Hageners realised that Europeans did not value shells in their own economic worlds and that these shells therefore enclaved them away from those worlds (Strathern & Stewart 1999a). However, they also used money in contexts similar to those for which shells had been used, making a double step of abandonment and reappropriation. This in turn geared their own exchanges to the introduced, externally driven worlds of cash-cropping and marketing, and set in motion a particular dynamic of escalation in factors of change. Competition for land and competition for money both led to killings and to the need for more money to pay compensation for the killings. By 1995, some leaders were calling for the abolition of compensation and the exclusive use of jail punishment as a way of settling conflicts, while at the same time bemoaning the growing selfishness and 'individualism' of a younger generation. Contradictions of attitude of these kinds all have their roots in the span of history since 1964 and earlier in which forces of change elicited one another dialectically: 'pacification' led to the flowering of exchange; shells were replaced by money; the exchange system was made dependent on the market; it went out of control; and this led to calls for its abolition. Yet, in 1998, we found that compensation payments were being used as vehicles for new political statements and purposes in an expanded arena of multi-ethnic relationships, geared to the symbols of the nation, the Western Highlands Province and modernity. Modernity as a local construction became the focus, as it had done before in different guises. In 1999, we found in our fieldwork that there was talk of reinstituting some further exchange activities as a part of a build-up to the next national elections. Tapes of exchanges obtained at various times up to 2010 attest to the continuous rebuilding of relations between groups via the deployment of wealth items, especially pigs. Social change and history are matters of flows of experience. Elements from the past are captured and reshaped as means of building the future. Equally important to consider are the ongoing changes and struggles connected with gender relations. Women are active agents in politics, even though men claim a monopoly over public power, and they participate strongly in debates regarding exchange, compensation, social control and the narratives of modernity, especially those developed within the rubrics of Christianity (see Stewart & Strathern 1998a, 2001a).

This synopsis of changes since the 1930s needs to be set alongside another part of the picture, the continuing history of violence. Exchanges of wealth never fully extinguished violence, and the interaction of local with national politics has meant that violence is now often associated with the cycle of elections for national political office. Considerations of these kinds turn original colonial 'wisdom' on its head. State structures themselves generate violence, and acephalous political systems have in the past been better vehicles for the resolution of conflicts than have state institutions in post-colonial circumstances. Indeed, this point was anticipated by the colonial-era British social anthropologists who worked in African contexts (for example, Middleton & Tait 1958).

Exchange in Mount Hagen

The literature on continuity versus change in the Highlands of Papua New Guinea is quite extensive. Most observers are agreed that the problems involved are complex and are not to be solved by deciding in favour of either continuity or change as an exclusive point of emphasis (for example, Brown 1995; Knauft 1999). Rather, we have to examine how these two elements are intertwined and how they merge into each other, blurring the boundaries of separation. This debate regarding Highlands historical processes goes back to the questions of longer-term prehistoric developments (Feil 1987; Wiessner & Tumu 1998), but it has mostly to do with the rapid changes set in hand by events from the 1930s onwards, when Australian explorers first entered the Central Highlands of what later became Papua New Guinea, bringing with them not just change in terms of material aspects of life but an entirely new psychology towards life that influenced the way the local people saw themselves, their transactions and their place in the cosmos.

Theories regarding the persistence of exchange practices tended in early anthropological writings of the 1960s to be balanced against accounts of the alacrity with which Highlands entrepreneurs took up the possibilities of business and economic profit (for example, Finney 1973). These studies were challenged by writers with a Marxist orientation in the 1970s, who discerned developing class structures, conflict and the emergence of 'big peasants' (Amarshi et al., 1979) – processes they sought to use to explain the outbreaks of group violence in the Highlands from the 1970s onwards essentially in terms of the theme of conflict between social classes. Such approaches in turn have given way to more nuanced analyses that emphasise cultural, political and economic factors as all necessary for a rounded standpoint on change. In the 1990s, the residual elements of the incomplete picture of the Highlanders as simply secular pragmatists were abandoned, as scholars came to better understand the rich ritual life that the Highlanders had, and which entered into their day-to-day transactional practices and expressed itself across the gender divide. In addition, the very early impact of Christianity on these Highlands societies had from the first years of missionary influence in the areas begun to be incorporated into and blended with indigenous patterns of thought and action (see Stewart & Strathern 2001a, 2009; Strathern 1984). The subsequent spread of evangelical Christianity further altered the ways in which transactions were conducted under the influence of new sets of moral codes.

In this context, scholars are provided with an opportunity to consider the basic wellsprings of action in these societies and the extent to which people within them are motivated by ideologies of exchange. At the outset it is important not to accept in a simple way any empirical opposition between gift and commodity as constitutive of the field of debate. This is because there is a long history of intertwinement of gift and commodity transactions in these societies, making it possible for gifts to be commoditised and commodity transactions to acquire gift-like aspects (compare Carrier 1992; and see Strathern & Stewart 2000a, 2000b, 2005). What we have to discern, instead, is the pattern of shifting strategies and meanings captured in exchanges and the major trends of history since the 1930s.

A mixed background of notions that combines together 'secular' and 'sacral' dimensions has more recently fed into the contemporary scene of discussions about change among the Highlanders themselves; and it is this scene that we propose to examine with some examples in order to pursue the point further.

Starting from these viewpoints assists in the interpretation of data from the outset since it avoids the imposition of typological schemes. However, a set of analytical ideas is needed to replace the typifications that have sometimes been employed. We use here a range of ideas: *substitution, transformation* and the *long-term trajectories of practices*. These are concepts similar to those that the people employ in their own reflections on their histories. We focus on a familiar theme, that of historical changes in the items used in exchanges, as seen in indigenous commentary (see also Stewart & Strathern 2002a; Strathern & Stewart 1999a). The commentary was given to us by two of our research collaborators in the Hagen (Melpa-speaking) area of the Western Highlands Province in 1999.

Both men were old enough to have seen many of the changes they described, although not to have witnessed the first arrival of the Australians in the early 1930s. We asked them to explain how the use of different items in the Hagen system had changed over time.

These objects had been used in brideprice and in the system of exchange known as *moka*. *Moka* is a general term for the delayed exchange of wealth items such as shell valuables and pigs or pork between individual partners or groups, marked by a principle of giving more than one has received in a previous phase from one's partner (Strathern 1971 [2007]; see also Stewart & Strathern 1998b,

2005b; Strathern & Stewart 2000a). This system of exchange has been on the decline since the 1990s and is considerably altered in tone from its earlier form. The items used have also shifted somewhat, according to a logic of indigenous perceptions that has been modified, or perhaps even produced in some instances, through transactions with outsiders, as the narratives will show. The significant point to bear in mind is that these valuables were also instruments of wealth for making peace.

For the Hageners, the pearl shell (*kokla kin*; also described in Tok Pisin as 'kina', a Gazelle Peninsula word from the northern coast of New Guinea) was the most admired and sought-after valuable from at least the 1930s until its demise as a valued exchange item in the 1970s. Many other shell types were given up as currency earlier than the pearl shells, while still used variously as forms of bodily adornment. These included the baler (*raem*), cowrie ropes (*ranggel*), nassa shells (*nuin, pikti*) sewn into mats (*pela öi*) with a central diamond called a navel (*uklimb*) from which the shells radiated outward in a design, and green snail (*kötö, örpi*), used largely as ornaments, attached to the ears and ringlets of hair, primarily by women (Strathern 1971 [2007], p. 102). These shell items had been dropped from *moka* exchanges prior to 1964, perhaps in the late 1950s.

Pearl shells began to lose their place in *moka* after the mid-1960s. For the Kawelka people of the Dei Council area, the first beginnings of the use of state money in *moka* were observed in July and August of 1964, at a new kind of event known as a 'tobacco-*moka*', indicating its initial lack of symbolic importance in the order of things. In 1999, seeking to elicit some retrospective reflections on the historical passage of shells, we asked two senior Kawelka tribesmen of the Kurupmbo sub-clan, R— and Pug—, to outline their views on this general topic of changes in the use of valuables. R— spoke, checking from time to time with Pug—, who also prompted him on occasion. It is important, though, to note that R— was in fact casting around to put his thoughts in order about a topic that to him clearly appeared antiquarian by this time. Nevertheless, the events and processes he described had played a significant part in his own life. It is evident that in his account he was producing a meditation on the character of historical change and on discourses of 'modernity'.

Narratives of change

> Pearl shells were the most important. After them in importance came cowries, nassa shells, balers, and finally green snail. Pearl shells continued to be used after the cowries and nassa shells were given up. The White people did not bring many of the cowrie and nassa shells with them, so we dropped them because we saw the Whites did not see them as important and we decided not to consider them as valuables any longer. When paper and coin money came we stopped using these smaller shells. We saw that we could use money to buy pearl shells [these were sold at tradestores during the colonial years alongside sacks of rice, tins of fish and packets of cracker biscuits].
>
> At first we thought that money was just a means to obtain pearl shells. So during the 1950s and early 1960s we used both money and pearl shells. Subsequently, we got Local Government Councils – we became members of the Dei Council. The Kiaps [Australian Government officers, placed as Council Advisers at this time] said that money would make the Council work efficiently. So the people began to think that shells were unimportant and they gradually gave up the use of them. It was not as though some one person made a speech and said, 'Let us give these shells up'; it just happened gradually as money was used more frequently. The people saw by then that pearl shells did not produce anything [they could not be used to purchase the same sorts of things that money could] and only money produced

things. Previously it was true that pearl shells had work in brideprice payments and other payments, but from that time forward they did not think that they had work anymore. In the past there were hundreds and hundreds of pearl shells with resin boards, but where are they now? They are not to be seen at all!

As for the shape of the pearl shell, the top is the 'head' (*peng*) and that is what bore the shell. This 'head' was broken off. It is not shiny, so it was removed when the shell was processed for use. They took the part with the good yellow colour and fixed it on a board with tree resin, but if they wanted the shell as a neck decoration then they would cut it smaller. The edge of this coloured part that is used is called the 'tongue' (*anmbil*). [See Strathern & Stewart 1999a for a full description of this manufacturing process.]

We had stopped using the small shells (cowrie and nassa) in the 1960s. We remember this because this was around the time that there was a big sickness and people were using money instead of shells at this time [for small transactions; the date should probably be the 1950s]. Early in the 1970s we gave up using pearl shells because at that time there was plenty of money and we saw that the money could be easily carried to other places and used to purchase food and things that we needed. We did not complain about giving up the use of shells. We are not sorry for these shells or nostalgic about them. Now we have money and we can use it to buy pigs or as brideprice.

R— was a man well into his fifties in 1999. In 1965, he was engaged along with his father in partnerships involving pearl shells and pigs that belonged to an elaborate sequence of *moka* prestations between the Kawelka and their neighbours the Tipuka people (Strathern 1971 [2007]). At this time, R— was in his very early manhood and newly married to his first wife. He therefore recalls the whole sequence of events at least from the 1960s onwards. Overall, it is clear that he sees the transcendence of pearl shells and their replacement by money as a mark of historical progress. In their views of history, the Hageners have seen themselves as reaching out to the external world, grasping it and incorporating or 'pulling' it into their own spheres of action. This is how in fact an older generation of male leaders saw the expansion of the *moka* system itself and the later influx of shells brought by the Australians. R— continues in this broad tradition of thought, with a discourse about change having to do with the media of exchange, at each stage of which something new is taken in, substitutes for an earlier item and is transformed while itself becoming an agent of internal transformation. Since wealth items continue to be central to identity, the past in a sense repeats itself; and since each historical situation is different, the past is also in another sense always left behind while the imagination incorporates the present into the future. The types of shell valuables are historical markers of these transitions in people's narratives of change.

In organising his account, R—, with Pug—'s help, systematised the different shells in terms of their remembered importance. In fact, in the earliest phases of direct contact with the Australians, Hageners were keen on all types of these shells and manufactured them into impressive valuables. Cowries, however, were used in the colonial context for smaller transactions between the outsiders and the Hageners, and so came to be identified as of 'less importance'.

His account makes it clear that the Hageners from the 1960s onwards saw state money as having more expansive power than shells. The perception coincided with, or closely followed, the opening up of the Highlands for travel and labour migration, and the new senses of identity that came with this process. Money was an efficient medium for inter-ethnic exchange. It could be used to obtain food. Just as the first white explorers had used shells to break into the Hageners' world by offering them these wealth items in return for food and labour, so the Hageners could use money to break across their own social horizons. In Tok Pisin, R— said that shells did not 'bear food', *i no kariim kaikai*, with the wider sense that there was no further profit to be gained from using them at this time. Mimetic appropriation of the 'white-men's' ways thus took over, coupled with a feeling of overcoming what, again retrospectively, was seen as the trickery of the whites in at first withholding their own 'true' money. But it is also true that the Australian Government itself had a program to switch the people to state money over time, as its own means of incorporating the Hageners into the state structure through local government council taxes and cash-cropping, mostly the planting of coffee bushes by indigenous small-holders. Both sides, therefore, in fact participated (for quite different purposes) in the same transition, each feeling that they were taking the initiative either to grasp at new opportunities or to impose a new economic order. R—'s rejection of any notion of nostalgia for the past is interesting and stems from his views of progress and the changing objectifications of self and culture that go with such a view, also enunciated by other senior men such as Ongka-Kaepa (Strathern & Stewart 1999b). Shells were first identified with the new order of colonial life in the 1930s, then were themselves seen as transcended by a further new order in the 1970s (see also Merlan & Rumsey 1991, p. 229). The narrative of shells and money thus becomes a means of self-reconceptualisation over time, a gathering of perceptions of change into a form of shifting historical consciousness.

R— omits from his account any stress on the fact that state money was introduced into *moka*, displacing shells (Strathern & Stewart 1999a). This move of 'involution' runs counter to his own narrative of change as 'evolution', but it has been an important part of the overall history of change, begun, as we have noted, in mid-1964 with a *moka* event among the Kawelka people. Accounts of these kinds are not common in the ethnographic literature, and we now describe this event in further detail.

A tobacco-*moka*

The genesis and execution of this *moka* show the incremental and improvisatory steps by which money entered these exchanges. Various reasons were given for the event, which was dubbed a *rok moka*, a *moka* for tobacco, that is, by meiosis something unimportant or trivial, having to do with the casual exchanges of younger men and comparable to their sharing of tobacco for smoking while playing at card games. Another version was that the two groups involved, neighbours and closely intermarried, had stolen pigs from each other and the *moka* was to put an end to this. One middle-aged man declared that he had paved the way for the *moka* by tying up a pig belonging to a clansman of the other side that had given the first sum of money, and had returned the pig to its owner, establishing a pact of good behaviour. The groups were the Minembi Yelipi and Kawelka Kundmbo clans in the Dei Council area, and the Yelipi Councillor, the son of a traditional big-man, had initiated the sequence by giving money to the Kundmbo. Ndamba, a senior and respected Kundmbo big-man, said that the money *moka* was also to forestall any poison-sorcery from being made on the young men of his clan who were going around playing cards (gambling for money) with their Yelipi peers (compare Chapter 2, this volume, on sorcery fears). Young men at this time spent much time gambling and on chasing the winners in a particular game from place to place in an attempt to play again and win back their stakes plus a profit. Older men such as Ndamba saw the conversion of all this money back into *moka* as a device for stabilising the younger generation's activities and for reasserting some of their own control as leaders in the group, an interpretation that older leaders made once again in later years, explaining why in the 1970s they encouraged women to contribute money to the purchase of large commercially reared pigs for *moka* occasions (Strathern 1979). Ndamba also had aims of peace-making or sustaining peace in mind.

Not only young men were involved. The older men, including the leaders, had joined in also, and all combined in providing a small feast of cooked food, including new items such as chickens, cabbages, tinned fish, dripping and rice for the visitors. The Kundmbo were the donors for the event, which was staged on 4 August 1964 at the Möimanga ceremonial ground, where later in 1973 the Kundmbo performed the Female Spirit fertility cult (Strathern & Stewart 1999c). They attempted to divide up both contributions and recipients according to clan subdivisions known as men's house groups but found the arithmetic and accounting complex. At this time the Australian currency was still in pounds and shillings. Each men's house group or sub-clan was supposed to add an extra amount to the sum the Yelipi had given earlier. The chief Kundmbo recipients had divided out what they previously had received to their sub-clansmen and now these were expected to provide a return plus increment to bring about the *moka*. For example, in Ndamba's sub-clan, the Kiklpuklimbo, a total of 12 men out of 20 in the group were said to have received £51, and now added £36 in order to make a total of £87 to give back (on the form of currency here, see Chapter 4, note 2). Older big-men tried to direct the proceedings, but younger men crowded round the money, engrossed in the actual work of counting it. The amounts of money were tied up in handkerchiefs and presented as bundles to Yelipi recipients. One young man shouted out that all this was the fruit of business and coffee-growing. The Yelipi Councillor was prominent among the recipients, and he attempted to get some of the totals down on paper, while the Kundmbo laid out the money in three rows, the first row to acquit the debt, the second row to add something to this (referred to both as 'profit' and as *poroman*, that is, 'companion' money), and the third 'new money' (*ku kont*) to stimulate the Yelipi to make returns. This performative act of laying out rows of money as though they were shells indicates the transfer of the people's mindset between one cultural schema and another, and shows how money truly was slotted into the place 'vacated' by shells – on later occasions money was laid out in rosette formations that resembled in size and shape pearl shells mounted on resin boards (see Strathern & Stewart 1999a, for photographs). At the same time, the introduction of a written record indicated the mimetic context, in which the accounting practices and techniques of the whites were being followed by a new generation of leaders within the council system, set up in 1962, only two years earlier. Meanwhile, older leaders such as Ndamba either quietly supervised the practical arrangements, trying to fix them in their own minds, or made overarching remarks. A—, for example, a leader in a sub-clan different from Ndamba's, declared that the big-men were not involved in the event since only the young men were giving, but everyone needed money to pay their council taxes before the year's end, so the Yelipi should make returns quickly. (In fact, A— himself had received earlier but is not recorded as contributing to the returns, which may explain why he found it difficult to get a hearing for his remarks.) The overall total recorded as presented was 317 pounds and ten shillings, a very considerable sum for that time.

Presenting saucepans of food along with the gifts was a part of the new style of this *moka*, and K—, a Lutheran mission evangelist (*mitiman*) who came from A—'s sub-clan, the Kumbambo, said a Christian prayer to bless the food, adding:

> Money is strong and comes from Jesus, who is our big-man (*wuö nuim*) up above, so you can make *moka* with it. Later, when the Yelipi make returns, you Kundmbo can use this money to build a church here. This money is being given to end the stealing between the Yelipi and the Kundmbo. We do not have much

business in our place, we are short of money, so you Yelipi must make returns to us quickly.

The whole event shows the complex performative ways in which money was socialised into an existing order and how this order was itself changed to accommodate and to express something that was new. The participants' horizons of consciousness included the demands of the new council system, so that the nexus between an old institution and a new one was made quite explicit. Finally, the Lutheran evangelist spoke of funnelling the returns into a further new institutional investment with God, legitimising money itself as the blessing given by Jesus and implying that a return gift to the church was needed for this. At the very start of the entry of state money into the *moka* we see an instance of the sacralisation of money in a context of gift-giving and also an early foreshadowing of developments in the late 1990s, when the *moka* system overall was in decline and further transformations had taken place, so that in 1998, 35 years after the prayers at the event detailed here, a new sort of *moka* was planned in which money was sought through local relational ties in order to build a new Assemblies of God church at R—'s settlement place (Stewart & Strathern 2000a; Strathern & Stewart 2000c). The church was to be of permanent materials with a metal roof, replacing the first building with its thatched roof and woven cane walls. In return, God would, it was hoped, increase his blessings to the community, returning the gift of the building 'with interest'. In addition, the attempt to domesticate and sacralise money indicates that peace-making and avoidance of trouble were also at play as motivating factors.

Commentary on historical processes
This observation regarding the sacralisation of state money in the context of a local political event also enables us to elucidate further

our analytical scheme of substitution, transformation and long-term trajectories of change as objects of analysis. First, outsiders bring a greatly increased supply of pearl shells. These shells carry established aesthetic and ritual values, and their increased availability is seen as an enrichment of cultural life. They *substitute* for all the other types of shells used before. The perceptions that they arouse in people are also *transformed*, because of their new association with the outsiders who have now brought them and the fact that they are obtained through transactions with vegetable foodstuffs and pigs, and in return for labour. The pearl shells are commodified items but they also belong to the ancient world of the gift. They are seen as items whose power depends, at least in part, on a new magico-religious or hegemonic link with powerful incomers who themselves introduce the people to new forms of transactions that are extensions of earlier patterns of external trade between Hageners and others at the edges of their social world. As the outsiders become the sole new source of these shells, so the shells come to express (again, in part) a dependency on these outsiders and a transformation of the outsiders partially into insiders – extending the network of what we have termed relational-individuality (see Stewart & Strathern 2000c). The Hageners' notion was that shells were 'whitemen's wealth', and that these new incomers' ideas were miraculously coincident with their own idea about shells as valuable items. But this transformation contained within it the seeds of a longer-term trajectory of further change. When Hageners realised that shells simply enclaved them in their own world rather than truly allowing them to tap into the world of the outsiders, they were disillusioned. Hence, at the instigation of the colonial Administration, they substituted again and adopted state money, in turn transforming it into a valuable by employing it in *moka* and using it in brideprice payments, and for compensations used in peace-making. (All exchange transactions in a sense belonged broadly to peace-making.)

Pearl shells were in the past sacred to the Female Spirit (Strathern & Stewart 1998a, 1999c), who was also seen as an exogenous power, coming to the Hagen area from Tambul in the south-west, roughly the same direction as that from which pearl shells came in trade networks. When state money was adopted, it was quite predictably regarded as something that came from the new deity (the Christian God of the outsiders) as well as the new government (which had also emanated from the southern coastal city of Port Moresby). By this logic of substitution and transformation, the society as a whole was set on a pathway of further change, since if money was to be used in ritual contexts for exchanges it had first to be obtained in new economic ways. The gift exchange system was therefore harnessed to the labour market and to the small-holder production of cash crops. It was precisely, therefore, the intertwining of gift and commodity in a nexus of values and conative aspirations that drove the *ongoing trajectory of change.* Furthermore, the presence of commodity exchanges in pre-colonial contexts of external trade had played an initial part in the transformational processes set in hand by the arrival of the first colonial explorers. But equally important was the ritual or sacred linkage of wealth with the powers of ancestors and the spirits. This facilitated the eventual absorption of money into the *moka* system, revealing the enduring links between 'economic' exchanges and 'ritual power'. These two are not fully separate categories but are closely interrelated. In addition, brideprice payments, which reaffirm cosmological links with powers of renewal and fertility, incorporate into themselves money as *moka* exchanges did. In 1998, one of our Hagen field collaborators explained to us while we were attending a brideprice occasion that, although *moka* exchanges were not held as they had been previously, brideprice occasions were still considered to be an enduring aspect of local life. But this practice too has altered significantly over time, as has *moka* (Stewart & Strathern 1998a). For example, brideprice occasions now incorporate separate gifts of money to the bride, contributed as a kind of 'tax' or generalised donation by men and women kinsfolk of the groom.

Anthropological categories of commodities and gifts, 'big-manship' and 'greatmanship' (see, for example, Godelier 1982 [2009]) are best seen as elements in an interrelated series of historical processes over time and space. These distinctions were never completely firm, and the movement of change carries these elements along with it in a complex set of interrelations, which the Hageners, as their words suggest, understand quite well.

Emergent dilemmas

The revalorising of money in the context of *moka* exchanges over time caused these exchanges themselves to undergo historical shifts. First, people had to be involved in the cash economy in order to obtain money. This in turn exposed them to the buying power of money itself, a point that R— makes clearly in his account. As new desires for consumption enter, and as forms of socialisation into the values of group solidarity and communal ceremony loosen their grip on succeeding generations, the linkage point between money and local ritual enterprises is threatened. Renewing it by diverting it in the direction of a novel prestigious activity such as church-building represents an attempt to strengthen the link again. But the very 'strength' of money – its association with outside powers – that led people to want it in the first place imperils that link.

Older leaders, perceiving these trends clearly, work to reharness money for church purposes that are also intimately linked to political functions within the communities. These leaders also try to get people to invest another kind of valuable in feasting activities for the opening of new churches. This is the pig, which has maintained its fundamental place as a store of prestigious value throughout all the fluctuations in the use of shells and state money. However, pigs require a considerable investment of food and labour, and in Hagen women have traditionally supplied a great deal of that labour. Within the context of the old *moka* activities, their efforts were harnessed to a relatively unitary system of values. The decline of *moka* has meant that women are no longer as keen to undertake all the work of rearing pigs, and men are even less inclined to pick up the jobs themselves. Women are also more able to earn money by doing other kinds of work. This money in many instances is more highly valued because of the immediacy with which it can be transformed into other goods or enter into various transactions.

In future, there may emerge a system that is based entirely on money, in which money alone is used to purchase goods for feasting purposes. For many years, since at least the early 1970s, the purchase of 'freezer meat', mostly sides of beef but also 'lamb flaps', and tins of corned meat or canned mackerel pike, has formed a part of feasting occasions. If the rearing of pigs becomes less popular, feasts will become more expensive affairs in terms of immediate cash needed to obtain goods. This will represent another remote point on the long trajectory of unanticipated changes initiated by the relatively smooth substitutions and transformations of earlier years.

Hageners perceive these processes as creating dilemmas for them, centring on money itself. They adopted money in order to mimetically appropriate the world of outside powers and have since learnt that this world is full of problems of its own. Two parallel and contradictory discourses about money coexist uneasily, the one condemning it as bad, a cause of strife and dissolute behaviour, linked to alcohol consumption, criminal activity, prostitution and the corruption and violence that goes with political bribery, as well as most recently a realisation that AIDS has made its way into a number of Hagen communities. People relate the entry of AIDS into their lives on the one hand with the wrongdoings of individuals (rich persons and sportsmen, who travel outside Papua New Guinea and come into contact with the disease), and on the other hand with fears that this disease may be a sign that God is punishing people because of their failure to observe proper rules of behaviour.

These fears reflect deep concerns about the ways in which people should be organising and leading their lives. The discourse on money reflects the dilemmas of deciding how money should be used: for longer-term communal ends or for more immediate personal and group consumption. The dialogue on this issue extends and reverberates between men and women, and between members of different generations. Some of the older male leaders criticise younger people for their unwillingness to work to produce wealth that can then be put into community enterprises. Younger people declare that the older people are perhaps too interested in controlling things and keeping wealth for themselves. Exchanging the world of proper participation in events for the world of personal consumption is seen as potentially leading to a dissolution of social bonds as such, and this is clearly connected with the role of wealth goods in peace-making. These concerns become most evident when stressful events occur such as in the following story.

Early in the year 2000, in the first days of January, two middle-aged men died among the Kawelka Kundmbo clanspeople at Kuk, raising questions about the present and future in a sharp way. First, the deaths were taken by some as possible omens of the feared impending world's end because of the fact that they happened at the turning of the new millennium. Second, the men died of severe disease conditions that were apparently not well understood by the doctors but which caused the wasting away of their bodies over a relatively short time. And third, their deaths at about the same time produced a strain on people's organisational capacities to stage and manage the contributions of food and money to the funeral feasts that form an integral part of cycles of exchange and in the past have been tied in with *moka*. During the speeches made at the funeral feast there were complaints that people were not contributing enough to the event. There were expressions of factional divisions between sub-groups. In addition, there were expressions of conflicts of interest between clansfolk living at Kuk as against those living in the more remote Kawelka territory at Nggolke (Strathern & Stewart n.d.). Further, complaints emerged about the people at Kuk having to deal with the corpses of men who died in urban centres away from home and whose bodies were always brought from the nearby airport at Kagamuga to Kuk rather than being taken on the longer and more difficult journey straight to Nggolke. Meanwhile, some older speakers protested their loyalty and commitment to the funeral prestations themselves. Finally, in a remarkable series of discussions, great confusion arose as to how exactly leadership was to operate on the occasion itself. The major division was between church leaders and those seen as outside of the church. The church leaders were also at odds with one another because of the divisions between the Catholic, Seventh Day Adventist, Lutheran and Assemblies of God churches in the community, and they debated with each other on how best to conduct the funeral proceedings. Gender issues arose when some of the male church members suggested that perhaps female leadership should also be recognised. Leaders outside the churches wondered how church affiliations would fit with the old, established system of division into clans and sub-clans seen as men's house groups (*manga rapa*). A debate about what the local social structure actually was or should have been took place on this occasion in the public speeches. Partial resolutions were declared so as to move the event forward without too many people becoming disgruntled and leaving.

Such a debate is part of a process in which people are coming to terms with the confusing circumstances of change. Comparable organisational discussions were foreshadowed in the 1964 arguments about how to make a money *moka*. Then, the problem was seen in substitutive terms; in 2000, it had to do with long-term trajectories, brought fully into people's consciousness. And the underlying dilemmas which the debates reflected, and reflected upon, were those we have delineated here: how to make people contribute to events once the overall frameworks of society have begun to alter; and how to decide who is to be in charge of and responsible for events. The church leaders represented a new version of sacralised control but without the old knowledge of how to organise and motivate people; whereas the leaders outside the church knew how to organise matters in accordance with the old social structure but lacked now the element of sacralisation. The result was an attempt to combine both, in search of a new hybrid form not yet developed: a form that combines sacred and secular, and binds commodity and gift together again, as happened previously in recursive processes of history. Pearl shells and state money were at successive historical moments introduced and incorporated into an ongoing holistic matrix of activities, which was underpinned also by the ritual complex of fertility expressed in pig-sacrifices and other ways. Money and Christianity have since brought with them further dilemmas of choice, leaving the Hageners to consider how to achieve a form of social structure that can resolve these difficulties and reinstate a balanced cosmos. (For some African comparisons see, in general, Hutchinson 1996.)

Conflict and violence

This account of changing exchange practices in Hagen might suggest a gradual and graded set of peaceful, if problematic, transformations away from patterns of violent activities. However, we have presented only one side of the picture. The other side is that the potential for violence was never eradicated, and that new circumstances have in fact aggravated its scope. The history of this process has been given in a number of other publications (for example, Strathern 1974, 1977, 1992, 1993a, 1993b; Strathern & Stewart 2000a). Here, therefore, we give a selection of points that bear on our main themes.

First, there is the context of earlier colonial practices in the Highlands, from the 1930s to the 1950s. The colonial intruders brought with them the two basic tools of 'empire', coercion and seduction, in the forms of guns and valuable shells. They used the guns to defend themselves against attacks, and to shoot their way out of threatened attacks. These attacks were sometimes aimed at gaining access to the supplies of trade goods, including axes and shells, which the incomers brought with them. At other times they were generated by earlier occasions when the intruders had shot people. Because of the tremendous appeal that both axes and shells had for the local people, recourse to shooting was needed less than it might otherwise have been. In this regard we might argue that the Hageners, and other Highlanders, pacified themselves rather than simply being pacified, because of their own desires for the goods the incomers brought with them. Clearly, both coercion and seduction were involved. In the 1960s, older Hagen men remembered keenly how administration officers had brought in their native police and had put people in 'jail' for wrongdoing. A vivid account of these happenings is given by the Kawelka leader Ongka in his lifestory (Strathern & Stewart 1999b). Ongka's account is valuable also because it details how leaders such as himself, who were young adults at the time, seized on the trappings of power (afforded them by being appointed as minor colonial officials) to establish new forms of domination for themselves in their own communities (pp. 7–9). It was in this context of coercion, exercised by the colonial field officers and aided by local officials, that fighting among groups, and also isolated killings, declined and the indigenous emphasis on *moka* exchanges developed and thrived to the mid-1960s.

Pacification, self-induced or coerced, did not, however, mean the end of conflict. Fights between sets of persons, escalating into the involvement of others of their groups, continued in the 1950s, and field officers regularly intervened and jailed participants in these. However, such conflicts were encompassed by the widening remit of the circuits of exchange of wealth that preoccupied the new generation of leaders who grew up in the shadows of colonial control. People were also kept busy with compulsory labour on road-building and the construction of 'rest-houses' for visiting colonial officers, and with the introduction of coffee trees as a source of monetary income.

These patterns of change and development were interrupted by some unforeseen consequences. The administration sponsored the introduction of local government councils, joining together several large groups into single deliberative bodies with powers of local taxation and disbursement of funds for projects. Councillors and their associated committee-men became important new parts of the political and administrative apparatus in the 1960s. From the mid-1960s onwards, also, political electorates were constituted for elections of members of a House of Representatives, the forerunner of the national Parliament that was set up a decade later when Papua New Guinea gained its independence from the colonial power, Australia. These electorates often, though not always, coincided with council areas or were amalgamations of such areas (see Chapter 4). In such cases, the effect was to create new political bodies, composed of an uneasy amalgam of differing groups, some with longstanding enmities towards one another, which stood potentially opposed to other such units in a political configuration much larger in scale than the clans and tribes that had operated in the political domain in pre-colonial times. We have already delineated such a process in some detail in Chapter 4. Further, people from different groups and electorates travelled more into one another's areas, for example to buy coffee, or on government service, or to visit kin, or to campaign for political causes.

The net result of these changes of scale and content in social and political relations was an increased potential for conflict and violence, one that was hard for the expanding exchange system to keep pace with. The introduction of vehicles and roads, with their potential for accidents, and the opening of taverns at which local people could consume alcohol, made the situation more explosive. Settlers from other provinces short of land for coffee-growing were also brought into the broad expanses of the flat Wahgi Valley around Hagen. Labourers were imported to work on expatriate-owned plantations. Goods became available for purchase in towns, leading to desires for the money needed to buy them, and possibilities for quarrels and fights in the urban centres themselves. The introduction of Village Courts in the 1970s was intended to give back to local leaders the powers to settle disputes, including those involving violence, in communities that had over time been eroded by colonial control. These courts had some success; but they were plagued by their inability to enforce their decisions, by corruption and by a rising tide of indifference to the authority of the magistrates. In more serious cases of assaults or actual killings, 'Trouble Committees' were appointed, consisting of local notables, to arbitrate disputes and decide on compensation payments.

The late 1960s and the 1970s already saw an escalation in tensions between groups, and in the Dei Council area of Hagen in late 1986, the killing of a young Kawelka Kundmbo clansman in a drinking spree with some contemporaries of his among the Minembi tribesmen (who included ancient enemies of the Kawelka as a whole) escalated, through the non-payment of compensation, into a series of major collective hostile encounters, fuelled for the first time by the use of guns. The numbers of those killed in conflict accordingly increased, and a wide area of group territories was embroiled in fear, distrust, ambushes and open armed engagements for a period of two years, leading to partial devastation of coffee crops, tradestores and dwelling houses as well as direct killings by gunfire and the rape of women in enemy territories. The establishment of peace was uneasy and difficult, notably aided by the erection of a memorial including a Christian cross at an interchange point between the territories of the Kawelka and the Minembi at a place called Ekit Kuk near to Nggolke in the Dei Council area. Many of the Kawelka left their territories and dispersed to other places. Since then, however, major fighting on this scale has not broken out again on these particular fronts (up to 2011). This cross is sometimes pointed to as a marker of the peace-making process that enabled its erection at Ekit Kuk. It is clearly a symbol of considerable significance and must have marked a consensus not only between the groups but also between the Lutheran and Catholic Christians on opposite sides of the conflict.

A further account of this phase of conflict is given by Strathern (1992, 1993a). Like all other conflicts, this one had its immediate precipitating causes and its longer-term historical background. This historical background is the reason why settlements of disputes are difficult to make. Here, the cross-cutting ties that social anthropologists of the 1960s tended to view as conducing overall to peace or resolution of conflicts (for example, Gluckman 1955) could, if the balance went that way, lead to an exacerbation and escalation of violence that is progressively intractable to settle even by means of compensation payments.

Furthermore, immediate and long-term causes are intermeshed, not separate. A young man of the Kawelka Kundmbo clan in their territory at Nggolke (alt. sp. Golke) went to drink beer with some age-mate companions of the Minembi Yelipi clan: precisely the kind of dangerous and unpredictable context that the old leader Ndamba had envisioned in sponsoring the money *moka* between Kundmbo and Yelipi in 1964 described earlier in this chapter. The 1964 attempt at peace-making already indicated that there was a problem between these two neighbouring groups. There were rumours of pig-thefts and arguments over individuals cutting gardens in forest areas on their borders. Both groups were in a sense interstitial between the two major political blocs of tribe-pairs in Dei Council, the Tipuka–Kawelka pair and the Kombukla–Minembi pair. The Yelipi were historical refugees, originally paired with the Papeke clan of the Minembi tribe, major enemies of the Kawelka as a whole (see Appendix). Their more distant origins related them further away again to the Ialibu area (Lelip, Yelip) far to the south of the Melpa-speaking region: ambiguous outsiders. The Kundmbo were themselves at odds with the other two main clans of the Kawelka, the Membo and Mandembo pair. There was quite serious fighting in the pre-colonial past prior to the 1930s between them and the Kurupmbo, a section of Mandembo. And they had a fairly close alliance with another Minembi clan to their west, the Kimbo, many of whom were in fact Kundmbo by ancient agnatic ties, incorporated into Kimbo by a maternal link some generations earlier. Ndamba in the 1960s had sought to strengthen and extend ties with his neighbours among the Minembi through intermarriage and *moka* exchanges, all as a part of peace-making. And the Yelipi were also ambiguously a part of the Tipuka–Kawelka complex because they had been given land as refugees by kinsfolk among the Tipuka Kengeke clan when they broke with their own pair-clan the Minembi Papeke and fled when defeated in internal warfare with this group.

This structural background may seem complex, but it was a part of everyday embodied awareness and practice among the groups involved. Consequently, when the young Kundmbo man went to drink with Yelipi companions, it was clear that things might go wrong. He himself probably felt safe, because his mother came from the Yelipi group. He was their sister's son, a privileged tie, an intertext in the narratives of conflict and violence between groups. Alcohol, however, can bring out the worst in people, and after a fisticuffs encounter he was abandoned and died on the side of the steep and rutted precarious road that was made as a part of the 'modernisation process' between the Kundmbo and Yelipi in the 1950s and early 1960s when Dei Local Government Council was established.

The Kundmbo, led by Ndamba, from whose lineage the dead youth came, demanded compensation, and in the manner of the times, an inter-tribal Trouble Committee was appointed via the local government structure, and provisional agreement was reached on the numbers of pigs and amounts of money to be handed over. However, at this point men from more distant Minembi clans, opposed as major enemies to the Kawelka as a whole and without the cross-cutting ties of peace through marriages engineered by Ndamba, entered in and urged the Yelipi not to pay (a reversal of the earlier narrative given in the Appendix). This was tantamount to a provocation of war. These Minembi clans had old scores of their own to pay off through revenge, and they had also stockpiled a set of new weapons: guns. Sensing a potential advantage, they incited warfare because they thought they could win. The Yelipi were perhaps persuaded because they were afraid of the Tipuka–Kawelka bloc and thought they might get back into the larger bloc of Kombukla–Minembi. The two blocs were also due to come into conflict soon over an upcoming general election, in which the sitting candidate (P—) from Tipuka was opposed by a Kombukla rival. Solidifying hostility between the two blocs would act in favour of the Kombukla candidate, because his bloc was the more numerous of the two.

So the fighting began, and each side made raids against the other, taking advantages by swift killings and ambushes, killing so many that no adequate compensations could be paid and reinstated the implacable major enemy relationship between them dating back to pre-contact times.

The most extraordinary feature of this history is that it was brought to a close by a Christian-influenced ritual, a cross erected as a memorial to the dead and a mark of reconciliation between the groups, standing at a commanding crossroad overlooking the valleys of the Minembi and the Kawelka. Where compensation could not be made, a new ritual was established that stood outside of the inexorable patterns of revenge and could be adopted on a new basis of shared identity. It remains an unusual, but important, case. In Chapter 7 we will look at recent theories of 'ritual efficacy' in the context of peace-making in general.

Exchange and conflict

Parliamentary politics themselves contributed to subsequent patterns of conflict. Members of Parliament were granted large sums of money to spend on projects in their own electorates, and this stock of money made the position of parliamentarian highly valuable, increasing the competition and animosities between candidates for elections. National politics began to be a causative factor in local conflicts, just as earlier colonial administrative decisions to set up councils and electorates had been (see Ketan 1998; Standish 1992 on the Chimbu/Simbu area; Strathern 1992, 1993b). In the 1990s, politics also began to be re-entwined in the networks of exchange themselves, since the sponsorships by politicians of particular payments of compensation for killings between groups can be seen as ways of seeking political support in elections. Violence before and after elections reflected the high stakes. (See the material in Chapter 1.)

These effects of nation-state politics on the Highlands have been matched also by the effects of large-scale commercial enterprises, especially mining, which have brought huge, uneven, rapidly spent influxes of cash into certain areas as a result of royalty and compensation payments to groups. Conflict over the division of these monies is endemic. Groups whose members feel aggrieved at being left out hijack vehicles and block highways. Since the 1990s the blocking of highways by criminals who threaten and sometimes kill travellers has been commonplace. These phenomena are frustrating, upsetting, worrying and expensive for the local populations themselves.

What is known as the 'raskol' problem (see Stewart & Strathern 2002a, pp. 72–82, with references)[1] has become endemic to the Highlands. Declining coffee prices have worsened things further. Small wonder that millenarian movements and ideas regarding end times circulated widely in the Highlands around the year 2000 (Robbins, Stewart & Strathern 2001; Strathern & Stewart 1997a). The elaborate *moka* chains of the past disappeared and were replaced by isolated large-scale compensation payments for killings. Among the Kawelka, one such payment was made in 2001 amounting to some K26,000. A newspaper report named another payment of more than K100,000 in the same year, made by one Central Hagen group to another. The principle of compensation, and the fear of revenge killing, go on in the midst of a hugely transformed world; but it is a far cry from the expansive rhizomatic *moka* of the 1960s, inspired by the colonially induced lull in fighting and the emergence of leaders under the colonial aegis who effectively bound past and future together.

These two narratives, of exchange and of conflict, seem hard to fit together. Yet they both belong to the historical experience of the same people and their region. The overall narrative is one of the dialectical engagement of forces for nonviolent change and forces that induce violent action. At a systemic level, these forces can be seen as uneasily counterbalanced. In other ways, they have produced each other. The growth of the coffee business, for example, has fuelled local animosities between people over land and led to violent altercations between them. Christian churches preach against violence, but the division between churches and sects can exacerbate local tensions. And parliamentarians promote 'law' and 'development', but their distributions of funds cause jealousy, distrust and severe local competition. Those leaders who operate as peace-makers in these changed circumstances face many problems, as we explore further in the next chapter.

*

We have moved a long way from a discussion of the relatively benign and adaptive processes whereby Hageners altered some of their exchange practices to an ever-widening set of themes indicating the causes of conflict and violence in a post-colonial world marked by both small-scale criminal actions, inter-group fighting and the conflicts that large-scale economic enterprises such as mining bring with them. Historical changes and experiences of these kinds have deeply affected people's senses of themselves in their world. In the next chapter we discuss this process further, looking at the problems faced by peace-makers.

CHAPTER 6

The problems of peace-makers: intermediate sovereigns

Introduction

This chapter discusses further issues of peace-making in Hagen, and goes on to examine relations between 'intermediate sovereign' groups and the state in Papua New Guinea. The inter-group patterns of relations in Hagen were disrupted by the imposition of colonial control. The resulting problems appear in events and processes within the post-colonial state. The state's sovereignty is contested at times of crisis both by separatist or micro-nationalist movements and by individual clan groups who occasionally oppose state control over land, forestry or mining resources. Compensation issues run through each of the historical periods considered, from the pre-colonial to the present. Attempts by state authorities to impose solutions by force or to negotiate with groups are construed as models of ways in which states may approach 'intermediate sovereign' groups. Settlements made with such groups are likely to work only if they satisfy the group's wishes at multiple levels. This chapter, therefore, looks at peace-making practices via the concept of 'intermediate sovereign' in political fields. We use the Hagen area for our primary examples, but present some of the propositions derived from study in that area in more general, or generalisable, form. The argument of the chapter is thus continuous with previous chapters while seeking to place the materials in broader contexts.

Inter-group relations and sovereignty

One branch of contemporary anthropology concentrates on historical change and narratives of change. However, our knowledge of how political groups operated in pre-colonial contexts is complicated by the fact that most actual observations began in colonial times. With this caveat in mind, it is worthwhile to begin by recapitulating how anthropologists studying parts of Africa, 'Melanesia' and elsewhere have modelled these societies through concepts of 'ordered anarchy' and 'segmentary political systems' arising out of British social anthropology (see Evans-Pritchard 1940, pp. 139–91, for more information on these concepts). For the purposes of this chapter, an initial comparison between inter-group relations and sovereignty is necessary. In such a comparison, tribes and clans may be seen as comparable to sovereign groups between which international relations existed (see, for example, Watson 1983).[1] The comparison is, of course, imperfect. We are not arguing that such groups saw themselves entirely as 'sovereignties'. In the first place, they were not hierarchically organised as clearly bounded entities with a formalised politico-legal structure. Nevertheless, an analogy of this kind is useful for understanding how states and intermediate sovereigns interact. Within a wider ethnic or linguistic group, individual major political units existed, numbering from several hundred to several thousand persons. These groups could combine for war against other groups and could also collaborate in order to bring about peace. Group leaders orchestrated such collective processes through exhortations of solidarity and appeals to self-interest.

While we cannot speak of 'government' within their units, we can speak of them as presenting a united front to outsiders and as not recognising authorised control by any political power beyond that within their own group.

How, then, did international relations proceed between groups of this kind? Such groups interacted through trade, intermarriage, negotiations and compensation payments for killings if these were enjoined by the 'local international rules'.[2] Between certain groups no compensation payments were made. In such cases, the absence of a regular expectation of payment anticipated permanent hostility between the groups involved. Yet, even in that case, trading and intermarriage might continue to occur. The resulting networks of kinship and friendship would partially mitigate hostility and provide pathways for negotiation over the disputed issues. This process could lead to informal alliances between segments of the tribes, dissolving their absolute hostility. Such international relations did not proceed through legally established frameworks; however, this is not to say that no framework at all existed, since the process involved was political and economic in character and motivated by mutual perceptions of self-interest.

Tribes, for example, could be paired with each other in Hagen because they shared a single divination-substance (called *mi*) used to test the truth of assertions in disputes.[3] They also had a material interest in the children of intermarriages because ritual divinations might proceed through the bodies of persons so related. A sister's son might swear an oath on his mother's group's divination-substance in order to establish the innocence of his own (that is, his father's) group in a dispute over a killing. International relations in that case were mediated through human bodies that constituted and represented the relations in question. Mechanisms of this sort are specific to a kinship-based polity and are not readily evident or considered plausible to those who operate in a bureaucratically organised state structure.

Segmentary social systems

The tribes described above were not unitary groups but were divided into segments that could oppose each other at one level, yet unite in the face of an enemy at a higher level. Existing hostilities within tribes were mediated by intermarriage, exchange and the intervention of secular and religious leaders who represented values shared by the contestants. The processes of opposition and cooperation could be much more complicated in practice than a simple, regular, segmentary model would suggest.[4] In all cases, these processes were not automatic but depended on circumstances and negotiations, and, above all, on the material flow of wealth goods.[5] Nevertheless, processes derived from the segmentary principle allowed for the creation of colonialism and state control. Thus, it provided an easy ideological vehicle for the subsequent creation of intermediate sovereigns.

Modalities of settlement

Inter-group rules provided a framework for the articulation of force, diplomacy and exchange within the segmentary scale of relations. In his autobiography, Ongka, a leader in the Kawelka tribe of the Mount Hagen area in the Western Highlands of Papua New Guinea, depicted how these rules operated in pre-colonial times (Ongka grew up shortly before Australian explorers and government officers first entered the Highlands area in the early 1930s):

> Now I want to talk about how we fought. Sometimes we fought with sticks. If a woman was raped she would scream out and come home covered in mud, then her menfolk would go out together and seize pigs from the nearest house of the rapist's group or wait for them behind a turning and set on them with sticks (*tembokl pöyö*). These were big long cudgels which each man cut for himself and put aside. When they used them they

all ran forward together in a row, the sticks poised above their heads, it looked like the rafters of a house or the long supports to which we bind sugarcane stalks. Heads and arms could be broken. We of Mandembo clan in Kawelka tribe fought with the Membo clan in this way, we pushed each other to and fro back into each other's territory. We did the same with the neighbouring Tipuka clans, chasing them as far as the banks of the Möka river in the valley, and then they raced back at us and chased us back up the hill to home.

There were no courts of justice then. Only the big-men could step in between the fighters, call to either side to keep its distance and arrange for pigs to be paid as compensation for wounds inflicted. Each side had to pay out this compensation to its own supporters, and many pigs were spent in this way. The blows could even be fatal.[6]

Ongka's colonial experience colours his account. His people first encountered the Australian explorers in the 1930s and were brought loosely under governmental control by about 1945.[7] Ongka was made a 'boss-boy', headman (tultul, luluai) and Local Government Councillor up until and after Papua New Guinea's political independence from Australian rule in 1975 (see, generally, Woolford 1976). He notes that in pre-colonial times only local leaders or big-men, who acted as financiers and diplomats for their groups, could intervene in fighting and begin the peace-making process through compensation. Significantly, he does not say that big-men instigated or controlled the actual fighting or that they were involved in the incidents leading up to it.

Ongka describes the combat between the two Kawelka clans, Mandembo (his own) and Membo, as a means to protect and gain territory. However, in other contexts, these two clans were close allies who joined forces to fight and oppose the third clan, Kundmbo. This dynamic conforms to the general expectations of the segmentary model.[8]

Ongka's account also pinpoints the major modality of peace-making: compensation. Killings between groups in a segmentary kin-based polity can lead either to a continuous blood-feud, in which further killings erupt into occasional warfare, or compensation payments. In the most densely populated areas of the Papua New Guinea Highlands, forms of compensation were highly developed and evolved into processes that over time could theoretically convert hostility into alliance. Two forms of payment for killings were used. In one form, the killers directly compensated the kin of the person killed. In the other, the instigating group paid reparations to its allies for the loss of warriors who died in support of their cause. The first method, direct payment, was utilised within a tribe or within an alliance-circle only when allies had fought among themselves. The rules of 'scaling' were thus fairly clear. Failure to pay automatically meant the assumption or resumption of hostilities. Between allies, a unilateral compensation payment could be transformed into the complex two-way set of reciprocal exchanges known as *moka* (see, generally, Strathern 1971 [2007]). In this case, peace-making by compensation was not just a single event. It was a historical process that needed to be maintained. This point is important in the present discussion (refer also to Chapter 3).

This particular modality of peace-making articulated and facilitated a processual vision of peace-making over time. First, a single medium was used. The payment or exchange of wealth focused the groups on a common value, symbolically equivalent to human life itself. Second, the payment or exchange took place at multiple levels as gifts passed through big-men's hands and were distributed widely. Third, individuals could extend these payments further by making individual exchanges. Fourth, over time, compensation payments could convert hostility into competition over the sizes of gifts made between parties. A single modality of exchange practices sufficed to achieve all these ends.

Functions of settlements
The various functions of settlements included payment for killings, payment to allies and compensation for a sexual offence, theft, misuse of a piece of land, verbal insults or failure to prevent a death (see Strathern & Stewart 1998c). Settlements could also be used innovatively to effect positive changes, such as setting up a new alliance. On the whole, however, they were a means of restoring or enhancing an existing status quo. This occurred because each group's basic sovereignty/autonomy was already recognised. Generally, settlements were not made to give new recognition to a group, but to re-establish a stable relationship between groups. In this regard, the functions of settlements are distinguishable from those involved in state and intermediate sovereign conflicts, in which the intermediate sovereign (IS) seeks to establish itself as an independent power. This difference pinpoints the obvious difficulty that recognition of IS sovereignty poses for the state. The enclaved IS threatens the state's own sovereignty. This threat is paralleled by the challenges posed to a new nation-state, such as Papua New Guinea, by dissident clans or tribes and regional separatist movements. The difference in a settlement's functions also indicates why a particular settlement may be harder to arrange today if it depends on rearranging rather than reaffirming the overall political structure. Inter-group fighting, however, does not necessarily involve a conscious challenge to the state as such, beyond a wish that the government would leave groups alone to sort out their own conflicts by force.

Forms of negotiation in settlements
Negotiations between hostile groups might involve the invocation of mystical sanctions and processes as a way to bridge the gap between

them (see Strathern 1972b). In the Papua New Guinea Highlands, a ritualised pattern of communication between groups complemented the controlling influence of sanctions. In Mount Hagen, as Ongka's account makes clear, groups placed tremendous emphasis on the rhetorical abilities of big-men in mediating political disputes and converting force into persuasion (see Strathern & Stewart 1999b). In moots (community meetings to discuss disputes), the two sides, arriving with spears, bows and arrows, would be carefully separated. People were expected to listen quietly as orators told their versions of history. Orators tempered their accusations by expressing themselves in 'veiled' or 'folded' speech, an indirect way of speaking that only leaders on the opposing side might fully understand. They also used other forms of symbolic communication. For example, a group that had lost a member in a fight would arrive caked in yellow mud as a sign of mourning and protest. Their attendance at a moot indicated their potential willingness to accept compensation as well as their marked grief at their loss. After settlement had been reached, orators would break into a particular style of speech, known as 'arrow-talk' (*el ik*), indicating that a ritualised agreement was about to be reached.[9] The strong ritual constraints on both verbal and non-verbal expression reveal the potential fragility of peace-making through negotiations. Modern uses of such ritual forms, when extended to higher levels, are more likely to break down because the rituals are unable to constrain the behaviour of groups too remotely interrelated to respect each other. The next section exemplifies how the issue of scale is significant in dealing with intermediate sovereigns.

Colonial and post-colonial contexts of change
Many of the problems currently present in Papua New Guinea and other parts of the world mirror the problems that existed during colonial times. For many years, the literature in political anthropology

has analysed these dynamics. A classic study of this order can be found in the anthropologist Evans-Pritchard's work among the Nuer of Africa, in which the prophet figure played an indigenous intermediate sovereign role (see, generally, Evans-Pritchard 1956). The Nuer prophets held spiritual powers that were highly venerated by the Nuer people. The role of these prophets as IS leaders has more recently been studied by another anthropologist, Sharon Hutchinson (1996, pp. 338–45), who has shown that Nuer prophets continue to perform the duties of peace-makers as well as fighters.

In the 1990s, a Nuer prophet named Wutnyang Gatakek raised his own army, which joined the Sudan People's Liberation Army (SPLA), the remaining portions of the Anyanya II Army. The united forces delivered a powerful surprise attack upon, and temporarily captured, the Sudanese government-held town of Malakal. This same prophet also 'repeatedly sought to defuse intensifying intra- and inter-ethnic conflicts, [arising] between various Nuer communities and between them and their Dinka, Anyuak, and Uduk neighbors' (pp. 338–39, citing as comparative authority Johnson 1994, pp. 348–51).

The SPLA is an IS that began to assert control over the Western Upper Nile during the 1980s, when it prevented further Arab militia incursions into that region. The SPLA rose out of, and modelled itself after, the resistance formed against the northern-based Anglo-Egyptian Sudan that Evans-Pritchard studied earlier. Since the time of Evans-Pritchard's fieldwork in 1930 and the end of the Condominium in 1955, the Nuer have been drawn into a web of 'government authorities, district councils, party bureaucracies, regional assemblies, and national parliaments – all of which were constantly being reshuffled, reorganized, and disbanded' (Hutchinson 1996, pp. 25–26).[10]

Dealing with non-state collectivities poses similar problems for modern governments as it did in the colonial era. The collectivities may operate like tribes with warlords acting in the role of tribal chiefs, or they may operate as parts of a wider segmentary group diffused across the landscape. Difficulties arise in dealing with collective groups when they do not have a single leader who might speak with one voice for the group, and when the power of the collectivity is diffused. During both colonial and contemporary times, mining companies that have attempted to negotiate with local groups have sometimes misunderstood the diffuse power structure and asked to speak to the area's group leader. This is an attempt to create an IS-type figure with whom the company or government officer can interact in a procedural manner that conforms to one with which the company is familiar and provides a context where its personnel understand the rules of engagement. Sometimes a group that does not perceive any merit or immediate gain from interacting with the officer elects an unimportant or non-powerful person to interact with the company. In this way, they either deceive the officer and gain better control of the situation, or at least distance themselves from the officer. If the newly appointed indigenous official gives them orders, they conveniently ignore them (see, for example, Strathern 1984, pp. 53–69).

Contested sovereignty within PNG

Papua New Guinea's independence came without any concerted struggle against the colonial power, Australia; but it has been followed by many struggles that the anthropologist Robert Foster has called 'nation making' (see, generally, Foster 1995). These struggles have taken two forms: the effort to create a national consciousness through the use of symbolism that transcends local contexts, and the effort to deal with groups that actively oppose the state in its role as peace-keeper and guardian of law and order (see p. 18; see also, for example, Gordon & Meggitt 1985, pp. 71–91). The distinction that anthropologists customarily draw between nation and state is crucial here. The state of Papua New Guinea was created out of two colonial territories with different histories and formal statuses, the northern territory being New Guinea and the southern, Papua (see Woolford 1976, pp. 1–3). Straddling these two territories, within the valleys enclosed by central mountain cordilleras, are the Highlands Provinces, which were opened to the outside world in the 1930s, much later than most regions. In 1975, Highlanders were reluctant to accept independence since they feared that it would result in the withdrawal of Australian resources and personnel, and domination by the more highly educated coastal populations. The new national government, led by coastal politicians at the time, thus began with a legitimacy problem: it did not represent 'the nation'.

Since then, party politics have focused on the creation of ad hoc alliances that enable one bloc to hold a majority within the Westminster-style parliamentary government. Highlanders have achieved great prominence in politics since 1975, but there is still only a weakly developed ideology of the nation as such, and allegiance to the nation cannot invariably stand counter to tendencies to oppose the state over pragmatic issues. Lack of national development as an imaginative construct, in historian Benedict Anderson's terms, easily fosters opposition to the state whenever a group's perceived local interests do not coincide with those of their co-nationals (see, generally, Anderson 1983 [1991]).

This point is relevant because it indicates that the formal concept of sovereignty has to cover more than one base in order to be effective. Sovereignty may be defined as a legally independent status vis-à-vis outsiders, but it cannot operate effectively unless there is some sense of the legitimacy of authority within its borders. States use the rhetoric of nationhood in order to confer such legitimacy on their formal powers. Unless the state can invent an adequately ritualised form of symbolism, however, it may find that creating internal legitimacy is difficult without the assistance of an external enemy, especially if the local form of sociality is tribal.

The situation in Papua New Guinea constitutes the segmentary variant of the violation of political scientist Stephen Krasner's (1995/96, p. 115) 'Westphalian principle', referring to the autonomy and territoriality of the state. Krasner points to several instances in European history where, for practical reasons, states have accepted diminished control over their domestic affairs and/or their boundaries (p. 117). This exemplifies the trade-off between the state and its constituent units, which can occur when these units deny the superior power of the state and thus deny aspects of its internal sovereignty. State authorities may decide to tolerate this denial if it does not lead to a threat of overall secession and is context-bound. Alternatively, they may decide to oppose it and risk stimulating even greater opposition. The overall problem may be called the 'internal Westphalian dilemma'.

Creating a nation based on an amalgam of diverse local groups is obviously more difficult when a great diversity of cultures and languages exists, as is the case in Papua New Guinea. Forceful imposition of national authority further impedes the state's endeavour to attain internal sovereignty. The role of the Papua New Guinea police in quelling tribal battles in the Highlands is a case in point.[11] The warriors tend to view the state authority as an interloper, interfering with their right (or at least their inclination) to fight each other. However, those who are not directly involved may welcome the intervention, arguing that it can restore order to an area where life is disrupted. Police raid villagers as a reprisal for fighting, burn down villagers' houses, confiscate putatively stolen property and jail relatives of the fighters as hostages. The power of the state is impressed upon local people in ways that are reminiscent of colonial times, but not conducive to post-colonial nation-making. In turn, the police may themselves be ambushed and killed in revenge for their killings. As a result of the re-scaling of segmentary principles, all of the police force may be situationally seen as enemies and potential targets. This may implicitly produce a cycle of vengeance between the police and the public. This cycle is contrary to the need for the police, as an arm of the government, to appear as impartial mediators in a conflict between groups. Consequently, the government loses legitimacy through the application of the very force that, in a sense, sustains it. What the state gains, the nation loses. If the people continue to resist, the process that Gregory Bateson called 'symmetrical schismogenesis' sets in (see Bateson 1958, p. 177). If their resistance subsides, the schismogenesis is complementary but does not lead to any genuine acceptance of legitimacy (p. 177).

Similar considerations may apply to relations between sovereign states and an IS. Force by itself may be necessary or may be exercised by both sides, but it is not a basis for peace-making. Neither nation-making nor international peace-making can proceed simply on a basis of force.

Micro-national and other resistance movements in PNG

The forerunner to the revolutionary Bougainville Freedom Movement (BFM), supported by the Bougainville Revolutionary Army (BRA), began by organising local opposition to colonial administration policies. One early segment of the movement, the Napidakoe Navitu, was established in 1969 to protest the Administration's proposed resumption of plantation and mining lands. Acting as an IS, Napidakoe Navitu represented local villagers in two settings. While initially unsuccessful in their legal action against the Administration's resumption of land, they succeeded in negotiating compensation payments. The group's main objectives were political autonomy, better education and the economic, social and political development of

Bougainville. Napidakoe Navitu was generally hostile to the Administration and later advocated Bougainville's secession from Papua New Guinea. Conflicts over royalties from the Bougainville copper mine and the environmental effects of this mining project became major factors in the development of the secession movement (see Griffin 1982, pp. 113–38).

In March 1997, the Papua New Guinea government was planning to hire 'mercenaries' to act as advisers in training their army to fight the BRA more effectively. The BFM exemplifies an IS that produced a revolutionary situation which was very difficult to resolve.[12]

A similar movement, founded in the same year (1969) as the Napidakoe Navitu, was the Mataungan Association. It was formed to protest the Administration's decision to form a multiracial local government council on the Gazelle Peninsula. Soon after its formation, the association's interests spread to include land issues, economic enterprises and the preservation of cultural heritage. After the association made various demands of the Administration that were not satisfactorily met, it announced that it would break away from the rest of the territory of New Guinea unless these demands were satisfied. The Administration initially reacted with a show of force but later introduced legislation designed to create a new type of local self-government for the Gazelle Peninsula that satisfied the association's demands, relieving its desire to seek a secessionist split. In this instance, an IS withdrew demands to become a sovereign entity and subsequently integrated into the state system as a small political party allied with others (see Grosart 1982, pp. 139–76).

Another IS was the Papua Besena movement, which failed in its attempt at separatism. This movement emerged explicitly to oppose the Australian Government's commitment to grant independence to a unified Papua New Guinea. The movement lacked a coherent organisational structure and chose to work through already established Papuan organisations. Its first leader was Josephine Abaijah, previously an employee of the Public Health Department, who charged the Australians with neglecting Papua, a former British colony. The claim of financial neglect was not substantiated, but it appealed to local sensibilities in the face of failed development schemes in the region. Abaijah also opposed the presence of immigrant labourers from the Highlands region in the capital city of Port Moresby because they competed with coastal and hinterland Papuans (such as the Goilala people) for unskilled jobs. Papuan public servants who held a dominant position in the bureaucracy prior to independence supported Abaijah's movement because they feared they would lose this position over time. While appealing to the idea of underdevelopment and neglect, the movement was based on a temporary coalition of interests at a particular historical period. However, it was eventually engulfed by the overall drive for unification of the two colonial territories under one parliamentary government, led to some extent by politicians from the populous groups on the northern, New Guinea, side of the divide.

Interestingly, in the absence of a 'ready-made' ethnic identity, Papua Besena invented one, through statements such as the following made by Abaijah: 'I am a Papuan. That makes me different from other people. I feel I have a nationality, a name, and a common future with Papuan people' (McKillop 1982, p. 329, quoting Steinbauer 1974, p. 32). The 'other people' are the 'New Guineans', and the contextual reference is thus a colonial one couched in the mythopoeic 'othering' terms of nationalism. Precisely because this primordial basis was actually fairly weak, Papua Besena took on the trappings of a kinship polity. In fact, Besena means 'clan' or 'tribe'. However, this particular IS failed because it lacked a strong basis, and Papua merged with New Guinea to form a single country (see McKillop 1982, pp. 329–58). This was also in accord with wishes or plans of the Australian Government. Papua Besena's sense of a separate identity was to some extent based on a consciousness deriving from early British colonial influence there.

Clan and state: compensation in a new world

Local systems of compensation in the Highlands of Papua New Guinea have also gone through a series of marked changes. The introduction of government courts for criminal and civil offences, characteristic of state government, has not greatly contributed to inter-group adjustment in the post-colonial context. Punishment and incarceration of individuals do nothing to solve the social problems that follow killings and assaults at local levels. By and large, these problems must still be settled through compensation practices. The state may intervene in the process as well. For example, it may require the establishment of special purpose Trouble Committees to determine amounts of compensation (see, for example, Strathern 1993a, p. 155). While the state's intentions are laudable, they may result in reducing discussions to haggling over amounts rather than expanding such discussions to achieve reconciliation between the groups themselves. The Committees' deliberations take a commodified and reified form, reflecting new forms of capitalist economics that have become prevalent. The state may also require individuals to pay a fine to the police, which merely reduces the amount of wealth available for the compensation process proper (see Gordon & Meggitt 1985, pp. 25–26). Further, a jail sentence acts not as a solution, but as a timebomb, as people may simply wait until offenders return from jail before exacting revenge. Local Village Courts established by state ordinance help to resolve minor disputes but lack the legal powers to punish killings or tribal fighting. They have also run into many problems since their first early post-colonial introduction (Strathern 1984, pp. 122–42).[13]

Compensations are also much harder to organise if killings occur between unrelated groups brought into contact through travel, migration and urbanisation. Yet this is precisely the context in which killings occur frequently today (see, for example, Strathern 1992, p. 234; see also Levine 1996). At local levels, the enmities between groups are exacerbated by an escalation in killings caused by the introduction of guns, by alcohol consumption in village taverns (see, for example, Strathern 1982a) and by a curtailment or diminution of the elaborate *moka* exchanges or other comparable forms of exchange which used to channel competition between groups into contests of prestige obtained through displays of generosity. Competition is increasingly focused on parliamentary and provincial elections since power is concentrated in the new political positions. However, politicians are unable to control conflicts at the local level unless they also attempt to foster practices of compensation between groups. In fact, elections themselves are surrounded by political conflicts that bring about killings and destruction of property, partly through intimidation and chicanery in the voting process itself.[14]

In the economic arena, clan and state may be even more explicitly pitted against each other. This new context of demands for compensation arises from enterprises of economic development, especially capital-intensive mining projects for gold, copper, gas and oil (see Strathern 1993d; also Strathern 1997). In these contexts, political associations, based on an expanded clan ideology, tend to emerge as IS or quasi-IS in relation to the central government. At issue here are the rights of locally defined interests vis-à-vis the wider state interests. From the point of view of the central government, sovereignty may include the residual rights over mineral resources, but local groups do not see it that way. Local groups do not generally accept that the state has a legitimate eminent domain right to resources either above or below ground surface. In fact, the national government has sometimes left it up to international companies to negotiate terms with the local people, implicitly abandoning its sovereign role.[15]

Local groups treat companies as they treat the state, refusing to grant sovereign rights to either. When they demand monetary compensation that excludes benefits to other groups in the nation-state or forcefully hold up projects by blocking roads or threatening workers, they are clearly acting as a rival IS. Such situations can be defused only by a combination of 'generous' payments and a great deal of time spent in diplomatic discussions. Such conversations attempt to lower the levels of suspicion between the local population and the company personnel. As one Australian liaison officer for a mining company put it, 'The Enga [in whose territory this mine is] are sure that the company is cheating them in general. From time to time they think they've worked out exactly how, and that's when we can expect trouble and have to get into some hard negotiating'.[16] In this case, the company had built a large round house, in traditional style, but with open sides (called a *haus win* in Tok Pisin, meaning a house with access to the air) – right inside the mine headquarters. It was used for meetings to defuse hostilities and to rearrange compensation packages between the company and local leaders.[17]

Local groups have also banded together as quasi-IS in order to oppose the putative pollution of their rivers and garden lands by mine effluents.[18] It is doubtful if any scale of compensation will ultimately be able to satisfy these demands, especially since both Australian law firms and European Commission lawyers filed suits or began to take an interest in documenting deaths of people and livestock or wildlife from river pollution.[19] Environmental issues formed a powerful symbolic element in the case mounted by the Bougainville Revolutionary Army against the mine on Bougainville Island (compare Havini 1990; see also, generally, Strathern & Stewart 1998b). These issues, dealing directly with land and its resources, can prove to be the most difficult to mediate in the long term. If land issues are at stake between a state and an IS (or between states), then we may always expect peace-making to be difficult.

Once again, we may compare this situation with 'international relations' in what we can call Old Melanesia (see, generally, Brookfield & Hart 1971).[20] In the old context, land was not usually directly at stake; or, if it was, a victorious group would drive out another and occupy some of its land, but might later set up mutual compensatory exchanges to restore friendship and intermarriage. More commonly, disputes stemmed from injuries to the person, such as killings and rapes. These disputes were solved or their solutions were marked by exchanges of wealth goods and often by arranged intermarriages, bringing the dispute into the ambit of the kinship polity (Strathern 1982b). Such options are simply not available when the local group deals with a company or the state. In this context, relations may become polarised and the local group emerges as an IS. This occurs because there is no effective modality through which negotiations can proceed as long as the two sides are fundamentally at odds, as is exemplified by the historical confrontation between Bougainville separatists and the central government of Papua New Guinea.

The Bougainville case also illustrates why peace agreements may be very difficult to make as well as subsequently difficult to maintain. In this case, the separatist movement had a far more powerful set of symbols on which to draw than had Papua Besena, as Bougainville is an island clearly set apart from mainland Papua New Guinea (see, generally, Griffin 1990). Its peoples share many cultural practices with their southern neighbours in the Solomon Islands, which were formerly administered by the British. They point to their distinctive dark skin colour to distinguish themselves from the lighter-skinned mainlanders. While the huge copper mine in their midst brought economic development, it also brought influxes of outsiders and environmental pollution. Like the Mataungans and the Papua Besena, Bougainville attempted to declare its independence from the rest of Papua New Guinea during the 1970s but was initially pacified by the introduction of a decentralised provincial government system from 1979 onwards.[21] The original main supporters of the BRA, the Nasioi people, are the ones whose environment has suffered most from the mine (see Oliver 1991, pp. 166, 205).

Killings between the Papua New Guinea Police/Defence Force and BRA fighters caused a vengeance situation that was hard to settle by compensations. The central government tried to stress the benefits of a settlement for the ordinary population, but they found it difficult to successfully negotiate with the BRA, which remained committed to separatism. This is a clear example of how neither the modalities of negotiation nor the rhetorical forms employed may be effectively able to overcome adverse circumstances in order to produce a lasting peace settlement.[22] Meanwhile, to recoup its losses of mining royalties, the central government encouraged large-scale mining projects elsewhere, which led to gains in revenue, but also to new confrontations with clan and regional groups, as noted already.

The most important lesson here is that if an IS (1) begins itself to use 'statist' terminology to describe its activities, especially by calling itself an 'army' (compare here the historical use of the term IRA in Northern Ireland), and (2) killings take place which rouse 'primordialist' senses of violation but are not dealt with in 'primordial' terms such as ritualised compensations, then the conditions for peace-making or peace-keeping become very problematic.

Douglas Oliver provides an excellent account of the negotiations between the central government and the Bougainville separatists up to 1991 (see, generally, Oliver 1991). He includes a picture of an October 1989 ceremony at the Arawa township (the town created to serve the mine), which is captioned: 'Prime Minister Namaliu (left) joins hands with Joseph Kabui [the Nasioi Premier of the Provincial Government and also chairman of the Interim Government of the Republic of Bougainville delegation that met with the central government at Honiara in the Solomon Islands in 1990] over traditional pig and food assembly' (illustration opposite p. 245). Both leaders bowed slightly in the picture as they extended their right hands over a large slaughtered (sacrificed) pig and a bunch of plantains to be cooked for a feast. A crowd of urban people stood at a short distance watching. The symbolism in this ceremony expressed an air of equality and reconciliation between the leaders. However, one pig was clearly not enough, since the conflict continued. Ritual can play a creative role in bringing about peace, but perhaps only in conjunction with many other factors. We explore this general point further in Chapter 7.

What works, and why

This section will summarise the implications illuminated by the case studies. Voluntary bilateral peace-making can work only on a basis of mutual respect, understanding and shared goals. Such a sharing of aims can proceed only if there are forms of language and action by which to express them. Further, peace arrangements will work only if their terms are adequately shared among the sections of the populations served by peace-makers.

Comparing conflict and peace-making in the 'old international context' with their counterparts in contemporary situations, we have found that the roots of contemporary IS-style movements can often be traced to colonial times. However, this does not mean such movements are simply to be 'explained' in colonial terms. The contrast between old and new highlights the inherent complexity of contemporary political affairs under which confrontations involve more levels and scales of interest. Today, the state enters into affairs at the local level and vice versa. This inherent complexity makes settlements more difficult, although sometimes it is used creatively to facilitate them.

Modalities and messages
In the Old Melanesian context, Highlands social leaders employed the single formal mechanism of compensation to settle a range of disputes over a range of segmentary contexts. Compensation was, and remains, a modality with many functions. It was accompanied by ritualised actions of appeasement and reconciliation that reinforced the outcomes of verbal rhetoric by leaders. The compensation was itself both medium and message, and it was accepted as the way to make peace or to mark it. In contemporary events, the principle of compensation remains, but the context has changed. Compensation may take place between unrelated groups or between local groups and the government. These contexts mean that shared values are no longer strongly operative. The Papua New Guinea state was able to absorb several IS-style movements at and shortly after independence; but at least one group, the BFM, evolved into a full-scale IS entity. The BFM claimed its own sovereignty. Ritualised messages work only if the medium to convey them is available and is appropriate in this scale to fit the political context.

Shared values
Nevertheless, tribal groups have made interesting attempts to find new shared values through the symbolism of place and of the nation. The following section focuses on cases involving gender symbolism.

Women have played, and continue to play, many roles in peace-making processes. Some of these are changing with shifting societal circumstances.

In the 1980s, an issue arose in the Central Hagen area that might have given rise to combat between two groups, but this was evaded by various peace-making strategies. The two groups, the Elti and the Penambe, are neighbours, closely intermarried, and historically paired as allies. An Elti man had launched an attack on one Penambe man's house and killed a brother of another prominent Penambe man. The Penambe organised a demonstration march of mourning in which the mourners were caked with yellow mud as is the traditional practice. Women and children were positioned at the head of the procession, indicating that their group as a whole was going to behave 'like women', that they would seek peace not war. The march took place in Mount Hagen town even though such demonstration marches traditionally would have gone forward on open land in the countryside. This movement into the city, the seat of the Provincial Government, symbolised a new awareness of the Government's role as a link to the wider nation.

Another example of women acting as peace-makers occurred in the Nebilyer Valley, where women's clubs (*amb klap*) began forming in early 1982 and continued to gain popularity over time. On 13 September 1982, one of these women's clubs played a pivotal role as peace-maker between opposing tribal alliances. In an unprecedented action, women from the neutral Kulka tribe's women's club, supported by the Provincial Government in Hagen town, marched out onto a battlefield between the opposing sides, carrying the Papua New Guinea flag, the symbol of unity. After distributing cash crops (European vegetables, such as onions and cabbages), soft drinks, cigarettes and 100 kina (Papua New Guinea currency) from their club funds to both sides, they planted the flag on the battlefield and told the warriors to go home, which they eventually did. The Kulka women's club's intervention preceded the compensation event that took place on 14 August 1983. The women were allowed to make public speeches at the event, a context in which usually only men would be allowed to speak (see Merlan & Rumsey 1991, pp. 156–97).[23]

The women's speeches emphasised that fighting was not an action that conformed with the women's club's goal of improving the living conditions in the community through pursuing 'bisnis' or cash-producing activities. One woman clearly stated that the club's technique of marching onto the battlefield carrying the Papua New Guinea flag and distributing food to both sides equally was a means of mediating a resolution through the action of exchange itself (p. 172).

These women used a mix of male and female oratory to effect a peaceful resolution through their speeches. Utilising *el ung* (arrow-talk, *el ik*), a form of male oratory, these women incorporated stylistic elements that would not traditionally have been used by women, while working within the framework of typical negotiations (see, for example, pp. 194–95).

A more traditional way in which women have served as peace-makers is through intermarriage. However, this practice is changing. In a reported article, an 18-year-old woman was offered as a part of a compensation payment by her group to another group in a Minj custom known as 'head pay'. In this practice, a female from one group was given in marriage to and went to live with a man from another group. Although this practice had persisted through history to the 1990s, in this instance the woman refused to be treated in this way as part of a payment and her case went to the Mount Hagen National Court. The judge found that the woman's 'rights to freedom of choice of a husband and thus her general constitutional rights to freedom were violated' (Dorney 1997, p. 13). The judge also held that the custom violated her right to equality since it 'targets only young women, not eligible men' (p. 13).

This situation reveals the conflict between the modern nation's guidelines for human rights protection and the cultural practices of many local people who view the state as an interloper, interfering in indigenous peace-making mechanisms. It is also apparent that human interests and perceptions may divide along lines of gender and age and that the state-based ideas of personhood conflict with those of the indigenous kinship polity. Interestingly, the spokesperson for the kinship polity in this case, Dr John Muke, previously a lecturer at the University of Papua New Guinea, in Port Moresby, with a PhD from Cambridge University in England, was a product of the new education system within the post-colonial nation-state (p. 13).

Making it stick

IS movements have problems in making their programs 'stick', as do states in dealing with them. One theory explaining why the BRA on Bougainville declared unilateral independence from Papua New Guinea is that its leaders Francis Ona and Sam Kauona were concerned that they might otherwise lose control over their movement to others or that the populace might not continue to give them support (Oliver 1991, p. 244). Where an IS is an unstable entity, making any agreement with it as a whole is obviously hard to do. Creating durable peace arrangements between clan groups involved ongoing historical processes. The peace was not just made and then left to happen. It had to be remade constantly by continuing exchanges; otherwise, it could revert to hostility. In this sense, there was no clear legal framework for peace. Peace was a social and historical, not a legal, construction. Nevertheless, compensation was the 'high road' followed in entering into the processes. In dealing with an IS, a state may have to assist in stabilising it in order to deal effectively with it, but this process can obviously backfire.

Satisfying wishes at multiple levels

As previously noted, satisfying the group's wishes at multiple levels is an important criterion for peace-making. First, participants have to agree on what the wishes and shared values are. For example, differences in such values may arise between different generations or genders, as the Mount Hagen Court case exemplifies. If only the leadership is satisfied, rival leaders are excluded or the interests of a populace diverge from those of the leaders, the collective wishes will not be fully satisfied. The functions of peace-making are involved here. Where these desires have to be met in many modalities, not just one, negotiations will be complex and vulnerable to cross-cutting aims. Diplomacy may involve more trade-offs and loose ends, and lasting settlements without the use of force may be hard to obtain.

Force versus diplomacy

While force or a threat of its use has a part to play in diplomacy, its use in the Papua New Guinea context has proved problematic and has led to a hardening of local opposition and to vengeance situations between new categories, such as people and police. In the old contexts, diplomatic speakers had to combine statements of their strength with a recognition of the strength and the equality of their opponents. In today's situations, the contexts are often putatively quite unequal, as when a conflict occurs between a clan as an IS and the government. If the government uses force, it is also weakening its own legitimacy while increasing its power. The diplomatic rule then is to conceal inequality as much as possible. When that cannot be done through rhetorics of nationhood, the state may reveal its hand, as can be done by passing legislation that outlaws certain compensation demands against the state by clan groups over (for example) mining issues.

Outcomes

The effect of such a ruling may be either to quell the movement or to escalate its resistance to the point where it explicitly challenges the state's legitimacy, as happened in Bougainville. In general, we can recognise two quite different outcomes of state versus IS encounters. Either the status quo will be reinstated or it will be overturned, depending on the power available to either side and their aims. If the aim is to set up viable international law in state–IS dealings, the rule of diplomacy must be to maintain attitudes of mutual respect and to try to create a meta-pragmatics of shared values that can then translate into agreements and rules. Without a ready-made ideology, such as compensation, to construct a meta-pragmatic code of this sort, it is evident that the problems of peace-makers are indeed considerable.

Compensation and its ritual underpinnings have remained central features in many of our discussions in this book. We turn in the next chapter to the topic of ritual and its place in peace-making.

CHAPTER 7

Transcending violence: the place of ritual

What part can ritual processes play in the establishment of peace, especially in situations of protracted conflict?

To answer this question, we need to begin with a working set of ideas about what the term ritual means. Anthropologists and others have discussed this matter extensively. For our purposes we do not have to propose a universal definition that will satisfy everyone. We do need, however, to pinpoint certain features of ritual as a form of action that will help us to delimit it as a concept for our present theme, including the role of the imagination in peace-making.

Features of action that help to mark out ritual sequences of action from a more general flow of actions include the following points. First, ritual sequences are phenomenologically and existentially set apart from the general flow by explicit or implicit *framing devices*. Typically, these devices are clear, for example the ringing of a bell, a mass lining up, a verbal announcement such as 'let us pray', or an act such as the inception of a special speech style like the *el ik* ('arrow-talk') that marks the closing of a *moka* occasion in Hagen. Second, rituals typically involve some kind of *symbolic action*, in which an aim or a value inherent in the structure of the ritual is expressed or represented in a condensed or striking way. An act of baptism, for example, entailing the use of sacral water by a ritual officiant to bring a child or adult person into a religious community of persons, depends on actions, gestures, words and the use of a symbolically charged medium, water, which together constitute the efficacy of the ritual itself. Third, ritual actions often, if not invariably, have a *unique function*, that is, they accomplish, or are designed to accomplish, something that other modes of action do not or cannot bring about. For example, this is the case in baptism, if only because this ritual is institutionalised as a part of the intersection of an individual life cycle, a family network and a religious congregation. Fourth, and in line with the institutionalisation of cultural forms, ritual acts tend to be *prescribed* both by being *authorised* and by taking place in relatively *invariant ways*, although over time and through space they may also be creatively or unconsciously altered. They may further be consciously invented or reinvented and then become unconsciously or naturalistically accepted as 'traditional'. Hence, fifth, rituals tend to be marked by claims that they are *traditional*, or they feed into a conscious creation that is intended to become traditional. Sixth, and finally here, the symbolic element in ritual noted in the second criterion above is often accompanied by its position in a wider perceived *cosmos* comprising the landscape, spirit entities and human persons among other living beings. This *positionality* of ritual acts gives them their wider significance and assists in the production of their overall efficacy.

These six features – framing devices, symbolic action, unique functions, prescription and invariance, traditionalism, and positional connection with a transcendental perceived reality, the cosmos – can help to give us working guidelines to identifying and assessing the place that rituals may have in contexts of peace-making. We have discussed definitional matters of this sort at length in earlier publications, in particular in our 2010 co-edited work, *Ritual*, published by Ashgate (Stewart & Strathern 2010b), in which we adduce examples from the work of a long lineage of theorists, highlighting the synthetic representations of Roy A Rappaport and Catherine Bell. What we have listed above is a further condensation of these more lengthy discussions. (See, for example, our Introduction to the *Ritual* volume, and selections 1 and 2 from the work of Rappaport (1999) and Bell (1997), respectively.)

Some further preliminary remarks are in order here. Our title for this chapter does not refer only to ritual. It also mentions that transcending violence may have to be the objective, or one objective, of ritual action. This is deliberate: if ritual has a special, or unique, function in the whole process of peace-making, it is plausible to suggest that this may lie precisely in the capacity of ritual to lift action to a symbolic level at which other actions are transformed, encompassed or transcended. Prayers for peace certainly fall into this category irrespective of their perceived efficacy.

The mention of transcendence also brings us to the question of the imagination. Why is imagination important? Precisely because imagination also has the potentiality to be transcendent, to lift people in thought above and beyond their immediate difficulties and concerns, to look backwards and forwards and to project a vision of what could be in a better life-situation.

Furthermore, ritual, because of its intimate connection with the embodiment of thought in symbolic action, is in principle a highly appropriate medium for the expression of such imaginative ideals and for connecting them with senses of order and power that are enshrined in folk models of the cosmos.

So far, we have cited factors that look as though they would give ritual a privileged place, indeed, in peace-making. Two difficulties must be acknowledged, however, that will give us pause and indicate why conflicts sometimes are protracted and are not easy to settle, even where imagination and ritual are brought effectively into play.

The first difficulty is that ritual and imagination are involved just as much in the production of violence as in the production of peace. Imagination (as in Benedict Anderson's (1983 [1991]) career-making phrase, the 'imagined community') works to bind people together beyond the immediacies of daily face-to-face interaction. By the same token, it binds people even more strongly when they engage in collective, embodied, ritual activities, the existential foundations on which Emile Durkheim (1915) built his house of theory relating to religion and society. The rituals of communal solidarity that Durkheim saw as basic to the totemic rituals of indigenous Australian cultures could clearly be in principle directed to any one of a number of social or political aims: they could promote either conflict or its resolution, war or peace. In one of the classic delineations of a New Guinea ritualised cosmos in which rituals equally marked the onset of war and the construction of peace, Roy Rappaport (1967 [1968]) showed for the Maring people (Tsembaga group) that both fighting and peace-making, historically contingent on the sizes of pig populations and numbers of killings achieved to revenge the deaths of kinsmen, were crucially brought into being by a congeries of rituals culminating in the pig-killing festival known as the *kaiko*. In this ritual cycle, then, peace-making rituals did not exactly transcend violence. War and peace were ritually balanced in relation to each other, taking their turns in the overall ritualised cycle of politics, demography and garden production. The symbolism of peace-making ritual was, nevertheless, interesting. Peacefulness, or rather a taboo on engaging in full-scale conflict, or war, was marked by the planting of special cordyline bushes in a group's territory. These cordyline bushes were known as *yu miñ rumbim*, 'men's life-stuff cordylines', and Rappaport noted in his ethnography that 'every adult male of the subterritorial group participates in this ritual by grasping the *rumbim* as it is planted, thus symbolizing both his connection to the land and his membership in the group that claims the land' (p. 19). As long as these *rumbim* remained rooted in the territory, the men who had planted them could not engage in warfare. In terms of our various criteria of ritual action, it is clear that Rappaport's example fits perfectly. Exploring the meaning of the *rumbim* further, we may note that in times of peace men's life-stuff is kept safe in the land. Men, like the *rumbim*, are planted, emplaced, alive. Once their life-stuff is uprooted it becomes mobilised for hostile purposes and is vulnerable to death; it is floating, volatile, like the spirit of anger and revenge that motivates warfare itself. Does peace, then, transcend war or not?

The second difficulty that we must mention is that rituals do not necessarily or automatically succeed. They can, indeed, fail, as a whole volume of studies has recently been dedicated to showing (Hüsken 2007). When we say 'fail' here, we mean primarily to refer to the views of the participants in rituals themselves. There is a body of literature in anthropology, stemming from the rationalism of Sir James Frazer, that tends to take it for granted that a class of rituals described as 'magical', including many rituals of healing or sorcery rituals to harm others, cannot work as they purport to do and therefore by definition fail to do what they claim to do (see, for example, discussions in Tambiah 1990). Leaving aside for the moment the intricacies of this particular argument and its sources in Frazer's seemingly ethnocentric and misplaced assumptions about ritual action, we repeat our point that we are here concerned mostly with the evaluations of the actors themselves. People do clearly recognise the possibility that a ritual, like any other action, may fail in its aims. They will, for one thing, judge its failure in terms of subsequent events. If a rain-making ritual is not followed by rain, they, like the skeptical outside observer, will say that the ritual failed, but not because it inevitably must fail, rather because a technical mistake was made, not enough resources were used, the wrong spells were cast or the wrong experts chosen (as happens when economic predictions fail in capitalist economies: the whole 'science' of economics is not thereby rejected). In the instance of peace-making by compensation payments, our type-case for the New Guinea Highlands, the entire sequence of giving and receiving the payment must be recognised as 'the ritual' in question. If the number and size of the pigs are not sufficient, the ritual will fail, because people's feelings, which it is the objective of the ritual to change from bad to good, depend on the quality or context of the gift, including its timing and the speeches that orators make at the occasion. Rappaport (1967 [1968], p. 217) notes that at the *konj kaiko* festival he witnessed among the Tsembaga during 1962–63, Tsembaga men handed out portions of belly fat from pigs to honour in turn those who had helped them in a previous bout of warfare. While this occasion passed off without incident, he notes that Andrew Vayda witnessed in 1962 a case in which allies who were left until last in the list of those who were called out to receive pork in this way took umbrage at this and 'not only refused their pig belly but departed early' (p. 217). Friends could thus become enemies next time round. In each case, therefore, we have to examine how and to what extent a ritual is held to have succeeded or 'failed' and what the consequences are of both success and failure in this sense.[1]

The embodiment of metaphor: Huli, Duna and Melpa

Conflicts and their settlements tend to be embedded in narratives that depend on certain kinds of root ideas or metaphors (like our use of the term 'root' itself here). Indeed, in the Melpa language of Mount Hagen a term for both dispute settlement and finding out how to deal with persons' illnesses is 'digging out causes' (*pukl öki*), where the term for cause is literally 'root' or 'base'. Such an idea of 'base' is important in many domains. Kinsfolk are said to share a 'base' (*pukl*, origin in this instance) in Melpa. Among the Duna the same idea is expressed in the term *tse*. *Tse* also refers to responsibility in Duna: *wei tse* is the fight-initiator who is responsible for making reparation payments to allies for the deaths of their kinsfolk in fighting to support the initiator in disputes (Stewart & Strathern 2000b; Strathern & Stewart 2004b).

Laurence Goldman has investigated the use of metaphors in dispute settlement among the Huli based on his fieldwork of 1977–78, carried out during the early years of Papua New Guinea's independence. A dispute is generally referred to as 'talk' among the Huli, and the same is true for the Melpa, among whom the phrase *ik ti petem*, 'there is some talk', means 'there is an issue, a dispute, people are saying things', and talk in these contexts means trouble because people are upset. So important is talk to the Huli, Goldman (1983, p. 281) notes, that there is a special kind of magical spell which is designed to bind up the talk or mind of an antagonist in a dispute. The first part of the spell is supposed to strengthen one's own speech; the second is concerned with destroying that of the opponent. Talk itself can be a form of aggression, as seen in the Huli expression about hitting an opponent's lips, neck and eyelashes (*inter alia*) in disputes (p. 281). The disputant attempts to stop or 'still' the speech of the other side.

Interestingly, in a phrase that Goldman took as the title of his whole book, there is a saying among the Huli that an opponent's talk can never really be finished or 'stopped'. For the Huli, 'talk never dies' because there is always some bit of unfinished business: *bi kugi*, talk left over' (p. 282). Melpa has the same idea: *nit kel ti petem*, 'there is a small notch/mark or indentation', that renders a situation open to further talk. Because of the open-ended, complex and aleatory character of disputes pursued in relatively egalitarian argumentation between equals or near-equals, disputes themselves are seen as generally refractory to settlement by words alone. Gifts must be inserted to make closure. The primary metaphor that Huli use of dispute settlement shifts from words to the body. A dispute is seen as like an illness or a wound. The anger and shame of someone who feels wronged are both seen as a sort of sickness. Goldman writes: 'The objectives of the settlement system in Huli are, I shall argue, the restoration of a physical state free from afflicting illness' (p. 282). Earlier in his book, Goldman notes that both talk and illness are said to 'strike' (*bara*) people or to 'eat' (*nara*) them. 'Pain, like bad talk, must be "pulled out"' (p. 209). If some truth is concealed, pain will result, because the talk has not been pulled out. 'When one holds onto the talk the other person will get pain' runs one line of a speech that Goldman provides (p. 217). An unsettled dispute is left like a scar within the local clan group (p. 217). 'Restoration of order is a restoration of heath' (p. 218). Reflecting oral discussions with one of the present authors (Andrew Strathern), Goldman notes (p. 218) numerous parallels with Melpa expressions, although the specifics of the Huli metaphor regarding pain mark out Huli ideas.

In line with these observations, Goldman suggests 'that compensation is here a symbolic application of "medicine", a healing rite' (p. 283). *Abi*, in Huli, meaning 'compensation', may be a contracted form of *dabi*, meaning 'to heal' (p. 283). *Nogo nigi* means 'ally indemnity payment'; *nogo* means 'pig'; and *nigi* means 'a type of healing leaf', *Laportea*, of the Urticaceae family. Then there is *nogo damba*, which Goldman translates as 'the pig to close down, cover over' an issue, pigs given to the kin of a man who has been killed, or for land, or as 'brideprice' (p. 284). In any such payment, 'head pigs', *haguene*, must be killed and consumed by the complainants, to recognise that the trouble has been put to sleep, finished (p. 286). Goldman argues that these metaphors do not necessarily signify reconciliation between litigants, only that 'health' has been restored to the complainants (p. 286). However, at the very least we can say that this is a way of ending the 'pain' of a dispute. In the terms of our own current analysis, it is evident that this whole metaphorical complex, centred on the body, wounds and sickness, represents a set of ritual actions that uniquely signify how violence can be transcended. (Perhaps, also, shame may be seen as like a wound, as in the English expression 'wounded pride'.)

Two further observations can be added here, from our own fieldwork. The first is that the Huli term *damba* is obviously a close cognate of the Duna term *tamba*, also a general term for compensation for a death or injury, although not, in any usage with which we are familiar, for ordinary brideprice payments (on Duna marriage, see Strathern & Stewart 2004b, pp. 37–52). For the Duna we have recorded, transcribed, translated and discussed a set of speeches about *tamba* collected from leaders (*kango*) in the Aluni area south of the Strickland River (Stewart & Strathern 2000b). We do not have an indigenous exegesis stating that *tamba* means literally 'closing'. However, 'closing' is an expression used for settling a compensation case in speech T1 in our case study. The speaker here declares that the case must be 'closed' at different locations within the landscape. He names seven different places (half of 14, a 'complete' number in the Duna counting system) where the issue needs to be dealt with, perhaps ones on pathways between the two groups involved, along which fighting could develop if the issue is not settled. The seven places are literally those within the parish of the men from whom compensation would be requested, but perhaps also ones with a strategic significance in fighting, as we are suggesting here. In other speeches, the orators make use of further tropes, for example by indicating that there is no ancient (that is, intractable) cause of enmity between them and those with whom their kin have fought through the statement 'The *yawa* greens do not have a bone, the *yaki* grass does not have a bone, the *tundu* grass does not have a bone'. This repetition of terms belongs to a genre also found in the *pikono* sung ballads (see on these, for example, Stewart & Strathern 2005a). By repeating various terms for types of things the speaker adds emphasis to the statement itself. The usage is homologous with that found in speeches and proverbs among the Huli people, which Laurence Goldman (1983) refers to as *kai*, 'praise' terms, or honorifics. Not all of these usages are directly honorific regarding the items named. What is actually being honoured is the relationship between the two sides in a dispute, which the speakers have indicated they wish to be peaceful. The naming lists are followed by other expressions, suggesting that the two sides can be neighbours, can plant gardens together, can cook food and share it together, and will even 'light the fires for courting houses together or light the fires of spirit-sacrifice houses together':

Keno yekeanda haruru kiranda kone
Okoanda haruru kiranda kone (Stewart & Strathern 2000b, p. 31)
Finally:
Keno uanda riya ayu ho pero laya koyana nga.
'Our faces will meet again and we will sleep together' (p. 32).

'Sleep together' is the final image of peace. The expression about seeing each other's faces again is exactly paralleled from the Melpa (Hagen) context, where a term for wanting to make peace or at least a ceasefire or truce in fighting stated that the people wanted to see each other's faces (*koembketa köneimon*), and so they would institute discussions about compensation for deaths.

The second observation is that the Huli embodied metaphor of disputes being painful and equivalent to an illness in those who are aggrieved finds its etiological counterpart in the Melpa discourse on *popokl* ('anger') (Strathern & Stewart 2000a, 2010a). Here, the idea is fully embodied, because *popokl* arising out of a person being upset over an issue (a dispute over land or pigs, for example) is traditionally held to result in that person experiencing sickness. The sickness in effect is held to be sent by the spirit of a dead kinsperson, who marks the sufferer out in this way so that their living kin will take notice of the problem. After divination, the appropriate response was for the person to say that their sickness resulted from *popokl* over a particular matter, which could then be put to rights, and in addition a pig could be sacrificed to appease the spirit that had been invoked. A spirit might be held to have made a person sick also simply because the spirit itself felt that its living kin were not sacrificing to it and enabling it to experience the smell of cooked pork. This whole complex of ideas and practices, then, conduced to the settling of disputes within small-scale family networks. Across the boundaries of enmity and hostility between groups, the ideology of compensation operated on analogous grounds. The death by killing of a kinsman aroused both *popokl* among the living and displeasure among the dead of the group. Revenge had to be taken to assuage this *popokl*, but gifts of pork and live pigs could be made instead to alleviate the *popokl* and so bring relations back to a peaceful state. While this might not amount to a full reconciliation, it would go a considerable way to achieving this end, which might subsequently be encompassed by making further gifts, followed by counter-gifts from the other side. These, in classic fashion, would emerge over time into full-scale *moka* relations, amounting to a stable alliance. The 'ritual plan', as we might call it, thus envisaged a number of staging posts along which productive relations could be built up if the two sides were willing, replacing in the end *popokl* ('anger') with *min* ('friendship') (Strathern & Stewart 2000a, pp. 21–41). Along the way, things could go wrong, for many reasons: further disputes, disagreements over amounts to be given, and impolitic remarks that might be made. But the ritual plan was available always as a pathway to which people could return. The image people used of the process depended on the idea of a road or path between people: a 'road of pigs' (*kng nombukla*) that constituted stable reciprocal relations among the partners involved.

Other Highlands New Guinea cases

These traditional kinds of practices were sorely tested and were often insufficient to settle hostilities in the post-colonial period after 1975. The Highlands societies became proverbial in the news and in the analyses of observers for periodic outbreaks of fighting and destruction between groups, often greatly compounded by the presence of large-scale development projects in the field of mining for minerals in clan areas. Robert Gordon and Mervyn Meggitt's 1985 book *Law and Order in the New Guinea Highlands* signalled this theme, as did Sinclair Dinnen's (2001) later work *Law and Order in a Weak State: Crime and Politics in Papua New Guinea* (compare Dinnen & Ley 2000). Applied studies were commissioned specifically to address the problem, for example the Wormsley and Toke 'Enga Law and Order Project', based on research carried out between 1982 and 1985, which provided 88 separate recommendations on how to deal with problems of violence in the Enga Province. Wormsley and Toke (1985, p. 23) say that they investigated more than a hundred tribal fights in 1982–85, in which 'dozens of deaths' and much damage to property occurred. Government police involved themselves in these fights in efforts to halt them, while the fighters themselves did all they could to hinder police from 'interfering', as they saw it, in this way. Wormsley and Toke list tribal fighting as the first of five problem areas for law and order, the others being 'Rascal activity' (p. 24), that is, criminal activity by gangs of male youths, 'assaults on women' (p. 25), 'corruption' and 'its relationship to the deplorable state of development in the Province' (p. 26), and in general 'disrespect for the law' (p. 27). (See also Carrad et al. 1982; Strathern 1997.)

The report provides admirable ethnographic backup for these assertions and is reasonably in line with the findings of Gordon and Meggitt's (1985) study, which, however, gives a more nuanced and distanced view of the issues, including a historical account of the 'decline of the Kiaps', ideas about the functions of speech-making, politics in general and 'the politics of spoils', questions of customary law, and a disquisition on Village Courts (from the Table of Contents).

The Wormsley and Toke (1985) recommendations all read as sensible and based on the authors' empirical findings and living experiences. They are wide-ranging and deal mostly with very practical matters: roles of police, how to handle criminal cases, how to reform the public service, how to protect the agents of the law, how to limit access to alcohol. The line is tough: prisons should be set up in unattractive areas in marginal locations (rec. 70, Appendix 1, p. 14). Prisoners should do 'physically demanding labour' if they have been sentenced to 'hard labour'. They could be used for roadwork (as the colonial Kiaps had done) (rec. 72, p. 15). Armed police should attend land court settings (rec. 67, p. 14). The government should not use the army to stop fights, and police Riot Squads (notorious for their heavy-handed approaches) should be withdrawn from the Province (rec. 27, p. 6; rec. 38, p. 8). Warring clans should pay a fine to the government, in pigs if necessary, and these pigs could then be sold by the government (rec. 35, p. 8; presumably not sold back to their previous owners).

Throughout all these recommendations there is no mention of peace-making, compensation payments or ritual at all. This is a state-based view of the situation, albeit a highly enlightened one and well ahead of the government policies at the time in terms of its anthropological insights. Recommendations 21 to 36 deal passim with tribunal fighting, arguing that police should be used only to contain fights (rec. 22), and, for example, that fines levied on warring clans could be used to pay for trained police to be stationed in fight areas (rec. 32). Nothing about the clans paying pigs to each other appears here.

Wormsley and Toke are rather critical of ideas that customary law' in general can be brought back into the contemporary (that is, the 1980s) situation (p. 34). They do recognise that customary conflict resolution in Enga included payment of compensation in a variety of contexts. They cite payments to maternal kin following a death, noting that failure to pay could lead to trouble, and suggesting correctly that this in itself was not a form of dispute settlement, but a way of avoiding a dispute by pre-emption (p. 36). This is obviously correct, but the wider interpretation is that such payments were a part of a great 'web of kinship' (borrowing this phrase from the title of one of the anthropologist Meyer Fortes's (1949) books) that stretched between groups linked by marriage and contributed in general to 'keeping the peace' between them. 'Keeping the peace' in this sense is in effect what we need to concentrate on rather than the state-based concept of 'law and order' in an abstract sense.

Wormsley and Toke (1985, p. 36) go on: 'Death payments made to the clans of allies killed in the service of one's military objectives were a social obligation.' They also note that failure to meet these payments led to disputes. They say further that the first response to a killing was to seek a payback death. Later, the two groups might wish to cease hostile relations and so compensation would be paid. They argue that such payments, however, did not resolve disputes in any lasting manner but were mechanisms for relieving tensions (p. 36) and were also linked to processes in the *tee* ceremonial exchange cycle (here they refer to the work of Feil (1980) and Meggitt (1977)).

These observations presumably underlie the avoidance in the report of any serious discussion of compensation as a form of making peace between groups among the Enga. We are left with the impression that the Enga themselves actually had *no* means of peace-making and many reasons for conflict. Naturally, then, there would be a problem of 'law and order' in the state-based system of government within a nation-state that was, in effect, a recent colonial and post-colonial imposition. For the Enga, their tribal fighting, it appears, *was* their method of dispute settlement. There is clearly some truth in this rather unpalatable inference, but it is unlikely to be the whole truth or indeed wholly correct in itself.

This part of Wormsley and Toke's text is lacking (at this point in their exposition) in any delineations of social structure. Was Enga fighting a case of war of all against all in the Hobbesian sense ('warre')? In Hagen and elsewhere we have seen that it is necessary to specify *contexts* of fighting. Were there no stable alliances among Enga groups? Did marriage ties and exchange not in practice mitigate hostilities? Second, if there were alliances, it would be overwhelmingly in the self-interest of groups to pay reparations to allies for deaths incurred. Not to do so would be military suicide. We have seen earlier for the Maring studied by Roy Rappaport (1967 [1968]) that the cycles of war and peace were ritually regulated, a way no doubt of stabilising political relations over time and space, and of allowing social processes a 'breathing space', as it were, in which to regenerate.

Meggitt (1977, pp. 133–44) devoted a whole chapter to 'peacemaking and homicide compensations' among the Mae Enga. He also notes, in an earlier passage, that the death of a prominent man in battle might be examined through divination in which a specialist directly questioned the dead man's ghost (p. 107), rapping an arrow on a branch held over the grave and noting when it swung backwards and forwards in answer to a question, putatively signalling answers from the ghost. Sometimes the divination would result in a verdict implicating someone of the dead man's own clan, in which case they might demand that the responsible person's sub-clansmen lead the process of contributing pigs to be given as an ordinary form of death-payment to the dead man's maternal kin.

Meggitt's narrative makes it immediately clear that *context* did matter, along a basically segmentary scale of relationships. If the groups involved are seen as fraternally related within the phratry (the widest level of grouping), then kinsfolk will urge those who are 'the owners of the fight' (the initiators of the fight) to end the violence by arranging compensation. If the groups are non-fraternal, such exhortations are likely to be ineffective, in fact 'pointless' (p. 113). Contingent tactics and circumstances determine the outcomes of peace discussions, among both current winners and current losers. Ritual dramatisations of grief in any case take place, in which clansmen may lop off fingers in mourning for land they have lost in the fighting (p. 115). Even if compensation is paid, Meggitt notes, 'the peace that follows is likely to be tenuous and short-lived' (p. 115). Big-men and notables are at all times closely involved. The process of peace-making may begin with the initial bringing of pork and valuable shells to a meeting, preferably in the form of an exchange between the two sides (p. 117). A good deal of dramatic expression of feeling ensues at such a meeting, in which leaders make strong claims for themselves and their groups, and kinsfolk of the dead at first refuse compensation, until they may at length be persuaded. Brawls and disagreements can easily occur, disrupting the whole process. Payments are spoken of as 'cause of origin settling' (p. 123); but even if the payments are accepted, Meggitt says, the aggrieved parties may still reserve the right to make a vengeance killing later. This point is a bit surprising. It would not hold for the Melpa, except in the sense that a party who felt that they were not properly included in the distribution of compensation items might hold such a view. And how often a killing might occur even after a compensation would be another issue.

Ritualised processes are important markers of stages in the arrangement of compensation (p. 129, but Meggitt does not speak of ritual here. The term is ours). The function of these ritual processes is precisely what Roy Rappaport (1967 [1968], p. 234; 1999, p. 96) has argued in general and for the Maring in particular: to turn the contingencies of process into the binary certainties of structure, via the medium of human agency within a perceived cosmos. The difference between the Mae Enga and the Maring cases is that the ritual process seems much less certain among the former than it is in the latter. In negotiating a settlement by compensation, Mae big-men (leaders) test the ground 'by thrusting rows of twigs into the ground to represent the stakes on the danceground to which the pigs will be tethered on the occasion' (Meggitt 1977, p. 129). While arguments and fistfights may swirl around the leaders, they continually try to deploy, re-count and rearrange these twigs to represent the outcome. Converting this a stage further, the leaders take their followers to a nearby hill and call out in chants to the other side that they are prepared to make a generous compensation for the killings that have taken place. The other side's men sing back. 'Both sides season their songs with metaphorical boasts and gibes' (p. 130). On the occasion itself, the leaders further define the situation for their use of formal oratory (p. 132). In accepting the compensation gifts a recipient 'should run round the lines of pigs and shout compliments to the donors, before embracing and praising the Big Man to signify acceptance of the offer' (p. 133). The ritual can fail if recipients are disappointed with the gift (p. 133).

These ritual stages and scenarios closely parallel those customarily followed by the Melpa. Meggitt also notes that the Mae put much effort into compensation of this kind, and that in perhaps three-quarters of cases their efforts succeed (p. 142). As for why this is so, he argues that the high population density of the area places a premium on the ability to negotiate such peaceful settlements and to avoid total conflict. The ritual steps involved play a crucial role in the attainment of this end. Population density alone, however, is not solely responsible, we suggest, because the same considerations and advantages of alliance by exchange operate in less densely populated areas, such as among the Tombema Enga studied by Feil (1984).

Wiessner and Tumu (1998, pp. 256 ff.) also testify to the importance of war payments to both allies and enemies (first to the former and then contingently to the latter) among the Enga populations generally. Taking note of what we may call the economy of killing and its self-limiting characteristics, they write: 'The high cost of war reparations when there were several allied deaths, together with fear that the wealth would be spread too thinly to satisfy anybody, provided a strong incentive to cease hostilities before many lives were lost' (p. 256). This viewpoint exactly meshes with our own overall argument that in systems of violence of this kind each violent act is shadowed by the possibility, indeed the desirability, of later making peace.

Wiessner and Tumu go on to delineate the stages at which reparations were organised. Their details parallel, again, very closely processes found historically among the Melpa (see, for example, Strathern 1971 [2007], pp. 94 ff.). Notable among these procedures is one that does not seem to form a part of Meggitt's account. The procedure is called *saandi pingi* in Enga. This consisted of 'optional, informal, initiatory gifts given in private by bereaved allies or by families in the clan of the victim to request reparations' (Wiessner & Tumu 1998, p. 256). Acceptance of such gifts constituted a promise to make reparations, perhaps preceded by gifts of cooked pork. This stage was followed by *kepa singi*, formal distributions of steamed pork by the 'owners of the fight', another, more formal, *saandi pingi*, and finally *akali buingi*, a formal large payment by the killer's to the victim's clan. This payment was expected to exceed the amounts of the initiatory gifts that had been received. Pigs raised for this occasion had their ears slit to mark their status. Ritual practices helped to remove the memory of the victim from his family's consciousness: someone would take away his bed, pipe, netbag and the like (p. 258). Feelings were very strong. Careful speeches were made, backed up by gifts of sugarcane and sweet potato (p. 261). Terms for making peace referred simply to cutting off, finishing fights or 'breaking the spear' (p. 260). Talk, and the use of indirect speech, metaphor and the like, were other important parts of the whole ritual process, as with the Melpa and the use of *el ik* (Strathern & Stewart 2000a). Marriages might subsequently be arranged on a formal basis between groups to consolidate positive ties. A *kauma pingi* ritual might be held to facilitate this process. The killer's clan would invite clansmen to send their young girls to the occasion, 'particularly those who had boyfriends in the clan of the killer. The girls were to be accompanied by a few young men from the victim's sub-clan who were shaved and dressed as women as an indication that they were not interested in revenge but would wait submissively, like women, for proposals from the killer's clan to pay reparations' (Wiessner & Tumu 1998, p. 262).

These details, culled from Wiessner and Tumu's extensive ethnographic materials, clearly illustrate the significant part that rituals played among the Enga in orchestrating peaceful processes among otherwise highly belligerent groups.

It is important to note details of this kind, because all too often they can be lost in the midst of complex discussions of 'modern' problems that tend to concentrate on national- or provincial-level activities, introduced politics, economic development and change, crime, police action, public servants – all the things that loom so large in the Wormsley and Toke report. Robert Gordon and Mervyn Meggitt's 1985 book is a careful discussion of many of these same macro-issues in an anthropological framework of analysis. A whole chapter (Chapter 3) deals with, for example, the 'decline of the kiaps'.

Kiaps were originally expatriates, often quite young, whose appearance and status in the colonial world marked them out clearly from the local people. They were expected to be field officers, often out on patrol, with powers to settle local disputes and to put people in jail. Kiaps themselves would often tell one of the present authors (Andrew Strathern) in the 1960s and the early 1970s that they had extensive on-the-spot summary powers to deal with trouble. They also had police to enforce their decisions. Gordon and

Meggitt (1985, p. 52) make the same point: 'If necessary, the kiap could arrest, prosecute, judge, sentence, and jail a person "on the spot", as it were.' They go on to make a number of other assertions, which are less applicable generally; that is, that Kiaps' patrols were infrequent and their power appeared to the Enga as 'arbitrary and irrational'. In other parts of the Highlands, and/or at other times, Kiaps patrolled frequently; some served in one area for several years; and their authority carried prestige and respect as well as (usually) being feared. (The cases we have in mind here include Pangia; see Strathern 1984.) A valid overall point that can be made is that the type of exclusive power, linked to the machinery of the colonial state, which Kiaps in their heyday exercised, was radically different from indigenous forms of leadership and dispute settlement. Nevertheless, Kiaps could, if they wished, follow indigenous methods, for example by listening for a long time to arguments in land disputes – the example here comes from Gordon and Meggitt (1985, p. 52) themselves. At another point in their book, Gordon and Meggitt also thoughtfully discuss the role of ceremonialism in the operations of Kiaps. They also use the appropriate term 'rituals of government' in this context (p. 179). They mention the following: 'the well-known and effective ploys of building "roads for peace", offering demonstrations of the power of firearms, and performing "spear-burning" ceremonies when patrols were engaged in peacemaking' (p. 180).

Dominance and deference were also induced by the Kiaps' different forms of dress, and by separating off their patrol spaces from the people at large (pp. 180–81). The Enga, like all Papua New Guinea Highlanders, with their stress on ceremonial dress as a way of marking out statuses and events, would be very sensitive to symbolic self-referential indices of this sort, we may note.

Moreover, the marks of dominance were connected with access to money. An older Enga man commented, 'Australian kiaps sat at the gate where the money flows in and everything worked smoothly.

We would buy more things with our money... but now the local kiaps block the way where the money comes in... These kiaps just don't care about us' (pp. 182–83). This somewhat counter-intuitive evaluation reverses the stereotype of dislike for colonial outsiders and preference for an indigenous élite; but it fits with similar evaluations made in the 1970s by older leaders among the Melpa speakers of Mount Hagen. In addition, the colonial Kiaps, according to Gordon and Meggitt, were perceived as having more autonomous power than their later indigenous replacements. Thus, 'the [Kiaps'] secular ceremonials [rituals] indicated and reinforced the autonomy of the kiaps, giving them a high-degree of self-control' (p. 187).

What about customary law and its potentially ritualised aspects? Gordon and Meggitt reviewed some of the literature on this topic and issued a number of cautions, including the familiar observation that it is a mistake to treat customary law as a system and that when it is written down it is transformed – and, in effect, therefore, made less rather than more viable (pp. 199, 202). Another point can be added: when such a codified set of 'laws' or rules is administered at local levels by Village Courts or others, it is bound to be bent in particular ways and sometimes is subject to outright abuse by those charged with administering it. The legitimacy of courts that deal with disputes at local levels therefore comes into question. At an earlier point in their book, Gordon and Meggitt note that: 'Some village courts in Enga also open their sessions with Christian prayers... [and] promoting the ceremonialism of village courts, commonly noted by anthropologists, is an effective strategy to enhance their credibility' (pp. 180–81). Credibility here contributes to legitimacy, and in turn to efficacy. A further chapter deals in detail with the 'rise of the village courts', and it is interesting that they report the views of Enga magistrates themselves corroborating this view, for example, asking for more regulatory visits from supervisory magistrates (p. 232). This request indicates a desire to be able to show connections with governmental powers, with a hierarchy of power and authority – a hierarchy that was very imperfectly maintained because of a decline in governmental diligence. (See, for example, the analysis of courts and recommendations in Strathern 1984, pp. 122–42.)

A further point, running parallel to, rather than counter to, these points is that indigenous moots, led by big-men, continued alongside village court procedures, and cases were sometimes brought to the courts only after a provisional agreement had been reached, or if such an agreement could not be reached and there was a risk of violence. In Hagen, this process was observed at work both in the 1970s and much later in the 1990s when problems of social control had increased, and village court venues became the occasional sites of rowdy confrontations and fisticuffs between disputants. The operation of either traditional or neo-traditional methods of settlement was thereby disrupted, and correspondingly there was little place for the creative adaptation of rituals. Indeed, such rituals to this day have survived only in contexts in which the cultural scenarios or scripts guiding compensation payments are adhered to. Compensation, with all its vicissitudes and risks, remains the sole high road to the ritualisation of aggression and its replacement by alliance relations. Whether the effectiveness of compensation payments could be reinforced or increased in certain contexts by national-level legislation is a difficult question that was discussed already via the Law Reform Commission in a volume published from Port Moresby in 1981 (Scaglion 1981; see Strathern 1981 in that volume; and comparable studies by Goldman (1981) and Sillitoe (1981) in the same volume).

Payback and its transformations: the work of Garry Trompf

Garry Trompf's (1994) major work on 'payback' covers a great deal of ground in a holistic analysis of 'Melanesian' society that deserves wide recognition. Payback is a term that covers both positive and negative forms of reciprocity, for example, the exchange of both wealth and sorcery. Trompf discusses 'peace-making and compensation' in contemporary and historical contexts as we have done here, and his enquiry under this heading begins with the observation that 'Where tribal (or clan) warfare is in evidence, the traditional machinery for peace-making is not necessarily intact' (p. 376).

Ritual procedures, he goes on to note, can be forgotten, and if they are remembered they cannot always produce firm conditions for peace (p. 376). This, of course, applies throughout the Highlands, although we have to ask if there is any more viable option and we may firmly reject the idea that sheer governmental force can slot in where compensation fails. These two modalities are incompatible and incommensurable. In an earlier passage in his book, Trompf gives an admirable account of how compensation practices, including those of the Mae Enga, were supposed to operate (pp. 107–12), and points out, much in line with our own interest in ritual efficacy, that compensation practices among the Enga were 'consciously acted out in the presence of the dead as well as the living' (p. 109, with references *inter alia* to Meggitt 1977, pp. 115–19, 138). The sacrificial aspects of compensation were, and are, extremely significant, and a major, classic, problem lies in the difficulties of combining such traditional aspects with Christian-introduced practices. Another difficulty arises from the expansion in scale of social relations (as documented in Chapter 4 of this volume, on elections, and discussed earlier in Strathern 1974). Trompf (1994, p. 377) refers to this, writing that with the introduction of money into payments of compensation for car accidents, for example, excessive claims are sometimes made. 'Trouble Committees' are often charged with settling on feasible amounts to be paid. As Trompf also notes, money acquires here a ritual or sacred value (p. 377; see Strathern & Stewart 1999a for a detailed historical analysis). The presentation of banknotes on occasions of this kind is highly dramatic and aesthetically orchestrated, making the money comparable to the pearl shells given earlier, an equation or analogy made easier by the fact that the national currency in Papua New Guinea was given the name used in the Melpa language of Mount Hagen for pearl shell, *kin*.

Trompf (1994) also collects some materials suggestive of the potential role for Christian morality and symbolism to enter into these compensation practices. He notes an example from the Huli area in which groups had begun to make apologies for killings, expressed in the Tok Pisin term *sori*, a practice Trompf says indicated Protestant mission influence in the area (p. 377). Emotional expressions of remorse were expected to accompany such apologies. Dramatic versions of such occasions might involve declarations of possession by the Holy Spirit. In the Hagen area, schoolchildren, according to a newspaper report cited by Trompf, turned up to demonstrate in support of a weapons-burning ritual at the Nebilyer Valley police station during 1981 (p. 378). The ritual was an attempt to make peace in a severe protracted conflict between the Ulga and Kulga tribes. These are cases in which an attempt is made to create a new ritual complex, blending a Christian ideology and affect with speeches and compensation payments that draw on pre-Christian patterns of conduct. The opposite approach, adopted by missionaries at early stages of their work in new areas, has involved not the blending of traditions, but their confrontation. Trompf records a statement by Seventh Day Adventist missionary Joseph Knoebel, who worked among Duna people at Lake Kopiago, that he had encouraged groups whose members wanted to become Christians to ceremonially smash their sacred stones, in a conflict of presumed ritual powers (p. 429). In our own fieldwork with the Duna we also came across narratives of this sort, told by the local people themselves. Acts of destruction of this kind might be seen as 'violent' in themselves. At later stages, when indigenous people try to find post-colonial solutions to problems of conflict, a more combinatorial approach often emerges. Our own argument would be that when this happens, it is not enough to utilise only one side of the equation. Asking for forgiveness and expressing repentance need to be accompanied by payments of compensation, with a recognition of the healing powers that wealth transfers. In this way, the spirit of 'totality' that Trompf emphasises for 'Melanesian' cultures can be preserved and built upon.[2]

CHAPTER 8

Conclusions and comparisons

The main thrust of our argument in this book has been to highlight the implications of a certain kind of violent act, in which the act of violence is always shadowed by the question of paying compensation for it. The focus of our discussions has been on communal politics in the Highlands of Papua New Guinea. A necessary feature for the argument to apply is that, in these cultures, certain wealth items (pigs, valuable shells, introduced state money) must be considered to possess a special symbolic equivalence to human life. Such items must be valued so highly that the promise of them can overcome the strong inclinations towards violent revenge-taking for deaths that are also deeply ingrained in the dispositions of people. Finally, in the simplified terms of our model, these valuables must be able to circulate through general networks of exchange, so that they can be feasibly amassed when they are needed for a particular occasion. These conditions simply summarise those that are basic to the actual historical practices of the Highlands societies, especially those, like the Melpa and Enga areas, where the exchanges of pigs and shells in the *moka* and *tee* cycles were predominant integrative cultural patterns, linking many other practices together.

Compensation payments are obviously not perfect vehicles for peace-making. For one thing, they begin with acts of violence, which people may remember and resent even after a payment of wealth has been made. This is because not everyone may receive a share in the payment that they think they are entitled to. Thus, there is a *nit*, as the Melpa say: a small notch or mark against which trouble can emerge. Furthermore, compensation works best within defined segmentary contexts. It cannot necessarily be expanded indefinitely. In Chapter 4 we gave an impressive early example of how the whole Dei Council area cooperated to make a payment for a death to Mul Council groups related to the driver who had been harassed inside Dei Council. The context was political need. With such needs, compensation can be deployed at widening segmentary levels, but it may not be infinitely expandable. The growing scale of social relations, and their greater differentiation with the development of social classes, may militate against the successful application of compensation principles. The politics of national parties, governmental offices, elections, voting and uneven development, as well as stresses that ripple out from large mining operations, conduce much more to outbreaks of violence than to easy processes of peace-making.[1]

Over the years since the time of initial self-government and independence both the national governments of Papua New Guinea (and other south-west Pacific nations; see, for example, Dinnen & Firth 2008 on the Solomon Islands) and Provincial governments have struggled with how to frame policies to contain violence, commissioning official reports on the problems involved. Such reports are well discussed, for example, in Gordon and Meggitt's 1985 book. The overall focus of these reports tends to be on governmental control (the stick approach) and secondarily on top-down sponsored development, seen as a way of transcending or deflecting violence (the carrot approach). Such a focus ignores the local-level potentialities for peace-making that the people themselves possess and government does not. Indeed, the intersection of parliamentary elections with tribal segmentary ethics of honour and competition has itself produced a potent site of troubles, as indicated in our Chapter 1. In spite of all these problems, no serious competitor to the payment of wealth as the road to peace-making can be identified. The vexing difficulties of making compensation work have to be understood against such a background.[2] Above all, compensation must be seen as a total social act, incorporating political, moral, economic and ritual facets. In Chapter 7 we further explored and stressed the potentialities of the ritual dimension of compensation payments. Ritual by itself, seen as an essence, cannot work. Instead, it too has to be seen as part of a whole ensemble of practices. But where ritual, like compensation itself, holds a vital key to success is in its symbolic amplitude, which enables ritual acts to operate as holistic condensations of value, affect, intention and supposition on the part of those who undertake it – which is why ritual is so important in both making war and making peace.

In this chapter, we go on to examine a number of studies from the perspectives we have just outlined, providing a further discursive exploration of what we called in Chapter 6 'the problems of peace-makers: intermediate sovereigns'.

We take first some studies from field sites that we have not so far been discussing.

West Papua, Solomons, East Africa
1. The Jalé
Klaus-Friedrich Koch (1974, pp. 27–29) listed six general ways of handling conflicts: negotiation without a mediating third party; mediation, in which such a third party does play a role; adjudication, by a third party with power to give a judgement; arbitration,

in which the principals agree to choose a third party who will make a decision; coercion, in which one side imposes an outcome; and avoidance, in which the conflict is shelved, perhaps temporarily. Among the Jalé people of West Papua (Irian Jaya) whom he studied, informal mediating roles were played by persons linked to both sides of a dispute, and these persons were usually ones with affinal links to one or both sides in a dispute. Accordingly, where such affinal links were tenuous or nonexistent, the likelihood that a dispute would result in armed combat greatly increased. Thus Koch concluded that 'coercive self-help' was bound to become institutionalised as a way of settling disputes (p. 35).

This model, however, does not actually indicate how disputes could be settled or at least terminated. These ways depended, as Koch notes in his concluding chapter, on the segmentary scale of social relationships. Between co-residents, the political solidarity of a men's house group was at stake. In conflicts between affines, their exchange relationships worked to conduce to settlements. In conflicts between parts of residential villages or numbers of villages, their place in a network of military alliances would influence them to come to terms. And, finally, there is a factor that links directly to materials from the Papua New Guinea Highlands context: 'the liability of a principal and his agnates to compensate their supporters for damages or injuries suffered in the course of any conflict may dampen a party's desire for revenge' (p. 159). We may call this the principle of indirect peace-making, since peace is brought about not by reconciliation or forgiveness between the principals but by their separate need to raise wealth in pigs and pay compensation to their allies. Peace in this sense means the halting of hostilities, for shorter or longer periods. As we have seen in Chapter 7, in Hagen this initial halting may be followed, contingently, by further processes, including direct payments to enemies or kin of 'accident' victims, or the establishment of rolling *moka* relations on 'the road of pigs'. As with Hagen, the Jalé marriage rules must have an effect on the incidence of cross-cutting ties between groups that conduce to peace-making. In the Jalé case, the whole population is divided into two exogamous, non-localised moieties, which assuredly requires a certain dispersal of marriage ties, but precisely how this worked out as a factor of 'social control' is not entirely clear. There is no equivalent of the *moka* among the Jalé, and correspondingly the stress on exchange and its influence on peace-making must be reduced by comparison with Hagen.

Koch's index to his book lists 15 passages where 'compensation' is discussed. The contexts are as follows:

1. Funeral exchanges, in which the kinsperson who undertakes to cremate a body gives a pig to an affine who has brought the body to the pyre and receives a pig in return (p. 45).

2. *Wergild* and pigs paid directly between agnates within village wards involved as allies of principals in a dispute. *Wergild* might be a live pig. Compensation would be to helpers or allies in the fight, in the form of cooked pigs (p. 97).

3. Compensatory payments between affines over property disputes (land, pigs) (p. 109).

4. A principal in a fight, 'man of the arrow's stem', is liable to pay compensation pigs for 'all injuries and deaths suffered by his supporters'. These pigs Koch translates as 'guilt pigs' (p. 120). (This is an exact parallel to the Huli case in Papua New Guinea and indeed is paradigmatic for compensation strategy generally in both West Papua and Papua New Guinea. See Glasse 1968, pp. 113–32.)

5. Complicated circumstances determine what happens in disputes between wards (Koch 1974, pp. 126, 130–33, 134).

6. 'Ear pigs' may be given in restitution for pigs that are stolen. If, however, the recipients think the ear pig is worth less than the one stolen they may steal another pig themselves, leading to further trouble (pp. 146–47).

7. An immigrant co-resident is more likely to be killed in revenge by the kin of a 'victim' than if he were a patrilineal member of the group (pp. 150–51). In all cases, both trouble and the potential to settle it rest with the 'man of the arrow's stem' (numerous references in the Case Histories section, for example, p. 183).

Throughout this discussion, Koch emphasises that settlements were contingent and circumstantial and that negotiations over compensation could easily turn into violence. Nevertheless, the only 'highway' to settlement was by means of compensation payments. The overall message, then, is the same as for all the other cases we have examined.

2. Choiseul

Koch, in his concluding chapter of the Jalé study, discusses the well-known work of Elizabeth Colson (1953) on the Plateau Tonga people (Gwembe Tonga of Zambia in Africa). Colson pointed out that in societies with segmentary lineages, social order depends not just on lineage interrelations but on interpersonal ties linking lineage members across lineage lines of division. (This, incidentally, is pre-eminently the case among the Duna, with their cognatic notions of group membership; Strathern & Stewart 2004b.) These cross-cutting ties preclude the development of vengeance activities for killings beyond a 'tolerable' point, according to this argument. Here again, from a New Guinea perspective, we can say that such cross-cutting ties operate through intermarriages and residence switches and are kept effective only through exchanges of material wealth items, especially in the normative guise of compensation payments, as has been our own major argument in this book. Considerations of this sort in general also underlie Max Gluckman's (1955) famous propositions on 'the peace in the feud'.[3]

Harold Scheffler took up this theme in relation to the inhabitants of Choiseul Island in the Solomon Islands, where he initially carried out fieldwork between 1958 and 1961, formulating an early version of his argument in an article published in 1964 (p. 803), followed by a book-length ethnographic analysis in 1965.

Scheffler's analysis of acephalous segmentary politics refers to a situation that had been in abeyance for a generation or so prior to his fieldwork, before pacification by British colonial authorities. This situation is comparable to that which held in the Papua New Guinea Highlands in the 1960s, when memories of pre-contact warfare and exchange were quite vivid.

Corporate cognatic descent groups, *sinangge*, among the Choiseulese held tracts of land. Leading men, or 'managers' as Scheffler (1964) calls them, influenced exchanges with shell valuables, known as *kesa* (p. 790). Clusters of *sinangge* formed 'regions', within which friendship and intermarriage were practised. The *sinangge* were not exogamous, and their resident members, linked by filiation to the *sinangge* genealogy, also had potential membership in other *sinangge* via cognatic ties. Agnatic descendants of a *sinangge* founder tended to be managers of their residential group, with some limited emphasis on primogeniture, balanced by differential ability (pp. 791–92) and competition.[4]

Considerable value was placed on prestige, and the pursuit of prestige through exchange determined actions rather than simple adherence to lineage principles (p. 793). Jealousy existed between *sinangge* members, resulting in suspicions of hostile sorcery among them, but persons were also held together within the group by complex obligations. Managers were committed to getting people to work together, so they would try hard to mediate disputes and persuade members to control their pride and accept compensation for theft or damage. While challenges to prestige had in principle to be avenged, compensation provided a way out, exactly as with the Enga described by Meggitt (1977).

Wealth, however, also provided another pathway (reminiscent of the Melpa *el klöngi* practice, the hiring of an assassin (Strathern 1971 [2007], p. 85). A man seeking revenge could recruit an agent to carry out the killing for him, promising a gift of shells and a feast in return. Preferably only the prime target would be killed, thus making it less likely that further violence would ensue, although this could not be guaranteed (Scheffler 1964, p. 796). At a wider level, if a killing was to be carried out by means of a raid, a *ruata* contract for assistance would be entered into – thus probably generating further conflict (p. 797). Losses by allies required further compensation with *kesa* (p. 797). As Glasse (1968) argued for the Huli, the more elaborate the alliance relationships, the more costly they would become, and this by itself brought a measure of limitation to the escalation of conflicts. We can see here the same principle at work as we have repeatedly stressed throughout the present book: if the cost of a violent act is already written into that act itself, it contains its own potential for closure. Particularly, in the Choiseulese case, Scheffler (1964, p. 797) noted that peripheral parties pulled in to a conflict tended to help find honourable ways of settling a dispute, because this suited their interests. In short, cross-cutting ties, combined with the necessity of finding wealth to pay compensation for killings, conduced towards the halting of conflicts and in that sense towards the creation of peace.[5]

3. East Africa
We step outside of the Pacific Island contexts to look at some classic materials on the so-called 'ordered anarchy' of acephalous political formations in a few parts of East Africa.

Two books on questions of violence include studies belonging to this theme, deriving from earlier work on 'tribes without rulers' (Middleton & Tait 1958). Suzette Heald worked with the Kuria people of Kenya from 1984 onwards. The Kuria, like the Nuer (Kelly 1985), had been an expanding pastoral people, pushing against neighbouring entities (Luo, Maasai). Raiding the cattle of enemies was a mark of masculine prowess. In more recent times, it became linked with smuggling, border theft and banditry, since the Kuria in Kenya are linked with clansmen in Tanzania (Heald 2000, p. 106). Raiders use guns to pursue their aims. Cattle owners resist with the use of poisoned arrows. Issues of revenge enter in. Elders with ritual powers attempt to control these activities and to put suspects through tests by swearing oaths, and by cursing offenders (p. 108). Young male raiders are seen as like gang members. (We may think here of raskol in Papua New Guinea.) Elders may also exert punitive sanctions against raiders, inciting popular assemblies to kill them (p. 118).

There is little sign of a role for wealth deployed for compensation here. Cattle raiding may have been a more balanced form of negative activity between groups in the past. With a link to transnational forms of smuggling and the availability of guns, it takes on a more deadly character, unmitigated by positive exchanges.

Jon Abbink (2001) provides a parallel case study, on the Suri people of Southern Ethiopia, near to the Sudan (see also Abbink 2000). The Suri are patrilineal agro-pastoralists like the Kuria. They practised various forms of ritually controlled combat and attack in raiding, stick-duelling and revenge-killing – but here Abbink (2001, p. 129) notes, in a passage that brings us closer to Papua New Guinea, that 'a revenge killing was in no way frowned upon if compensation payment had not been forthcoming after a (previous) homicide'.

However, at the time of Abbink's fieldwork, and writing, in 1991–94 and subsequently, restrictions on raiding practices between the

Suri and their neighbours had broken down. The Sudanese civil war led to extensive trading in guns. The Suri's neighbours, the Nyangatom, became more powerful, and drove away more of their cattle, provoking the Suri in some cases to shoot their own cattle. With other neighbours, the Dizi, the Suri had previously recognised the Dizi's overlordship of the land and their ritual rain-making powers (p. 130). Forced out by the Nyangatom, the Suri more recently began a violent expansion against the Dizi, with greater destructiveness than was ever seen previously. Clearly, ritualisation of peaceful relationships cannot hold against contemporary inter-regional pressures. Automatic rifles play their part in all this (p. 135). Ecological crises of famine also push groups to more aggressive activities. We see here a parallel to the effects of guns in warfare in the Papua New Guinea Highlands: if anything, with more severe results (compare Strathern 1992 on the transition to guns in Hagen warfare in the 1980s). Once again, compensation does not figure in the Suri story. Guns and globalisation come to the fore instead.

Our final case in this section is from Uganda in the mid-1990s. Mark Leopold made a re-study of the Lugbara, earlier studied by John Middleton and made well known by Middleton's numerous insightful publications (for example, Middleton 1960). Middleton's account of Lugbara politics was analogous to Evans-Pritchard's on the Nuer. Segmentary distance between lineages defined the degrees of violence expected and exerted between them, even though pacification took place in the 1920s (Leopold 2005, p. 143). Middleton's exact words, quoted by Leopold, say that what determined 'the nature of fighting and the means to end it and the type of reparation needed to settle it' was the 'social distance between the parties, expressed in lineage distance' (p. 143). Leopold points out that martial traditions among the Lugbara may have been magnified as a result of army recruitment in the Ugandan state (p. 145). The underlying thrust of this comment and others in Leopold's text at this point is that

Middleton followed a tradition of writing that contrasted centralised politics based on contract and consensus with uncentralised politics centred around force. Leopold quotes with approval David Turton's statement that anthropology in this way legitimised 'the state form of political organization' (Turton 1994, p. 21; quoted in Leopold 2005, p. 145). Leopold goes on to indict Pierre Clastres in this context, and to argue that violence, that is, the monopoly of control over it, has been equally made central to the definition of the state, at least in Weberian terms (p. 146). This is indeed true, and it explains why fighting appears as such an intrinsic threat to 'the state' in places such as Papua New Guinea. Leopold goes further, and points out that post-colonial war and hostile actions within colonial states are much more destructive than earlier versions of fighting in the acephalous context. His remarks resonate here with those of Abbink reported above, about changes in the violent activities of the Suri and the larger context or theatre of violence in which such changes have emerged.

Leopold goes back to Middleton's work and works forward from the observation that, besides lineage elders and rain-makers, 'notables' could have influence in peace-making between groups (p. 150). In the turbulent post-colonial situation, new kinds of notables have attempted to reconstruct the relationship between the Lugbara and the state, partly through the reformulation and dissemination of historical narratives (correcting, for example, misperceptions about tribes and their animosities and roles in state violence). From the point of view of our comparative interests here, it is interesting that Leopold highlights the fact that ritual was often brought into play in order to reset social relations, utilising the traditions of cursing available to elders in the past. Those who came as 'foreigners' (p. 154) and spilt blood were cursed in the past, but these curses could be ritually lifted, so that those guilty of killings could be forgiven and social relations could be renewed. The killings would have constituted 'bad deaths', and the rituals would also be designed to purify the land where the deaths occurred and the ghostly aspects of the persons killed who had not been properly assigned a place in the cosmos. (The formulation here is our own, not that of Leopold.)

Indeed, the upshots of the whole debate here are that certain indigenous or traditional ideas in the end prove to be the most fertile starting points for the recreation of peace, and that such starting points are encapsulated in ritual. One lead in Middleton's own exposition that is not followed up by Leopold is the reference to reparation. Could reparation of some kind be added to the lifting of curses? In our own argument we have stressed the wealth complex as also the peace-making complex. This is avowedly a model derived from the conscious model of the Hagen people themselves, and this is perhaps both its best justification and its greatest limitation: justification because starting from indigenous capacities to make peace is an implicitly plausible strategy; and limitation because the problem of scale enters: can reparations be extended beyond their original scales of operation, and, if so, how far? Answers to these questions cannot be given clearly, because the compensation option has never been seriously brought into contexts beyond the inter-clan or inter-tribal level (other than in the historic experiment of the 1960s between Dei and Mul councils and inter-Province occasions explored in Strathern & Stewart 2000a, pp. 138–46).

Warless/peaceful societies?

The societies we have been discussing have been those in which recourse to physical conflict is an accepted part of human interaction. The degree of conflict, its consequence, and ways of settling it make all the difference to how this recourse plays out over time. War is a special category of physical conflict, one in which the scale of conflict involves whole groups and in which more members of the group risk being killed in combat than in lesser conflicts. The anthropologist Raymond Kelly (2000) has made a careful investigation of the putative origins of war, beginning his study with a consideration of societies without war, which he labels 'peaceful societies' (p. 1).

Kelly's mode of analysis is sociological. It does not depend on assertions about 'human nature'. 'Peace' and 'peaceful' are of course themselves rather vague terms, subject to variation of meaning. It is easier to work with categories such as violence/absence of violence, avoidance of physical conflict, controls over levels of conflict and the like. Egalitarian band societies are the most likely candidates for the minimising of inter-group violent conflict, partly because of their small scale, widespread interlacing kinship ties and the ease with which people can move away from one another if they come into conflict. Further, homicide rates, which if high must surely preclude any idea that we are dealing with a peaceful society, do not necessarily indicate war as such. Bruce Knauft's (1985) study of the Gebusi indicated very high homicide rates for these people, based on vengeance activities carried out by raiding parties against persons identified by divination procedures as sorcerers. But such vengeance raids do not have to be seen as warfare: they resembled rather execution parties. Kelly (2000) proceeds to examine the uses of violent activity or physical force in social life among a number of peoples often described as 'peaceful', for example, the Mbuti, Siriono, Copper Eskimo, !Kung San and Semai. Only the Semai appear to emerge as actually 'non-violent' (p. 31), but a feature that is shared more widely is a relative lack of retaliation for homicides (p. 42).[6]

This finding enables Kelly to proceed with his argument, to wit, that a transitional shift to warfare signals a move from one form of 'collective violence' (p. 43) to another. Retaliation by killing an imputed killer is replaced by the possibility of targeting any kin of the killer, thus triggering chains of vengeance, either in feud (limited conflict) or war (broader conflict). This move correlates with the development of more solidary groups and concomitant senses of group liability, that is, with 'segmental societies' (p. 45). With segmental societies based on lineage principles, classificatory kin terms provide, Kelly says, a matrix in terms of which one group member can be substituted for another (p. 47). In contexts of violence, the initial killer may still be a preferred target, but other accessible group members may be killed if the first perpetrator is not available. With full-scale war, there is full group liability, although it should be noted here (and this is our own point, not Kelly's) that such liability is much reduced when there are cross-cutting ties of marriage alliance and kinship between the sides in the fights: as is the case universally throughout the New Guinea Highlands. These same cross-cutting ties, of course, are the vehicles for peace-making initiatives via payments of wealth, and they work all the better as such because the ties are multiplex (in the old term deployed by Gluckman (1955)), and compensation is *not* isolated from other pathways of exchange and shared interests, including the regenerative and reproductive nexus of kin ties.

An interesting problem lies in the causes of the transition between feud and war. First, we should note that these coexist in the same social formation. The implication is that if there was a historical transition it was seamless and analogical, becoming more digital and clear, perhaps, in cases in which considerations such as struggles over resources (for example, land) become more pronounced.[7] With full group liability, more people are exposed to danger, also, and there may be possibilities for conflicts either to escalate or to de-escalate when group members press for settlements on a basis of 'all for one and one for all'.

Kelly's category of warless societies, as we have seen, does not mean 'peaceful societies'. Of the societies he examines early in his book, it is only the Semai who seem to emerge as averse to violence per se. This picture is in large part due to the long-term ethnographic work of Robert Knox Dentan (1968). The Semai, as studied by Dentan in the early 1960s, practised extensive agriculture in forested regions, with a low overall population density of five to 25 persons per square mile. They had plenty of room in which to move around, including in cases of conflict (a criterion important in Kelly's scheme of warless societies). They were not a tiny population overall, however, numbering 12,748 in the 1965 census (p. 8). They hunted and killed animals for food but used a 'secret language' to refer to them, suggesting that if the 'real name' of the animal were used while they hunted it, the animal might hear this and evade capture (p. 39). Dentan suggests that this practice of giving secret names 'seems also to be a way of avoiding the consequences of aggression by concealing the fact of aggression' (p. 39). Alternatively, the Semai's own explanation may be accepted as what motivates them.

An important concept for the Semai, in Dentan's account, is *punan*. *Punan* is an emotion of unhappiness caused by someone frustrating the person's desires. *Punan* is thus homologous with the Melpa *popokl* concept in this regard. A person suffering from *punan* is held to be liable to an accident. To avoid this, Semai try to preclude *punan* from arising between people, or, presumably, to deal with it promptly if it does (p. 55).

Among themselves, Semai were not warriors. They would flee rather than fight. However, when recruited by the British authorities in Malay to fight against the Communist insurgency of the 1950s and ordered to kill their enemies, they did so with considerable violence (p. 58). Dentan assumes that Semai had aggressive impulses, but within their own social arena each person reined in these impulses. He reports that people say it is wrong to nag others, as it also is, however, to refuse a request; that people should not make difficulties for one another – if they do, withdrawal is the right response; and that they view with suspicion acts of rhetorical persuasion even if they recognise these as marks of intelligence. There is also a certain fluidity in social relationships, for example those of marriage, which reduces the likelihood of disputes over rights, including sexual rights. Their extended groups are simply bands of around 45 people, and usually not more than 100 as a maximum (p. 79). They are also eclectic in their responses to changes, willing to accept new ways without necessarily giving up the old (p. 94).

Dentan's ethography does not have any special section on fighting or homicide. Clayton Robarchek (1994) has also studied these people. He takes the view that the Semai see themselves as victims of a malevolent universe (p. 183). Robarchek and his spouse worked with the Semai in the 1970s. He discusses witchcraft ideas among them, ideas that in classic ways reflect the inverse of socially acceptable norms (p. 185). In addition to witches, the Semai generally fear outsiders, *mai*, and *mara'*, strange beings that are held to attack humans (p. 188). *Gunik*, by contrast, are spirits that have joined with humans, to help them, arriving in their dreams.

Ghosts, says Robarchek, are 'malevolent and homicidal' (p. 188), even though they were once kin, and hostility to ghosts is expressed in expeditions to 'kill' them (p. 192). Robarchek's discussions in this paper do not really explain what these ideas regarding hostile ghosts are all about. We may suggest, following his materials, that they are the split-off aggressive aspects of personality. But we should ask how, then, they are felt to impinge on social processes. It is apparent that the control over aggression among the Semai finds a psychological 'safety valve' in other directions. But are such safety valves really safe? The point that in other contexts Semai could become very aggressive might be interpreted as suggesting otherwise, as does Robarchek's brief report on changing interactions with outsiders and the emergence of aggression under strain among Semai in 1979–80 (pp. 192–94).[8]

Making and unmaking enemies

Making peace often seems hard, whereas making enemies may be easy. Günther Schlee's book of 2008 (pbk 2010) carries the title *How Enemies Are Made*. The subtitle, however, indicates that the scope is not universal or global (*Towards a Theory of Ethnic and Religious Conflicts*): rather, the book sets itself against oversimplified versions of ethnic conflict, for example 'primordialist' theories (p. 4). Schlee also negates the idea that ethnicity, or ethnic groups, are universal phenomena. This view is in line with his anti-primordialist stance, which permeates his whole analysis. The overall implication is that if ethnicity is contingent and historical, then ethnic conflicts are not immutable or irremediable, and thus they can be brought to an end so as to produce peace. When, at the end of his discussion, Schlee goes into the complexities of a role he himself took up in Somalia as a part of peace-making efforts, we rapidly see that actual matters are more complex than this summary allows, because it is not only 'ethnicity' that is involved, but conflicts over ecological resources (p. 113), between pastoralists and agriculturalists, between landowners and 'liberators' (p. 113), the roles of warlords, and the whole set of difficulties surrounding the existence of a 'weak state' (as found also in the conflicts in Afghanistan) (p. 114). In other words, even if ethnicity is contingent and created, it cannot easily be neutralised because it is bound up with many other intractable axes of conflict, throughout which Schlee acknowledges that the idioms of clanship are persistently important (p. 114). Many other players or stakeholders were involved: neighbouring states, non-government organisations, the European Union, the US, and most palpably the so-called 'warlords' (a terminology also found in relation to Afghanistan). Finally, 'Islamists' emerged as a force by 2006 (p. 168).

With all this, we see that the issue of 'ethnicity' is almost inextricably enmeshed in a huge complex of other factors. It is also evident that while the causes of conflict are abundantly clear, ways of making peace are not.[9]

An extreme case in which this last proposition is strongly exemplified can also be found in Are Knudsen's (2009) ethnography of intractable/protracted conflicts in Kohistan within the North-West Frontier Province of Pakistan, an area previously studied by Lincoln Keiser (1986, 1991). In his earlier study, Keiser emphasised the role of the introduction of guns in the escalation of violence in Thull, Kohistan (an observation picked up by Strathern (1992, p. 245) in a study of 1980s warfare in Mount Hagen), using the distinctions between action and passion, and seeing passion as an emotion central to definitions of existential identity. Knudsen's (2009) approach adds an important dimension to the idea of passion, that is, the idea of belonging to a group (p. 10). Among the Palas villagers whom Knudsen studied, belonging is not a stable or secure phenomenon but is often threatened, so they try to protect and conserve it. Patriliny determines the formal boundaries of a group, but support from group members can be at risk (p. 10). The people have also been affected by orthodox versions of Islam since the 1970s (p. 31), with bans on dancing, emphasis on reciting the Koran, and lay evangelisation (pp. 33–34). Although group membership is by patrilineal descent and in addition there is marriage with patrilateral parallel cousins within lineages, land boundaries tend to be blurred, and this, according to Knudsen, 'incites male posturing, leading to violent clashes and homicide, a problem that afflicts other acephalous societies too' (p. 154).

Knudsen comments that it is difficult to find an end point in conflicts (this is reminiscent of Laurence Goldman's (1983, p. 186) *Talk Never Dies* title on the Huli). In cases of killings, 'there is a strong moral obligation to retaliate, but also an obligation to accept mediation and pleas for truces and ceasefires' (p. 186). Revenge killing is also undertaken at the level of personal vendettas and does not extend to higher levels of grouping (p. 187). A stress on violence in general has, however, increased among men (p. 188). Vendettas often have to do with supposed offences against women (p. 189). Violent episodes reduce food supply and make contests over fields more likely (p. 191). Prior to the advent of orthodox Islam, extramarital sex relations were not a cause for murder and could be settled by compensation (p. 198). It is clear that the combination of guns and orthodox Islam has exacerbated conflict and made violent disputes more intractable than they were before, in large measure because of the loss of compensation as an acceptable way to mediate disputes.

Compensation and ritual: final words

The example highlights the significance of compensation as a mechanism of dispute settlement, especially in contexts of violent physical actions or actual killings.

It should be stressed here that discussions about compensation are finetuned ways of debating, negotiating and mediating. Occasions of arranging for compensation require enormous amounts of attention to social and individual details and concerns, with contingent results and risks of failure. Compensation is therefore a political art.

Because of the complexities involved, compensation payments also have to be strongly ritualised, and the ritual process has to mark waystations along a road to peace.

We take a final look here at peace-making rituals as described for the Maring and the northern Melpa, both essentially referring to pre-colonial conditions.

For the Maring, Rappaport (1967 [1968]) thought that peace-making rituals existed but were performed infrequently. However, after a *kaiko* festival was finished, two groups that had earlier fought might agree to make peace and to raise numbers of pigs in addition to those already expended on their respective *kaiko* events.

Rappaport had only sketchy materials on the details of peace-making but reported the following (pp. 219–20). The two sides would first have to agree that they wanted to make peace. This is perhaps the most important point of all. Then, each side would consult its own ancestors to make sure these also agreed. After that they would meet at the border between their territories and they would exchange the livers of pigs, perhaps from those pigs they had just sacrificed to their ancestors as a part of the business of consulting them. Pigs' livers in all three of the Highlands societies where we have carried out fieldwork are symbolically important. Men cut them into pieces and share them after they have been specially roasted. The Melpa term for liver is '*kaemb*', meaning compassion, pity, which can stand for good feeling in general. The liver among the Melpa can stand for a whole man: 'cooking the liver of a man' can be an expression for rejoicing over the successful killing of an enemy either in fighting or by sorcery. In the case of the Maring peace-making ritual, the livers were shared only among those whose mothers or grandparents came from the enemy group. The significance of maternal ties as vehicles for friendship is notably picked out. The other members of the groups would continue to observe taboos on sharing food, but the taboos would be gradually abrogated over four generations. At the time of peace-making, women were also exchanged or promised as brides between the two sides, and were clearly depicted as *wump* (= Melpa *mbo*), or 'planting materials', by which the dead persons killed in fighting between the groups could be replaced, ideally one woman for each man slain. At the same time, we may note here, new intertwining relations of maternal kinship would be created.

Every one of the cultural motifs or elements that appear in this Maring scheme could be easily paralleled among the Melpa. We see here the final transformation of wealth into persons, and persons into the sharing of food.

For the Northern Melpa themselves, the leader Ongka-Kaepa has given us a graphic account in his autobiography of the *el pint pint* ritual.

First, by mutual agreement the two sides would put barriers of leaves, along with pieces of broken shields and spears, on the pathways by which warriors travelled to fight one another (Strathern & Stewart 1999b, p. 63). So they closed off the roads of war.

Second, they planted cordylines as a mark of the 'peace process'. Cordylines are long-lived and would stay as enduring markers. (Further, this act is the same as the Maring planting of the *rumbim*.)

Third, they would work hard to make gardens and raise large herds of pigs, so that over about three years successive generations of pigs would grow up and feed on expanded sweet potato crops from the gardens. Sometimes, the pigs would not do well, and people said this was because of *el pint pint*, the 'dry things' of warfare (charcoal, *mara* leaves, cowrie shells, worn in war decorations). They decided to drive out these dry things.

Fourth, then, they would take to the special communal men's house that had been used for discussions on war leaves of some special plants which a ritual expert (*mön wuö*) had bespelled. They dressed up a tall man with charcoal and white and yellow earth, placed a gourd as a mask on his face and gave him a divided plume of a red bird of paradise, and also a tall tail of a marsupial (decorative marks of a warrior, increasing the impression of size in epideictic fashion). In his hand they placed an old dry spear, blackened with soot. He was thus made to look like a spirit being.

A cultural drama was then staged. The 'Spirit Man' climbed up a tree, and later the clansmen came and called out to him with various names, and the spirit figure came down with all his warfare paraphernalia on. The men greeted him and recited the names of all kinds of items connected with war, then told him to go away, back to the bush where he belonged.

At this point, young men clubbed pigs prepared for sacrifice. They also chased the spirit figure, pursuing him across the borders with some of their enemies, then erecting new ritual barriers at a big river near to the borders.

The spirit man took off his decorations, washed himself in river water and joined his clansmen, who placed sweet potato leaves at the noses of the pigs they had just clubbed. The pigs were then cooked along with sweet potatoes, and one tuber was given to each woman to take home and feed to her pig herd, to help the pigs to grow.

Then they gradually prepared to hold a big feast, a few years on. After some three gardening cycles they would hold the feast and call upon their allies to come and receive large gifts of pork, satisfying all obligations and saying: 'Now we have made an end of this old matter and we are going to start on some new work' (Strathern & Stewart 1999b, p. 65).

It is notable here that Ongka is describing an intricate and dramatic ritual to mark exit from a state of fighting; but this does not lead to direct compensation between enemies. Instead, the ritual recognised, as did the Maring *kaiko*, the ally relationship. Yet there is a sense in Ongka's account that this whole ritual could not occur unless relations of enmity were at least in abeyance, the nearest thing to peace in this context.

Here, then, we have two cases in which compensation or reparation payments were set into carefully orchestrated ritual contexts. Aside from the dramatic cultural creativity shown, perhaps especially in the example Ongka gave, one very notable feature here has to do with the staging of time. Peace takes time – and resources – to bring about, and what we learn from these examples is that it cannot be achieved by any single act but by the slow, careful movements of persuasion and inclination, under the signs of *festina lente* and imaginative practice.[10]

CHAPTER 9

Envoi: three themes beyond the local

In developing our central arguments in this book, we have deliberately concentrated on local contexts in which compensation practices generally operate and are still effective even in transformed circumstances. The sources of transformation have been discussed many times in previous publications, both by ourselves and by other scholars, beginning with the times of 'first contact' in the 1930s in Highlands Papua New Guinea. They include different historical phases: early processes of pacification from the 1930s to the 1950s (in some more remote places the 1960s); the consolidation of colonial administration and introduction of planned political change and economic developments from the 1950s to the 1970s, leading up to Independence in September 1975; and aftermaths and complexities, deriving from large-scale mining projects, intensified competition for political office and the electoral violence that goes with this, and correspondingly at national level the emergence of 'corrupt' practices in which power is both gained through the disbursement of money and maintained through siphoning off of funds into interpersonal networks, from 1975 to the present (2011 at the time of writing). Money, of course, in the sense of state money, has entered deeply into the transactions and the consciousness of people for many years. They have absorbed it into life cycle and political exchanges, to that extent 'domesticating' it, but also making themselves dependent on government policies and economic globalisation (see Stewart & Strathern 2002d; Strathern & Stewart 1999a). Since money is much in demand, the amounts of it needed for compensation payments have correspondingly increased, and this expansion in scale can threaten the viability of any particular payment. Comparable pressures, however, occurred from the 1930s onwards, when the people in Hagen, for example, began to find themselves in possession of an influx of shell valuables. Such valuables became instruments of peace-making as well as prestige-making when big-men seized the historical moment to extend the scope of their exchanges and to make peaceful inroads into social niches of their ex-enemies. The surplus was thus productively ploughed back into politics, and when the inflation in supply of shells became too great they were dropped in favour of money, that is, state money introduced first in the form of Australian currency in colonial times and from 1975 the national Papua New Guinea kina currency. The size of payments was from then on calibrated in monetary terms, although pigs, still largely produced by the people themselves, have always remained an important foundation of any successful payment. With the increasing scale of social relations and the mobility of persons, compensation payments for deaths have embroiled wider and wider categories of people, making it more difficult for payments to be economically, politically and ritually effective. They are still, however, the most effective ways of settling such disputes, because they are grounded in longstanding and enduring cultural attitudes, which by virtue of their persistence are also capable of being adapted for new contexts. They provide the substratum of established practice on which the further imagination of peace-making can be elaborated. They thus have the capacity to be extended beyond the local level. Three contextual themes, however, present challenges to the arguments in favour of the continuity and adaptability of compensation as a means of conflict settlement. These themes are: first, circumstances of the urban–rural divide; second, problems at national political levels and with large-scale industrial projects; and third, the impingement of terror, whether between local groups or between such groups and state authorities. The powers of imagination have to be brought into play in order to meet such challenges.

Urban contexts

It may be objected that our argument so far depends on the operation of residentially fixed local political groups and their leaders, among which compensation payments can be effectively structured and ritually marked. What, then, of the contemporary fluid and unstructured urban contexts, with their class inequalities, squatter settlements and cosmopolitan movement of peoples?

Obviously, in these contexts compensation payments cannot be a panacea. And in addition, parallel to the incidence of compensation payments there is always the operation of state and provincial criminal law and the courts. This incidence may be more obvious in urban contexts, but it applies also throughout rural areas. Michael Goddard (2005), however, has shown that urban Village Courts can play a very valuable role in settling conflicts that can otherwise lead to violence or in handling the aftermaths of violent sequences of action (compare also Goddard 2009). Goddard's (2005) discussion is illuminating in a number of ways. His fieldwork was in Konedobu, an old previous administrative centre in the capital city of Port Moresby, not far from Hanuabada, a historically Motuan community. One of the areas served by the Konedobu

Village Court was Ranuguri, composed mostly of migrants from the Gulf Province area of Malalaua (p. 57). Such migrants are commonly bi-local, urban-based but often visiting home or vice versa, and Goddard rightly notes that in their lives 'elements of urban and rural economic activities are integrated' (p. 57). One of the microethnic groups in Ranuguri is the Toaripi people, who have brought into the city a fear of sorcery, including in this expanded cityscape the sorcery of other cultural groups (p. 59). Indeed, this is a widespread feature of the results of the mixing of groups in the uncertain and often dangerous contexts of city life, where rumours and gossip about events pass quickly and are transformed as they traverse shifting contexts of cultural background and knowledge (compare Stewart & Strathern 2004). Goddard (2005) quotes the earlier work of Dawn Ryan, who remarked that when local Motuan landowners asked the Gulf settlers to leave or pay rent, the settlers refused and threatened to defend their homes either with physical force or by sorcery (p. 60). Goddard's findings were that sorcery ideas were still alive but there was a great reluctance to refer directly to them in Village Court cases. This reluctance seems to stem from a wish to avoid giving a negative stereotype to Ranuguri that might attract unfavourable attention from the police. The background here is that many settlement areas in and around the city are seen as hotbeds of crime, violence and gang activity. Ranuguri is not one of these settlements, and its inhabitants are keen to maintain a positive profile. Consequently, although sorcery is a contemporary issue, they do not refer to it directly, nevertheless arranging informal compensations, for example, for supposed false accusations of sorcery made between people (p. 65). Goddard's case history shows the creativity and imagination of people in both dealing with potentially inflammatory situations and keeping these 'under the radar' of external surveillance in a difficult urban context of life.

Another settlement area is Erima. We ourselves have been familiar with this place for many years, because clusters of people from the Dei Council area of Mount Hagen have from time to time lived there and we have travelled into it by a dirt access road to visit friends and acquaintances. Goddard points out that Erima contains ethnic enclaves and there is friction between these, at times exacerbated by consumption of alcohol (mostly beer) (p. 158). Such conflicts are restrained by the people's perception that they need to stand together against intrusive police raids. Consistently with this stance of resistance, the people also prefer to use what Goddard calls 'neo-customary dispute-management procedures' in preference to going to formal magistrates' courts (p. 159). This is an important point in comparative terms, because whenever this situation holds, we find a fertile field for self-help procedures to prevail. Church officials and leaders in micro-ethnic enclaves play parts in such processes, and Village Courts provide a slightly more formal structure into which customary values and practices can be fitted. One Village Court official whose work Goddard studied exemplified well the kinds of values that underpin local customary procedures everywhere, based on intense knowledge of circumstances and their history rather than any strict application of 'law' in the sense of external legal rules. This official's work contrasted with that of another (from the Southern Highlands, whereas the first official came from Milne Bay Province), who used bullying and bribes ('gifts') to get his way (p. 168). These two officials became locked in a struggle for power over time, with complex results for the Erima court. Goddard points out that the court's operations were also affected by branches of government and the state, showing how the state is enmeshed in the locality and vice versa. This again is a valuable point for comparisons, since it is precisely this process of mutual enmeshing that can either empower or disempower local methods of settling disputes. An overall point that one can add here to Goddard's discussions is that if we look at the kinds of sanctions that can be used in Village Courts, monetary compensation is a sanction that is available to magistrates, but in itself such compensation cannot achieve the complexities and subtleties of traditional compensation practices, which can flourish only outside of state-based frameworks.

Another general point that we would like to make here is that urban and rural contexts cannot in practice be separated. Instead, they form an extended field of social and political relations in which persons move between places and exploit opportunities but remain tied together by material concerns, including problems arising from violent deaths and/or sorcery accusations. In his autobiography, the Kawelka leader Ongka refers briefly to a case belonging to the 1970s in which a young man of a neighbouring clan died in the capital city, Port Moresby, far from Hagen, and Ongka's sub-clansmen were accused of having been involved in the death and Ongka himself was threatened with a killing for revenge if he did not organise a compensation payment to the kinsfolk. Ongka explains further that the dead man's kin stole pigs and cassowaries from him in a series of escalating threats. Short-circuiting, in a manner classic for his innovative style, the usual divide between 'custom' and 'law', Ongka reported the threats in the local council chambers, still presided over by an expatriate officer at this time, and had a fine imposed on the man's relatives, but then he turned round and raised a compensation payment to them, probably because their clan was a political ally of the Kawelka clans (Strathern & Stewart 1999b, pp. 126–27). The kinsfolk of the dead man had sent a deputation to the hospital in Moresby, demanding to know the results of a doctor's postmortem on the body. They were told that he had died of a diseased liver caused by alcohol consumption, but they remained suspicious. Back at home in Hagen the dead man's own cousins among the Kawelka, accused of having caused his death, sent the sacred divination sign of their group, a cordyline leaf, swearing their innocence. Contemporary and traditional ideas were thoroughly at work here, precisely in an expanded urban–rural field of relations. The same intertwining is shown in the fact that kinsfolk of the dead man from both the Kawelka and his own group drove a van to the site of his death at a busy corner in the Boroko suburb of Moresby near to midnight, when traffic flow was light, and whistled to his wandering spirit (*min*) to get on board and come with them to the door of the hospital morgue, where it could be reunited with his dead body, prior to its removal by plane back to Hagen for burial. Spirits do not like bright city lights, the Hageners said, so the operation for this transfer could not be conducted until late at night when traffic stopped. The case history also shows the creative improvisations that people bring to bear in their life-worlds to link urban and rural contexts together.

National-level contexts

Elections of the kinds discussed in Chapter 1 of this book provide the most obvious context in which the national and local levels interpenetrate. Most obviously, as many observers have pointed out at length (for example, Ketan 1998; Standish 1992), the gift mentality to which Goddard (2005, p. 168) alludes has greatly skewed the trajectories of politics in the Highlands Provinces. Candidates need money to gain support, and if they are elected they need more money to maintain support. Since their salaries and entitlements alone cannot meet all these claims on them, the pathways to the further appropriations of funds, especially if they hold ministerial positions, open up dramatically. This kind of pervasive process, an absolute product of locality–state relations, tends over time to weaken both local respect for leaders whose bribing activities are too obvious and the integrity of state institutions themselves.

We have previously examined this nexus in a chapter of a book devoted to the comparative study of the state, identity and violence edited by Brian Ferguson (2003). Here, we draw out a number of points from our chapter in that book (Strathern & Stewart 2003) in order to reflect further on the prospects for compensation as a way of making peace. To begin with, we noted that one problem for Papua New Guinea as a whole up to the 1990s is that it lacked a strong narrative of the nation as an imagined community, in the now time-honoured phrase of the historian Benedict Anderson (1983 [1991]; Strathern & Stewart 2003; compare Foster 1995). Historians variously point to the great linguistic diversity of the nation's groups, or to the fact that there was no great struggle for Independence from Australian rule prior to the emergence of Papua New Guinea in 1975 around which such a national narrative could coalesce. The pursuit of self and local group interest and the multiplicity of political parties also increased fears of violence over time, leading some politicians to settle their families in Australia to provide them with some safety.

In these circumstances, we proposed that a social contract model between politicians and their people might be put forward as a way of strengthening what was perceived early in the years following 2000 as a 'weak state' (Strathern & Stewart 2003, p. 302). We noted the positive roles that Christian churches played, or could play, in developing such a social contract idea (p. 302). The forces opposed to the development of a social contract ideology included those that we called forces of predation: organised gang crimes, violent protests against industrial installations, and inflated demands for compensation. Narratives of rape and assault sorcery fed into perceptions of predations on society by disgruntled and subversive agencies. The perceptions of danger and distrust arising from these images were increased by ideas that the police themselves were sometimes in league with criminal elements (p. 305). Compensation demands were sometimes made when the police shot persons who supposedly ignored police roadblocks set up to catch criminals. Roads came to be seen as both vehicles of 'development' and pathways of danger and military-style conflict. We cited a case in which a Kawelka Kundmbo clansman was ambushed and killed on the government highway between Mount Hagen town and Dei Council, in the course of a period of severe inter-clan conflict in the late 1980s. Both police and clan enemies set up these roadblocks. By the 1990s, passenger vehicles between the Southern Highlands and Mount Hagen were regularly held up and stopped by armed criminals.

Leaders, as we documented, made strong efforts to deal with the escalation of conflicts. One dispute (case 1, pp. 307–308), dating to 1998, involved Kawelka leaders in arranging compensation to people from the Chuave area in Simbu province, as a result of an altercation between a Kawelka woman and her Chuave co-wife that ended in the Chuave wife being stabbed and dying. The Kawelka leaders persuaded their kin to pay compensation for this death in order to maintain the name of the Kawelka (*Kawelka-nga mbi* in the Melpa language): meaning, however, not just reputation, but that if no compensation were paid the Chuave people would block the Highlands Highway running down to the coast and might kill more people, making the Kawelka responsible for further compensations. Compensation was duly paid. Another case (case 2, pp. 309–311) also involved a killing between two co-wives of different ethnicity, neither of them from Hagen but both married to a Hagen businessman. This case showed much greater involvement of church pastors, and the use of the lingua franca Tok Pisin, in the multi-ethnic milieu of the case. A procession of persons participating in the compensation also carried the Papua New Guinea flag. Pastors put the meeting in God's hands. Special welcomes were given to both 'lawyers' and traditional 'magic men' who might be present. Money packages for distribution were hung up on a dais in a netbag, like the body of the dead woman. The populace at large contributed more money as 'taxes' to pay members of the Trouble Committee that had mediated in the dispute.

Both of these cases shared what we called 'social engineering'.

They also shared the creative use of imagination, in which state-based images were pulled in and put to work for local purposes. Imagination made the bridges between these levels and compensation was the vehicle for this bridging.

Crucial to both cases was the fact that the issues were between local groups. Matters are more intractable when industrial companies (or possibly the government itself) are pitted against local groups of people. Numerous observers have commented on this context, which we have also frequently referred to (for example, Stewart & Strathern 2002b; Strathern & Stewart 2000a). Of these observers, Colin Filer has perhaps made the most trenchant commentaries, arguing in a series of publications that the compensation payments demanded and paid in conflicts between local people and multinational companies can have negative results (for example, Filer 1990, 1996, 1997, 1999, 2009). Filer has consistently emphasised the disintegrative, as opposed to the integrative, components and ramifications of compensation in these conflicts. One of Filer's (1997, pp. 160–62) arguments has been that the term compensation is itself stretched too far, made to cover too much, both conceptually and by way of the amounts of wealth demanded from companies, especially where 'landowners' as a category are involved. In his 2009 publication, Filer turns his critical gaze away from landowners and companies to international planning groups and the concept of 'bridging epistemologies' (p. 92). This concept takes into account the 'knowledge systems' of indigenous communities as elements of systems ecology (p. 93), rather than as embedded in politics and involved in hybrid constructions of policy. Filer argues against the metaphor of the bridge between epistemologies here, asking, 'What is underneath the bridge?' (p. 96) His answer is that there may be too many things underneath it that can destabilise the bridge itself, at the broadest level the question of ownership or control over the ecosystems in question (p. 90).

Filer's conclusions seem to be that many dangers are ignored in talk about bridging epistemologies or scales, especially in the quicksands of development processes. In our own, much more locally based discussion of compensation and the imagination we have not referred to epistemologies but more in terms of practices. In our terms, what is underneath the bridges built by compensation practices is the arena of conflict itself, and the bridges in question are the only available vehicles for transcending the conflicts. Where a dispute has too many power inequities and too many competing international interests, clearly any given attempt at compensation may fail. Where questions of scale are still manageable, the idea of compensation can quite flexibly be extended, but, for example, between a company and a clan, those questions of scale can destabilise both the practice of compensation and its results. Destabilisation can then lead to terror, the exact opposite of the basic purpose of compensation as a means of making peace.

Terror and the imagination

We turn back again here to the beginning of this book, and also to some earlier work of ours. Terror is an emotive and subjective term. Phenomenologically, it refers to gaps in experiential horizons into which fear and uncertainty enter and colonise the minds and bodies of people. Violence is one of the prime instruments of producing terror, precisely because of its capacity to cause such gaps, operating directly on the body. But terror also can go beyond its immediate embodied contexts when the imagination engages with it, multiplying the physical by the metaphysical realms of thought.

In the volume we co-edited with Neil Whitehead, *Terror and Violence* (Strathern, Stewart & Whitehead 2006), we added a process in which that multiplication typically happens, the process of rumour and gossip, which can gesture beyond the known to the unknown. Noting that acts of terror do 'suggest a world of meanings beyond the acts in themselves' (p. 6), we argued that the imagination in general is the chief multiplier (p. 7), and that 'the imagination also comes into play when violent acts are deliberately used to stimulate further violent acts' (p. 14). We then went on to show how processes of this kind are involved in the production of fears of witchcraft and sorcery, as well as suggesting that a sorcerer or witch figure who is seen as an intruder into social life can be compared to the figure of the terrorist in general and suicide bombers in particular – with this difference, we should add: that the suicide bomber kills himself or herself to kill others, whereas the sorcerer or witch is thought to predate secretly on others in order to enhance their own life power.

The point we wish to make here is from the opposite end of a spectrum of analysis. In Chapter 1 we noted, largely from newspaper sources, the distortions that have entered Papua New Guinea as a part of the downside of parliamentary democracy. The friction caused by the imposition of national onto local politics has certainly, at least in the Highlands, generated an atmosphere of occasional terror, associated with the inordinate spirals of exchange that are a part of contemporary politics. Yet there is a constraint. Elections do take place and politicians are elected. Electoral violence has not led to electoral revolution or the imposition of authoritarian government on a long-term basis. The horizons of terror are episodic. Anarchy threatens but does not take over. It is not that these episodes of electoral violence are themselves necessarily followed by restitutive actions. However, it is our argument that after electoral periods, the imagination of peace is able to reassert itself, simply because it is what most people want. And we have explored in Chapter 7 the significance of ritual processes in becoming the vehicles for such imaginative actions. In the examples we have further alluded to here we can also see how a cultural form of the imagination is brought to bear creatively on harnessing symbols that work to make bridges between the two sides of a compensation case. A netbag full of packets of money is a potent symbol indeed, combining an image of female transactions and male manipulations of such transactions. Gendered symbolism aside, what is at work in this example is the equivalent of Claude Lévi-Strauss's mythological bricolage – that is, ritual bricolage, based on the local Hagen 'theory of mind', the idea that people's *noman* or minds have to be made straight and in alignment with one another and symbols can reach effectively into the person to produce this result. The ideas of God, the ancestors, pigs, money, netbags and the Papua New Guinea flag: all these things can be brought into ritual play in the cause of peace. Imagination is the way along which this play can take place. Hagen metaphors or comparisons (*to*), like the 'tropes' to which Peter Dwyer and Monica Minnegal (2010, p. 634) have recently drawn attention in theorising social change, themselves make use of the ideas of a bridge and a road when they refer to the power of exchange: a *pol* or 'bridge' is a means of making a connection with others, and a 'road', *mon* or *nombokla*, is the term for the highways of exchange along which the traffic of peace can travel.

Appendix

How do cases – instances of 'poisoning' accusations – fit in with the ideal picture of relations among groups?

1. Within the clan

The ideal that one does not poison one's clansman and hence that one does not accuse a clansman of such an act is kept to well enough. But there are three exceptions.

The first exception is the incomer who is bribed by his agnates or others to poison a big-man of his clan of incorporation. It is a familiar enough stereotype. Men often said this was the only reason why in the past they were unwilling to take in refugees: *tin kopnant ruing pilpon ti nötitimon*: 'we felt they would poison us [strike us with *kopna*] and refused them refuge'. There is a strong dogma that an immediate sister's son would not poison or kill one, yet in practice these can be suspected, if they are regarded as *wuö korpa*, men of low status, also. The low-status man is expected to be open to bribery and also to be jealous of big-men and willing to kill them. One case represents a true mother's brother as poisoning his big-man sister's son. An agnate of the same lineage who was a *wuö korpa* would not be suspected in the same way, and there are no cases on record in which one was accused, or any of a more distant clansman who was of low status being accused merely on the basis of a presumed general disaffection or weakness of character.

Second, there is one case in which an accusation was made between two different sections of the same clan. These act in some ways almost like separate clans but do not intermarry and are together coupled as a single group paired with another exogamous group of their tribe. The pair is Membo–Mandembo of Kawelka tribe and the two sections are Ngglammbo and Kurupmbo. We explain this example in terms of the apparently incipient process of the two sections becoming separate clans. The cases date to early colonial times (1930s onwards).

The Ngglammbo suspected a Kurupmbo man, Kilwa, of poisoning the father of Kuklup, Poka. (Kilwa's son joined the Membo clan and no longer acted as a Kurupmbo other than in rare *moka* occasions.) Kilwa's sisters were married to men of the Kombukla and Minembi clans and it was suspected that he had been 'greased', that is, offered pay to do the poisoning. Ngglammbo Ndekane challenged Kilwa to eat the cordyline. (The *köya koema* cordyline is the *mi* or divination-object of the Kawelka and the two men were supposedly *wuö noimb tenda*, 'of one penis', so that the *mi* could act punitively on the accused if he were guilty.) Kilwa complied. Subsequently, his testicles swelled up and he died a painful death, so he was affirmed guilty. The Ngglammbo remained angry over this, but at first the Kurupmbo would not give them compensation. They came to blows, in fact, although without lethal weapons, and then exchanged cooked pig and pearl shells to make the peace between themselves. This sort of incident is much harder to uncover than are stories of poisoning sorcery between enemy clans, and it is probably not unique in fact. There seem to have been no such poisoning or sorcery fears between the two sections of Kundmbo clan among the Kawelka, which appeared in other ways to be more hostile to each other than were Kurupmbo to Ngglammbo. But in Kundmbo the sections are of more recent creation. Within the lifetime of old men in the 1960s they had changed from being sub-clans and the only named subdivisions of the clan. It seems likely that within the very extended exogamous units in some of the Hagen tribes – Kumndi and Nengka, for instance – incidents of hostility and poisoning between segments would be more common.

Third, owing to particular disagreements, agnates of the same clan might occasionally be accused. Only one case of this was recorded, and there were special factors at work in it. Moep, of Membo clan among the Kawelka, was 'isolated' genealogically. He had no close brothers and his father's father was not firmly linked to any other lineage set. His wife was seduced by R—, the son of the most eminent big-man of Membo, who belonged to the opposite sub-clan from Moep. R— was a young big-man himself, and not a few of these are rumoured to engage in sexual adventures because they are confident they can pay for them. Moep was furious, and more so when R— refused to pay, carrying his big-man status a little further. Soon afterwards R— died and there was a great outcry. Who had poisoned him? The natural suspects were the *el parka wuö* (major traditional enemies) who lived nearby, the Minembi Andakelkam, but Öndipi, R—'s father, had friendly relations with these. Suspicion was turned on Moep, but he fled to the protection of his father's father's mother's brother's son's son ('classificatory uncle'), Ongka, a luluai (Administration-appointed headman) of Ngglammbo clan section and a prominent leader. Ongka protected him as if he were an immediate sister's son, and Moep became his 'helper' (*kintmant wuö*). When some of the Kawelka moved to the Kumant, Moep went too, to look after Ongka's pigs. No more sanctions were taken against him, but he was forced to join the Ngglammbo and relinquish membership of Membo, and was regarded as not much better than a *wuö korpa*.

In those tribes in which exogamy is carried as high as the tribe section or the tribe itself, it seems more likely that poisoning-sorcery fears between segments of the exogamous unit could arise, but the dogma is that they do not. The question relates to terminological difficulties, depending on how 'multi-functional' in reference definitions of the clan, tribe section and so on can be.

2. Between pair-clans

The dogma here is that although pair-clans may fight each other with staves, steal from each other and threaten to fight with spears if their tempers are roused, they will not actually resort to warfare and will not poison each other. Practice is consistent with the dogma here, since it is only between pair-clans that have broken the rule of alliance and fought with weapons of war that accusations of poisoning spring up. Thus, there are doubtful references to poisonings between the Ndikambo and Wanyembo clan groups among the Tipuka; and there is a more specific case between the Minembi Yelipi and the Papeke, their pair-clan with whom they fought. The poisoning occurred in the context of pre-colonial warfare and feuding between the two groups, as follows.

When the Engambo Numering sub-clan fought the Yelipi, the Papeke seem to have deserted the Yelipi, and it is perhaps from this time that the hostile relationship between them dates, although trouble may have broken out before. The Papeke killed Yelipi Reipa in the fighting or else while he was gathering mushrooms in the forest that lies between the settlement area of the two clans. This led to blood-feud retaliation rather than open warfare, executed by a young man who later became a leader of the Yelipi, and another who was a well-known fighter. Papeke Mowa was killed in a raid into Papeke territory. It seems that the Kawelka Kundmbo, who had lost two men in warfare with the Papeke, approached the Yelipi and asked them either to join arms against the Papeke or to carry out a killing for them, and this was an extra motive. The two Yelipi men were Kambila and Lap. Later, Lap's own brother was killed by Papeke men,[1] and the Papeke offered to pay compensation in cooked pigs.

The Kundmbo came and urged the Yelipi to kill in return rather than eat pork as compensation. The Papeke arrived with a cassowary bone and asked for a pandanus fruit and a stone axe as solicitory gifts, but the Kundmbo offered to pay the Yelipi with meat instead. As the Papeke came, the Yelipi ambushed them and speared Mel, the father of Mowa, who had already been killed. The Papeke ran back for their weapons and the feud turned into full warfare (*el mam ekit urum*, 'a big fight started'). A Yelipi man, Tepi, married to a Papeke woman, was angry at the Yelipi treachery and went off to the Papeke to live with his affines, taking his two young sons with him. He brought them up and obtained wives for them there among their maternal kin. But later some poison was said to have been put into a bamboo tube of drinking water that he had collected during a heavy rain spell, and he died. This was not made the basis for an open accusation and resurgence of ill-feeling, but the Yelipi believed that the poison was put there by Papeke men, although not ones of the same sub-clan as his wife. One Papeke man of the Ngonyembo sub-clan had been killed, and suspicion probably lay in that direction. It is more likely that the Ngonyembo would be suspected of trying to gain revenge for themselves than that they would act as the executives of other sub-clans.

Between pair-clans in a less disturbed relationship than that of Papeke–Yelipi, there could be frequent stick-fights and disagreements over compensation payments, but no poisoning accusations. This was true, for instance, between the Kitepi and Oklembo of Tipuka and between Membo and Mandembo of Kawelka. Between the Tipuka Kengeke and Kendike, there was one case in which the daughter of a Kendike mother was accused of poisoning her Kengeke husband, but this was through persuasion of her mother's sister's son, a Kombukla man, not by her mother's brothers of Kendike. Yet in another case, a big-man of Kengeke clan, Rumba of Wölyembo sub-clan, who was in the 1960s spoken of as 'first' among the

Kengeke as a leader in his time, was supposed to have been poisoned by one of his son's wife's brothers of Kendike Milyembo sub-clan, and this became the basis for elaborate pig prestations between the two clans in the 1960s.

3. Between clans, other than pair-clans, of the same tribe, with whom 'minor enemy' relations were maintained

Between clans of this category, poisoning accusations were made frequently enough and were often made the signal for warfare to break out between them. Their relationships differed in no way from those between minor enemies of separate tribes. In fact, with some clans of a different tribe, there could be a more suspicion-free relationship since there might be no 'cause of war' with these and they might even be one's allies from time to time. This was the case between the Kitepi and the Membo.

Principals	Mandembo (Kurupmbo and Ngglammbo)	versus	Oklembo
+	+		+
Allies	Membo	versus	Kitepi

Membo and Kitepi were thus opposed only as allies of the two 'root men of war' groups, and this was constantly alluded to in speeches in the 1960s.[2]

Acknowledgements

The idea for a book of this sort is one that we have considered for many years. We wish to thank the Office of Dean N John Cooper, Faculty and School of Arts and Sciences at the University of Pittsburgh, for longstanding support of our research and publication work. Special thanks go also to the European Union Center of Excellence in the University Center of International Studies, and to its previous Director, Professor Alberta Sbragia, for support of our research in Ireland and Scotland over many years. Thanks go to Ms Catherine Rodgers for typographic assistance on some segments of this book. We also thank everyone at University of Queensland Press for their assistance and efforts in the production of this book. The extensive peer review set of comments on this work has helped us to strengthen it and we thank the five anonymous commentators for their suggestions.

For permission to reproduce material in this book we thank the following organisations: by kind permission of Continuum International Publishing Group, material from pp. 52–70 of Pamela J Stewart and Andrew Strathern, *Violence: Theory and Ethnography*, 2002; by kind permission of the Publications Committee of the National Museum of Ethnology, Osaka, Japan (Chief Director, Akiko Mori), material from pp. 7–16 of Pamela J Stewart and Andrew Strathern, *Speaking for Life and Death: Warfare and Compensation Among the Duna of Papua New Guinea*, 2000 (Senri Ethnological Reports no. 13); and by kind permission of the Editor-in-Chief, Andrew Orr, of the *Cornell International Law Journal*, material from pp. 681–99 of the paper by Andrew J Strathern and Pamela J Stewart 'The Problems of Peace-Makers in Papua New Guinea: Modalities of Negotiation and Settlement', published in vol. 30, no. 3, 1997.

Over the years there have been many people whom we have come to know and to benefit from in their conversation and their insights, observations, hospitality and activities in many parts of the world where we have spent time, from remote villages in Papua New Guinea to large cities in Asia and Europe, and we thank them all for their discussions and kindness.

Andrew Strathern and Pamela J Stewart
Cromie Burn Research Unit
University of Pittsburgh

Endnotes

Chapter 2

1. If a man is accused of thieving a pig or seducing the wife of a clansman he will be challenged to the *mi* divination test, that is, to chew or lick the sacred divination-substance of his tribe and eat pig-meat sacrificed for the occasion. If he is guilty, the ancestors, it is said, will kill him, because he has violated his *mi*. Although the *mi* is shared by members of a whole tribe, its use in social control tends to be restricted either to an intra-clan context or to special pacts between clans. (Compare Strauss & Tischner 1962, passim.)
2. For an account of spirit categories in relation to warfare and exchange, see, for example, Strathern & Stewart 2000a.
3. Some spells (*mön*) and ritual techniques are known to most people, but the most important ones could only be inherited or purchased. Even if purchased, they would probably be 'sold' only to a kinsman. A son wishing to learn spells from his father might have to kill a pig and present him with its meat as a solicitory gift. (On spells in the Female Spirit rituals, see Strathern & Stewart 1999c.)
4. This was comparatively rare. The two cases that were encountered in early fieldwork of the 1960s came from the Kopon area, home of the Kawelka and Tipuka tribes:

    (1) While the Tipuka Kitepi clansfolk were living at the place Munumb, the two sons of Tipuka Kendike K— were supposed to have poisoned Tipuka Kitepi Rulkembo Nd—. The Kitepi came along the path to Kendike territory and accused them of this. They burnt what was called the *mon* ('road, pathway') fire, fashioning it just like a fire inside a men's house, surrounded by a hardened ash rim. They asked the Kendike to cook pigs and give legs of pork to them. The Kendike denied they had done the poisoning, so the Rulkembo took up their shields and the other Kitepi joined in. Kendike Romba,

Engk and Kakl were killed in the fight; and Kitepi Rulkembo Mel was killed on the other side. An Oklembo Kundmbo man had joined in, and a Tipuka Kelmbo man who was living with his Kitepi mother's brothers. These too were killed on the Kitepi side.

In this case, then, the demand for compensation, made between two *el öninga* groups within the Tipuka tribe, failed, and fighting broke out instead.

(2) Two big-men of the Minembi Mimke clan were said to have been killed by poisoning. One of them, M—, used to live at his own ceremonial ground which he had made, and when he died he was buried there, along with some settlement-mates, wives and children, who also died. Earlier, Mimke R— had died also and when an autopsy was performed a sweet potato was found in his stomach. A woman (wife married in) confessed that she had been given the sweet potato by Kombukla E— and told to give it to R—. The Kombukla were then suspected of killing M— as well. This must have happened about 1940, that is, prior to pacification in the area, but it seems no war was made on the Kombukla Moggopokae (the small clan of the man who was the alleged source of the poison), who in any case live a long way from the Mimke. Nothing appears to have been done, in fact, for neither the Mimke nor the Kombukla spoke of counter-poisonings which followed, although the Kombukla Moggopokae are afraid of the two Minembi Andakelkam clans that neighbour them in the Baiyer, and these two clans are in the same major tribe section as the Mimke. Instead, a younger generation of Mimke men demanded an outright compensation for the deaths, and they were given 31 pigs, according to the informant (a middle-aged man of the Mimke group). This is further unusual in that the Kombukla appear to have admitted their guilt. In the first case, as was more usual, the charge was denied and fighting started. Historical timing is all-important here. Case 1 belongs entirely to pre-pacification times, whereas Case 2 stretched into the post-pacification times when groups were attempting to settle old disputes peacefully by means of exchanges, partly to facilitate the safe movements of plantation workers in the area, who might converge on a given company-owned plantation from a number of different clan areas.

5. The heads and tail-bones of pigs are considered both delicacies and especially appropriate for sacrifice to the ancestors, hence the mention of them here.

6. The big-man seems to be saying that the aim was to achieve equilibrium only, but fighting often went beyond this.

Chapter 3

1. Practices of competitive exchange were found to a high degree also among the Mendi people (Ryan 1961). Rena Lederman (1986) further developed and refined the ethnography and analysis of exchanges among Mendi groups. Paul Sillitoe has given regional specialists a series of exceptionally detailed monographs on the Wola people of the Was Valley west of Mendi government station (for example, Sillitoe 1979) and has argued about the roles of big-men in war in New Guinea (Sillitoe 1978). It is clear from these and many other studies that there is a complex range of variations in Highlands New Guinea areas with regard to the precise roles of leaders in war and peace (or conflict-generation and conflict-resolution), the characters of groups and the extent to which ideologies of descent and of segmentary structure apply to them, and their demographic and ecological circumstances, as well as their differential historical engagements with the outside world (see, for example, Strathern & Stewart 2000f). We concentrate here on exchange practices that are closely tied with, and typically are generated out of, compensation for killings. Rena Lederman (1991) pointed out that the alternating interplay between interpersonal exchanges and group-based exchanges in Mendi meant that collective action groups were occasion- or event-centred, produced in large part by the efforts of individual big-men, and cross-cut by inter-individual ties across group boundaries. One might comment that these two apparently opposed concepts nevertheless constituted a totality of dialectical relationships, resolved from time to time in massive displays and disbursements of wealth.

   An early discussion of the different logics and trajectories of exchange patterns in the New Guinea Highlands is to be found in Strathern 1969. Pierre Lemonnier (1990) provides an exemplary cross-societal comparative study, drawing on the large reservoir of ethnographic case studies and analyses available at that time. He specifically discusses peace-making and 'Big men' (pp. 96–97), peace and the societies without such big-men (pp. 98–104), and the activities of prominent men whom he sees as intermediate between the putative big-men and great-men categories deployed by Godelier (that is, 'leaders') (pp. 123 ff.). Lemonnier's thoughtful arguments remain very valuable, especially as they are based firmly on the details of empirical data, seen synoptically and in relation to theoretical problems of explanation, rather than on a priori totalising schemes of a purely classificatory sort (such as 'mediated' versus 'unmediated' exchanges). At one point in his exposition, Lemonnier notes the following (p. 145):

> On peut noter au passage que le Bigman tend à se rapprocher du contrôle du savoir rituel, celui-là même qui, dans des sociétés où la manipulation des richesses est réduite à sa plus simple expression... fonde le pouvoir, ou, tout au moins le 'prestige', des hommes qui s'élèvent au-dessus des autres.

Lemonnier goes on here to note that the transition to big-men leadership forms illustrates the political development *'de l'échange pacifique'* (p. 145). This crucial observation is much in line with our central arguments in this book. (See also Strathern 1970a, 1993c, on the important ritual roles of big-men in Hagen and elsewhere in the Highlands.)
2. Wiessner and Tumu (1998) provide an extraordinarily detailed and comprehensive set of materials on all parts of the Enga region, including much information on ritual practices, especially war reparations, which are central to our own exposition here, based primarily on the Hagen (Melpa) case (see, for example, pp. 245–64). It is notable that they take into account the creative roles played by the invention and recitation of songs in either generating or settling conflicts (p. 254). This is an arena of study that could be extended comparatively. (See also Strathern & Stewart 1999b, pp. 119–27 (Ongka's songs)). A particular strength of Wiessner and Tumu's discussions is their deployment of oral histories that provide temporal depth and an appreciation of endogenous changes in practices, including war reparations.
3. Wiessner and Tumu (1998, pp. 257–58), however, provide the testimony of an informant from the Wabag area (where Meggitt worked), who noted: 'You see, one of the fundamental features of war reparations was the additional or "profit" pigs given to individuals in the victim's clan.' Feil (1978, p. 49) notes for the Tombema area that although a profitable return on a *tee* gift is certainly hoped for, nevertheless equivalent returns are acceptable and can keep an exchange partnership going.

Chapter 4

1. An account of this 1968 election was given by Strathern (1970b); and of the 1972 election also by Strathern (1976). Strathern and Stewart (2000a,

pp. 93–112) review a span of Kawelka political history, including some of the events portrayed in greater detail here. (For a set of early discussions on conflict-settlement procedures, see Epstein 1974.)
2. In 1968 the state currency used in Papua New Guinea was the Australian pound, later changed to dollars. At Independence from Australia in 1975, the Papua New Guinea government opted to name its own national currency the kina and toea currency, instead of dollars and cents. The term kina was actually derived from a Tolai word referring to pearl shells and appeared also in the Melpa term for the same shell type, *kin*. Toea referred to the kind of armlet worn as a decoration by Motu speakers around Port Moresby on the southern coast. The intention was that the terms for the new currency should draw on traditions from both the north and south coasts and from the Highlands. Andrew Strathern was involved in giving advice to Michael Somare, the new Prime Minister, and the Papua New Guinea Parliament at this time.
3. See the illustration in Strathern and Stewart (2000a, p. 95, and other election images and discussions in that chapter).
4. This was the exact place where P— himself was later attacked in an attempted revenge for the incident discussed here, an attack that we describe later in the present chapter. (See also Strathern & Stewart 2000a, pp. 96 ff.; Strathern 1972a on the trial in Mount Hagen of P—'s attacker. Strathern acted as an ad hoc official court translator for the judge at this trial.) From an inter-group viewpoint, these ethnographic materials reveal the vulnerabilities and tensions that surround border areas, particularly where groups are interstitial and have ambiguous affiliations. The same situation holds between Northern Ireland and its borders with the Republic of Ireland (see Strathern, Stewart & Whitehead 2006).
5. These earlier terms, luluai and tultul, were derived from terms used by Administration officials in the Tolai area of the Gazelle Peninsula, New Britain, after Australia took over the control of New Guinea, the northern half of Papua and New Guinea. Indigenous luluais and tultuls had been given badges to wear on their foreheads as marks of their office and were part of an official colonial hierarchy, being appointed to their positions as we have noted above.
6. These observations do not mean that the rituals of compensation simply 'fail'. They do mean that the specific frameworks of ritual action are stretched, sometimes to breaking point (compare Hüsken 2007).

Chapter 5
1. These references include Banks 2000; Dinnen 2000a, 2000b, 2001; Goddard 1992; Harrison 1993; Hart Nibbrig 1992; Kituai 1998; and Sykes 2000, in addition to several works by the present authors.

Chapter 6
1. The phrase 'international relations' has been used in this context by the anthropologist James B Watson (1983, p. 6) writing about the Tairora people of the Eastern Highlands of Papua New Guinea.
2. 'Local international rules' were the local rules by which relations between separate, independent, politically organised groups were structured.
3. The single divination-substance (*mi*) was a plant, stone or living creature associated with a sacred origin story of the group(s) involved. It therefore represented a source of power. It was believed that the substance could act directly on the bodies of descendants of a group's founder. A sister's son shared in the bodily substance of his mother's group through his mother's blood and therefore could offer himself as a kind of pledge by swearing an oath over the substance. If he lied, it was thought that the *mi* would punish him with sickness or death. (See, for example, Strathern 1972b, p. 41.)
4. The segmentary model predicts that groups opposed at a local level of social structure will unite at a higher level against a common, less closely related, enemy. (See, for example, Evans-Pritchard 1940, pp. 143–47.)
5. Wealth goods could be cattle (in parts of Africa) or pigs and forms of valuable shells that circulated through bridewealth and compensation payments (in the Papua New Guinea Highlands). (See, generally, Strathern 1971 [2007], pp. 93–114.)
6. *Ongka: A Self-Account by a New Guinea Big-Man* 1979, trans. A Strathern, Duckworth, London, p. 49). This volume was subsequently revised and reissued as Strathern & Stewart 1999b. The citation here appears on p. 41 of that version.
7. See *Ongka: A Self-Account by a New Guinea Big-Man* 1979, trans. A Strathern, Duckworth, London, p. 130 (pp. 111 ff. in the 1999 edition).
8. The Kundmbo, however, had a cross-tribal ally (the Kimbo clan) in another tribe, the Minembi, which was otherwise a tribal group opposed to all the Kawelka. Intermarriage, propinquity and exchange of personnel led to this situation, which negated the segmentary model at one level while conforming to the principle of balanced power that underpins the model. (See Strathern 1972b, pp. 31–53.)

9. At this point, everything could backfire: a piece of 'folded' speech might be interpreted as a show or an admission of a previous killing, whether it appeared in the 'arrow-talk' or earlier in the moot, and fighting would then erupt (see Strathern & Stewart 2000a, pp. 71–82; for examples illustrating the force and aesthetic qualities of *el ik*, see Strathern 1971 [2007], pp. 240–42).
10. Most recently, the Nuer and Dinka must have been involved in the referendum by which the southern Sudan people voted to secede from the north and form an independent state of their own, and thus shifting from IS to sovereign status in early July 2011.
11. But compare work by Strathern (1992, pp. 229–50), discussing a switch from exchange to violence as a means to resolve disputes, and indicating that police action is accepted only if it is convenient.
12. However, Radio Australia broadcast news on 10 October 1997 that a truce had been declared in the nine-year civil war as a result of closed peace talks at the Burnam Army Camp in Christchurch, New Zealand, between officials of the different interested parties. The truce called for an immediate stop to armed conflict and for all parties to work towards reconciliation. See 'Papua New Guinea Signs Truce with Bougainville Rebels' 1997, Associated Press, 9 October, available in 1997 WL 488740. (For a full review and update to 2010, see Regan 2010.)
13. Handbook for Village Court Officials, No. 1 1976, Papua New Guinea, pp. 33–34. (For commentary on Village Courts, see Strathern 1984, pp. 122–42. See also Michael Goddard's work on urban Village Courts in Port Moresby, for example, Goddard 2005.)
14. See, generally, work by Strathern (1993b, pp. 41–60); also by Stewart & Strathern (2002a) and Ketan (1998) on electoral politics, violence and new coalitions among the Kawelka. (This thesis was later published by the University of the South Pacific, Fiji, in 2004.) William Standish's work in the Chimbu (Simbu) Province area clearly illustrates problems of violence surrounding elections there (see, generally, Standish 1992). Standish's work provided a unique historical perspective on politics in Simbu, and it is regrettable that his material has not yet appeared as a published monograph. (On electoral violence see Chapter 1, this volume.)
15. This happened, for example, in dealings between Chevron and local people in the Southern Highlands Province, and in the Enga Province between Porgera Joint Venture and the Ipili/Paiela people (source: field visit to Duna area, Southern Highlands Province, June 1994). (For extensive discussion of these matters, based on our fieldwork in the Duna area, see Stewart & Strathern 2002b; and compare also Strathern & Stewart 2004b.)

16. Interview by A Strathern with F Robinson 1994, Australian Liaison Officer, Duna area, Southern Highlands Province, June.
17. Field visits 1994, 1998, 1999, Duna area, Southern Highlands Province.
18. Ibid.
19. Ibid. (see also, generally, Kirsch 2006).
20. Brookfield and Hart (1971) use the term 'Old Melanesia' to refer to a historical reconstruction of the character of indigenous societies prior to the extensive effects of colonial change.
21. This government system was subsequently revoked in 1995.
22. However, 'accords' have been reached from time to time, and further talks were taking place in Wellington, New Zealand, in August and September 1997. (See also Griffin 1982.) A finalised Peace Agreement was reached in August 2003 and the first President of an autonomous North Solomons, Joseph Kabui, was elected in 2005. (For updates, see Regan 2010.)
23. This case study is based on Merlan and Rumsey's (1991) fieldwork in the Nebilyer Valley, in the area described by Melpa speakers as Kulir. The Elti–Penambe case study derives from fieldwork by A Strathern (1980s).

Chapter 7

1. Gordon Larson (1987), writing on the Ilaga Dani people of the Central Highlands of Irian Jaya (now West Papua or 'Papua') in the wider island of New Guinea, provides a very detailed and well-observed account of peace-making and reparations among these people. He notes that men were always ready for fighting and that each death in fighting could elicit acts of revenge; but indemnities could be offered instead (p. 164). Citing the Maring case as a parallel, he notes the idea that warfare and peace-making went in ritual cycles (p. 164), and that episodes of peace could last 'from a few months to a period of years' (p. 165). Indemnity payments to the agnatic group of a victim of killing were paid with live pigs, salt packs, cowrie shells and axe heads. If payment was not made, a phase of ritually controlled warfare was declared (p. 166). In this phase, ancestral war-making ritual paraphernalia were re-consecrated (as with the Maring), and shamans (ritual experts) were deputed to divine the will of the ancestral spirits. Fight-initiating groups were seen as 'owners of the war' (p. 167) (exactly as with the Melpa) and so were held responsible for indemnifying their allies for deaths incurred (p. 167). Smaller initial payments were followed by more massive ones, called 'paying for the cost of the war' (p. 168), in which pigs were slaughtered. Finally, *yewam* indemnity

payments were made, after gardens had been planted and harvested to fatten up more pigs. Very large numbers of visitors attended in festive dress (p. 169). The earliest distribution following a death was called the 'dead birds' distribution, which took place as a memorial for those who fell in fighting. The numbers of pigs corresponded to the numbers of men who had died, and these were presented to the owners of the war by agnates of the victims along with a feather headdress worn by the victim during the fighting. This preliminary gift elicited a promise of a much larger indemnity payment at the *yewam* stage, going in the opposite direction, from the owners of the war to the groups of the victims (p. 291). The structure here is exactly the same as held among the Enga and the Melpa. This is a comparative point of prime significance, because it shows the 'social contract' of 'the gift' in a process of evolution out of violence itself: death turned into transaction. As a particular point reflecting the organisational complexities and intricacies of Ilaga Dani warfare, alliances were extensive and built up into military confederacies, and there was a proportionate calibration of war payments. Fighting was not supposed to stop until the owners of the war had suffered more casualties than their allies, and the most peripheral allies should incur fewest losses (p. 262). Payments were made for wounds as well as deaths. Shamans used divination to determine when a loss of life would be met by revenge (p. 266). Ritual warfare could escalate into total war if the processes of payment for killings did not proceed, and in one case all groups turned on a single pair of patriclans, driving them out and forcing them to seek refuge elsewhere (as happened to the Kawelka among the Melpa speakers of Mount Hagen; Strathern & Stewart n.d.). The initiation of ritual warfare was controlled by secret actions of the war shamans, followed by 'ceremonial divination on the battlefield itself' (Larson 1987, p. 251), and all indemnity payments outstanding were suspended until the next round of peace-making. It is interesting that shamans were important among the Ilaga Dani as they were among the Maring, while they were perhaps less important in the Melpa case – perhaps a sign of incipient political differentiation in the Melpa case, where warfare was less clearly ritually regulated. For Ilaga, Larson concludes his account of peace-making with the killing of the 'peace pig' (*nggam*) (p. 317), which is slaughtered and eaten in concert with enemies as a sign that no more attacks or killings should be undertaken at the time (p. 318). The Ilaga data show the vital role of ritualisation processes at all phases of conflict and its settlement. Payments from 'victims' to 'owners' show how a contract of peace is built into violent death itself, mediated by pigs: exactly one of the overall arguments of this book. (For further comparisons, on the Bokondini Dani, see Ploeg 1969; for further materials, on the Hagen area, see Rumsey 2009.) Rumsey espouses the basic segmentary model outlined for the Melpa by Strathern (1971 [2007], 1972b), and notes for the Ku Waru area, as for the Melpa, that *moka/makayl* relations take their genesis from bouts of warfare, and the basic rule is that fight initiators indemnify their allies for losses.

2. The point regarding 'totality' is made by Trompf (1994) on p. 105 of his book, as well as in general throughout it. On p. 105 he warns against reductionist analyses that would reduce phenomena to 'power struggles' or 'social control', leaving out their religious dimensions. Curiously, by means of a very truncated and partial reference to a passage written by Strathern (1970a, p. 573), he seems to suggest that such a reductionist analysis appears there. It does not. The full passage is in fact devoted to making it clear that 'big-men', as leaders, in Hagen played important ritual roles, thus:

> From time to time larger-scale sacrifices were held, at which clansmen brought pigs to a clan cemetery-place and a leading big-man, holding the ropes by which pigs are led, would address a prayer to clan leaders and other clansmen of the past, asking for success in warfare and ceremonial exchange. Such a sacrifice might be held before an attack on another group was made.

As in war, so also in peace-making. The Hagen (Melpa) big-man and leader Ongka makes it clear in his autobiography that leaders took part in a ritual drama called removing *el pint pint*, which was a powerful way of making peace between enemy groups (Strathern & Stewart 1999b, pp. 63–65). We revisit this point in Chapter 8, drawing together a number of themes and extending our fields of comparative reference.

A news report in Papua New Guinea's *The National* newspaper (3 December 2010) records a peace settlement between the Kulga group in the Nebilyer Valley south of Hagen and the Togla–Wanka (Rokla–Wanika) alliance pair living in the Kulir area of the Southern Nebilyer. According to the report, these combatants had been involved in conflicts for almost 40 years, that is, dating back to the years immediately prior to Independence, when troubles were also breaking out in the Northern Melpa area (see Strathern 1974). More than 100 lives had been lost in these fights, the report declares. These numbers are far more than could be paid for by compensation payments themselves, but the peace settlement was established with a payment of 70 pigs and K30,000 in money. (The direction of these payments is unfortunately not specified in the report, but it seems that they were made by the Kulga to the Rokla–Wanika, since we are told that the Kulga leaders took the initiative in the peace settlement and persisted in spite of a killing of a Kulga man almost two weeks earlier.) The most significant aspect of the report, for our purposes here, is that the Christian churches were crucially involved. The event was organised by the Kulga for Jesus peace and reconciliation committee and was preceded in 2007 by a ritual in which the combatants had given up their guns (to authorities?) and had put a bag full of earth into a church to mark that their land/territory was now dedicated to God and that peace would endure. This was, then, a creative harnessing of ritual forms and a blending of Christian and indigenous ideas of the sacred and of emplacement. The Maring (Rappaport 1967 [1968]) would understand this form of ritual action, as would the Melpa.

Chapter 8

1. Regan (2010) provides an insightful long-term view on the conflicts in Bougainville following the demise of the Conzinc Riotinto copper mine there. Interestingly, in view of our overall argument in this book, Regan remarks on the significance of ritual in peace-making, including the breaking of spears and the use of Christian symbols, which he neatly refers to as 'hybrid reconciliation processes' (p. 37).
2. For a set of papers discussing all of these issues with their ramifications up to 1981, see Scaglion 1981. This volume contains a chapter by A Strathern (1981), 'Compensation: Should There Be a New Law?', which concludes with a set of ten specific points, suggesting that a new, but flexible, national law on compensation would help to strengthen it as a practice (pp. 20–21).
3. Colson (1995), in a later contribution, points out that it is a mistake to suppose that the outcome of disputes is necessarily the re-establishment of complete harmony between groups, as may be implied in phrases such as 'dispute settlement' (or 'peace', in fact). She calls into question the use of the term 'rituals' in this context if these are meant as devices to create such a harmony (for example, p. 67). She argues, following the work of Philip Gulliver (1979), that agreements between contestants are 'likely to include a residue of antagonism and sometimes bitter hostility between rivals' (Colson 1995, p. 66). These are well-taken points. Compensation rituals in New Guinea are events in which the participants are deeply conscious of the risks involved, yet they do proceed with their actions as the best way to find livable solutions.

4. Scheffler (2001, pp. 170–76) provides an important theoretical and empirical recension of the picture he gave earlier of these Choiseulese groups (the *singangge*). At issue is the balance between filiative and descent-based 'rules' of membership of these kinds of kin groups. In his later account, Scheffler tends to stress the importance of agnation for the Choiseulese, but he recognises also the significance in general of 'mother's side' ties among them. The Choiseulese structure appears to resemble closely that of the Duna, discussed by Strathern and Stewart (2004b, 2010c).
5. For comparable data and discussion, see again Rumsey (2009) on fighting and compensation in the Nebilyer Valley south of Hagen township among the people Merlan and Rumsey (1991) call the Ku Waru ('those who live at the cliff edges'). Rumsey's delineation of structures and processes follows quite closely that of Strathern (1971 [2007], 1972b), as well as the much later ones he refers to by indigenous Papua New Guinea scholars such as Ketan (1998). (For another earlier discussion of compensation and its contemporary problems, see Strathern 1997 in Toft 1997.)

In his 2009 discussion paper, Rumsey (p. 4) adverts briefly to the controversies about 'descent' in Highlands groups, noting that regardless of the intricacies of those controversies, the principle of complementary opposition provides a useful model for understanding segmentary political processes. We may add that descent as a political ideology (rather than a strict principle of recruitment) provides the clearest underpinning of such segmentary processes. Ketan (1998, pp. 73–125) also provides a re-discussion of the issue of descent and group formations. Using the very general term *reklaep* ('line') for 'groups', Ketan argues that it (the *reklaep*) is not based on descent. Conflating data from two different areas (Ku Waru and Central Melpa), Ketan cites the work of Merlan and Rumsey (1991, p. 37), in which they argued that sharing common apical ancestors was not important for Ku Waru groups, but that apical pairs of ancestral brothers were important, and hence 'brotherhood', not descent, was operative, at least at the level of the tribe. Ketan asks why this discrepancy of viewpoint exists between Merlan and Rumsey and Strathern, and passes to a personal viewpoint that there is no real difference between Nebilyer and Hagen. However, there is a difference: the Ku Waru groups tend to be small, to have been driven into their territories by warfare and to have remade alliances on a fluid basis. This helps to explain the different forms of genealogies that Merlan and Rumsey found.

In addition, when Hageners speak of 'brothers', they do so in an agnatic context, whether a 'father' is named or not. Ketan finally decides that descent is an ideology as a means of promoting group solidarity. Quite so: that was precisely the argument made in 1972 by Strathern (1972b). Influenced by 'descent theory' or otherwise, the distinction between recruitment and identity put forward in that book offered a crucial way out of an impasse in theory which is not to be settled by deciding that descent either 'is' or 'is not' important.

Ketan's clan among the Kawelka is the Membo. See Strathern's work (1972b, p. 48), on the agnatic genealogy of that clan from the apical ancestor Tilkang, according to the leader Kont, relating primarily to Membo Oyambo sub-clan. The Elpuklmbo subgroup of Köyambo sub-clan, to which the leader Nggoimba belonged, was not fitted into this agnatic genealogy. This is also Ketan's small group. Strathern notes that at these lower levels the ideology of the men's house (*manga rapa*) operates more strongly than the idea of descent (p. 48).

Ketan also argues that in the 1980s leaders as 'fight leaders' became very important and suggests that they might be more important than previously, as reported in the accounts by Vicedom (in the 1930s) and Strathern (originally in the 1960s). But Vicedom was closer to the 'pre-contact' society, when warfare was an overt part of life, than any other ethnographic observer; and Strathern's work has covered different periods, from 1964 up to the year 2000, including the 1980s (in collaboration with Stewart). 'Fight leaders' in the 1980s coexisted with numerous established leaders whose roles came back prominently into play in the 1990s as the organisers of exchanges and peace-making when these phases of warfare were halted, as must have happened often before.

6. On transformations in Gebusi society between 1982 and 1998, connected with the penetration of values from outside, including those of Christian churches, see Knauft 2002.
7. There is a debate in the literature about whether warfare in the Highlands was 'about land'. It certainly had implications for the occupation of land, as the history of the Kawelka (Strathern 1972b; Strathern & Stewart n.d.) and of Ilaga Dani groups (Larson 1987) clearly shows. That land was as dear to the hearts of the Mae Enga people as pigs were, and that indeed the fate of both was bound up together with that of people, is made abundantly clear by Meggitt (1977). It is a different question whether war was consciously waged in order to obtain land (rather than to protect it) or, if so, this was because of a level of land shortage and population density (see, for example, Brookfield & Brown 1963; Brown 1978, 1995). Again, big-men as fighters and exchangers might be involved in land issues, but this does not

mean they advocated war as a means of land acquisition. (See Sillitoe 1978 on these various issues.) We should distinguish in general causes, intentions and consequences. (See also Koch 1974, pp. 162–65, engaging with the ideas of Rappaport 1967 [1968] on the question of ecological causes of war among the Maring.)

8. For further discussion on the Semai see Edo, Williams-Hunt & Dentan 2009. This paper usefully follows changes in Semai practices over time with their incorporation into the Malaysian state context and the innovative actions of a Semai leader, Busu.

9. Schlee and Watson's book of 2009 contains many illustrations of this point, with illuminating contemporary ethnography. Hutchinson's (2009, pp. 49–71) chapter in that volume contains an interesting demonstration of the particular efficacy of ritual and sacrifice as markers of peace-making between Dinka and Nuer forces that had been locked in deadly conflict as a spin-off from civil war in the Sudan. The huge white bull sacrificed at Wunlit in South Sudan in 1999 was intended to cleanse the people of 'all the evils of the previous eight years' (p. 49) of fighting and killing. (On earlier Nuer–Dinka relations, see Kelly 1985.)

10. Castoriadis, in his seminal work, *The Imaginary Institution of Society* (1987, English translation), insists on the importance of what we tend to call the 'symbolic' in human action generally: 'Everything that is presented to us in the social-historical world is inextricably tied to the symbolic' (p. 116). Castoriadis also insists on the 'imaginary' or 'invented' component that enters into 'every symbol' (p. 127). Ongka's deft local account of the *el pint pint* ritual neatly falls into line with Castoriadis's general theory.

Appendix

1. It is not always possible to obtain names of protagonists and hence gauge degrees of closeness in the feud. The stereotype is that 'the Papeke', et cetera, as whole clans do the killings, but on the side of the avengers themselves the individual names are often mentioned. The information here all came from Yelipi men, so only their side of the stories was recorded.

2. The cases alluded to here go back in time, and for historical reference we have allowed a few names to stand in the text.

References

Abbink, J 2000, 'Restoring the balance: violence and culture among the Suri of southern Ethiopia', in G Aijmer & J Abbink (eds), *Meanings of violence: a cross-cultural perspective*, Berg, Oxford and New York, pp. 77–100.

—— 2001, 'Violence and culture: anthropological and evolutionary-psychological reflections on inter-group conflict in southern Ethiopia', in BE Schmidt and IW Schröder (eds), *Anthropology of violence and conflict*, Routledge, London and New York, pp. 123–42.

Aijmer, G & Abbink, J (eds) 2000, *Meanings of violence: a cross-cultural perspective*, Berg, Oxford and New York.

Amarshi, A, Good, K & Mortimer, R 1979, *Development and dependency: the political economy of Papua New Guinea*, Oxford University Press, Melbourne.

Anderson, BRO'G 1983 [1991], *Imagined communities: reflections on the origin and spread of nationalism*, Verso, London.

Banks, C (ed.) 2000, *Developing cultural criminology: theory and practice in Papua New Guinea*, Monograph Series no. 13, Institute of Criminology, Sydney.

Bateson, G 1958, *Naven: a survey of the problems suggested by a composite picture of the culture of a New Guinea tribe drawn from three points of view*, 2nd edn (original edn 1936), Stanford University Press, Stanford, CA.

Bell, C 1997, *Ritual: perspectives and dimensions*, Oxford University Press, Oxford.

Bourdieu, P 1977, *Outline of a theory of practice*, trans. R Nice, Cambridge University Press, Cambridge.

Brookfield, HC & Brown, P 1963, *Struggle for land: agriculture and group territories among the Chimbu of the New Guinea Highlands*, Oxford University Press, Melbourne.

Brookfield, HC with Hart, D 1971, *Melanesia: an interpretation of an island world*, Methuen, London.

Brown, P 1978, *Highland peoples of New Guinea*, Cambridge University Press, Cambridge.

—— 1995, *Beyond a mountain valley: the Simbu of Papua New Guinea*, University of Hawai'i Press, Honolulu.

Byrne, RMJ 2007, *The rational imagination: how people create alternatives to reality*, MIT Press (a Bradford book), Cambridge, Mass.

Carrad, B, Lea, DAM & Talyaga, KK (eds) 1982, *Enga: foundations for development* (vol. 3 of Enga Yaaka Lasemana), University of New England, for the Enga Provincial Government and the National Planning Office, Papua New Guinea, Armidale, NSW.

Carrier, J (ed.) 1992, *History and tradition in Melanesian anthropology*, University of California Press, Berkeley.

Castoriadis, C 1987, *The imaginary institution of society*, trans. K Blaney, Polity Press, Cambridge, UK.

Clark, JL 1985, 'From cults to Christianity: continuity and change in Takuru', PhD thesis, University of Adelaide.

—— 2000, *Steel to stone: a chronicle of colonialism in the Southern Highlands of Papua New Guinea*, C Ballard & M Nihill (eds), Oxford University Press, Oxford.

Colson, E 1953, 'Social control and vengeance in Plateau Tonga society', *Africa*, vol. 23, no. 3, pp. 199–212.

—— 1995, 'The contentiousness of disputes', in P Caplan (ed.), *Understanding disputes: the politics of argument*, Berg, Oxford, pp. 65–82.

Crehan, K 2002, *Gramsci, culture, and anthropology*, University of California Press, Berkeley, CA.

Dentan, RK 1968, *The Semai: a nonviolent people of Malaya*, Holt, Rinehart and Winston, New York.

Dinnen, S 2000a, 'Violence and governance in Melanesia: an introduction', in S Dinnen & A Ley (eds), *Reflections on violence in Melanesia*, Hawkins Press, Sydney, pp. 1–16.

—— 2000b, 'Breaking the cycle of violence: crime and state in Papua New Guinea', in C Banks (ed.), *Developing cultural criminology: theory and practice in Papua New Guinea*, Monograph Series no. 13, Institute of Criminology, Sydney, pp. 51–78.

—— 2001, *Law and order in a weak state: crime and politics in Papua New Guinea*, Pacific Islands Monograph Series, University of Hawaii Press, Honolulu.

—— & Firth, S (eds) 2008, *Politics and state building in Solomon Islands*, Australian National University and Asia Pacific Press, Canberra.

—— & Ley, A (eds) 2000, *Reflections on violence in Melanesia*, Hawkins Press and Asia Pacific Press, Annandale, NSW, and Canberra, ACT.

Dorney, S 1997, 'The constitution, change and custom . . . Miriam wins', *The Independent* (PNG), 14 February, p. 13.

Durkheim, E 1915, *The elementary forms of the religious life*, George Allen and Unwin, London.

Dwyer, PD & Minnegal, M 2010, 'Theorizing social change', *Journal of the Royal Anthropological Institute*, vol. 16, no. 3, pp. 629–45.

Edo, J, Williams-Hunt, A & Dentan, RK 2009, '"Surrender", peacekeeping and internal colonialism: a Malaysian instance', *Bijdragen tot de Taal-, Land-en Volkenkunde*, vol. 165, nos 2–3, pp. 216–40.

Epstein, AL (ed.) 1974, *Contention and dispute: aspects of law and social control in Melanesia*, Australian National University Press, Canberra.

Evans-Pritchard, EE 1940, *The Nuer: a description of the modes of livelihood and political institutions of a Nilotic people*, Clarendon Press, Oxford.

—— 1956, *Nuer religion*, Clarendon Press, Oxford.

Feil, DK 1978, '"Holders of the Way": exchange partnerships in an Enga Tee community', PhD thesis, Australian National University, Canberra.
—— 1980, 'Symmetry and complementarity: patterns of competition and exchange in the Enga tee', *Oceania*, vol. 51, no. 1, pp. 20–30.
—— 1984, *Ways of exchange: the Enga Tee of Papua New Guinea*, University of Queensland Press, St Lucia, Qld.
—— 1987, *The evolution of Highland Papua New Guinea societies*, Cambridge University Press, Cambridge.
Ferguson, B (ed.) 2003, *The state, identity and violence: political disintegration in the post Cold-War world*, Routledge, London and New York.
Ferguson, RB & Whitehead, NL 1992, 'Introduction', in RB Ferguson & NL Whitehead (eds), *War in the tribal zone: expanding states and indigenous warfare*, School of American Research Press, Santa Fe, pp. 1–30.
Filer, C 1990, 'The Bougainville rebellion, the mining industry, and the process of social disintegration in Papua New Guinea', *Canberra Anthropology*, vol. 13, no. 1, pp. 1–39.
—— 1996, 'The social context of renewable resource depletion in Papua New Guinea', in R Howitt, J Connell & P Hirsch (eds), *Resources, nations, and indigenous peoples*, Oxford University Press, Melbourne, pp. 289–99.
—— 1997, 'Compensation, rent, and power in Papua New Guinea', in S Toft (ed.), *Compensation for resource development in Papua New Guinea*, Monograph no. 6, Law Reform Commission, Port Moresby, pp. 156–90.
—— (ed.) 1999, *Dilemmas of development: the social and economic impact of the Porgera gold mine, 1989–1994*, National Research Institute, Boroko, and Australian National University, Canberra.
—— 2009, 'A bridge too far: the knowledge problem in the Millennium Assessment', in JG Carrier & P West (eds), *Virtualism, governance, and practice: vision and execution in environmental conservation*, Berghahn Books, New York and Oxford, pp. 84–111.
Finney, BR 1973, *Big-men and business: entrepreneurship and economic growth in the New Guinea Highlands*, Australian National University Press, Canberra.
Fortes, M 1949, *The web of kinship among the Tallensi*, Oxford University Press, London.
Fortune, RF 1939, 'Arapesh warfare', *American Anthropologist*, vol. 41, no. 1, pp. 22–41.
Foster, RJ (ed.) 1995, *Nation making: emergent identities in postcolonial Melanesia*, University of Michigan Press, Ann Arbor.
Glasse, RM 1959, 'Revenge and redress among the Huli', *Mankind*, vol. 5, no. 7, pp. 273–89.
—— 1968, *Huli of Papua: a cognatic descent system*, Mouton and Co., Paris.
Gluckman, M 1955, *Custom and conflict in Africa*, Basil Blackwell, Oxford.
Goddard, M 1992, 'Big-man, thief: the social organization of gangs in Port Moresby', *Canberra Anthropology*, vol. 15, no. 1, pp. 20–34.
—— 2005, *Unseen city: anthropological perspectives on Port Moresby, Papua New Guinea*, Pandanus Books, Canberra.
—— 2009, *Substantial justice: an anthropology of Village Courts in Papua New Guinea*, Berghahn Books, Oxford.

Godelier, M 1982 [2009], 'Social hierarchies among the Baruya of New Guinea', in A Strathern (ed.), *Inequality in New Guinea Highland society*, reissued with new preface by A Strathern & PJ Stewart, Cambridge University Press, Cambridge, pp. 3–34.

Goldman, LL 1981, 'Compensation and disputes in Huli', in R Scaglion (ed.), *Homicide compensation in Papua New Guinea: problems and prospects*, Monograph no. 1, Law Reform Commission, Port Moresby, pp. 56–69.

—— 1983, *Talk never dies: the language of Huli disputes*, Tavistock Publications, London and New York.

Gordon, RJ & Meggitt, MJ 1985, *Law and order in the New Guinea Highlands: encounters with Enga*, University Press of New England, for University of Vermont, Hanover and London.

Griffin, J 1982, 'Napidakoe Navitu', in RJ May (ed.), *Micronationalist movements in New Guinea*, Political and Social Change Monograph 1, Australian National University, Canberra, pp. 113–38.

—— 1990, 'Bougainville is a special case', in RJ May & M Spriggs (eds), *The Bougainville crisis*, Crawford House Publications, Bathurst, NSW, pp. 1–15.

Grosart, I 1982, 'Nationalism and micronationalism: the Tolai case', in RJ May (ed.), *Micronationalist movements in New Guinea*, Political and Social Change Monograph 1, Australian National University, Canberra, pp. 139–76.

Gulliver, PH 1979, *Disputes and negotiations: a cross-cultural perspective*, Academic Press, New York.

Harrison, S 1993, *The mask of war: violence, ritual and the self in Melanesia*, Manchester University Press, Manchester.

Hart Nibbrig, N 1992, 'Rascals in paradise: urban gangs in Papua New Guinea', *Pacific Studies*, vol. 15, no. 3, pp. 115–34.

Havini, M 1990, 'Human rights violations and community disruption', in RJ May & M Spriggs (eds), *The Bougainville crisis*, Crawford House Publications, Bathurst, NSW, pp. 31–37.

Heald, S 2000, 'Tolerating the intolerable: cattle raiding among the Kuria', in G Aijmer & J Abbink (eds), *Meanings of violence: a cross-cultural perspective*, Berg, Oxford and New York, pp. 101–22.

Hüsken, U (ed.) 2007, *When rituals go wrong: mistakes, failure, and the dynamics of ritual*, Brill, Leiden.

Hutchinson, SE 1996, *Nuer dilemmas: coping with money, war, and the state*, University of California Press, Berkeley.

—— 2009, 'Peace and puzzlement: grass-roots peace initiatives between the Nuer and Dinka of South Sudan', in G Schlee & EE Watson (eds), *Changing identifications and alliances in north-east Africa vol. 2: Sudan, Uganda and the Ethiopia–Sudan borderlands*, Berghahn, New York and Oxford, pp. 49–71.

Johnson, D 1994, *Nuer prophets: a history of prophecy from the Upper Nile*, Oxford University Press, Oxford.

Katz, PR 2005, *When valleys turned blood red: the Ta-pa-ni incident in colonial Taiwan*, University of Hawai'i Press, Honolulu.

Keiser, L 1986, 'Death enmity in Thull: organized vengeance and social change in a Kohistani community', *American Ethnologist*, vol. 13, no. 3, pp. 489–505.

—— 1991, *Friend by day, enemy by night: organized vengeance in a Kohistani community*, Holt, Rinehart, and Winston, Fort Worth, TX.
Kelly, RC 1985, *The Nuer conquest: the structure and development of an expansionist system*, University of Mission Press, Ann Arbor.
—— 2000, *Warless societies and the origin of war*, University of Michigan Press, Ann Arbor.
Ketan, J 1998, '"The name must not go down": political competition in Mount Hagen, Papua New Guinea', PhD thesis, University of Wollongong, NSW.
Kirsch, S 2006, *Reverse anthropology: indigenous analysis of social and environmental relations in New Guinea*, Stanford University Press, Stanford.
Kituai, A 1998, *My gun, my brother: the world of the Papua New Guinea Colonial Police 1920–1960*, Pacific Islands Monograph Series no. 15, University of Hawai'i Press, Honolulu.
Knauft, BM 1985, *Good company and violence: sorcery and social action in a lowland New Guinea society*, University of California Press, Berkeley.
—— 1999, *From primitive to post-colonial in Melanesia and anthropology*, University of Michigan Press, Ann Arbor.
—— 2002, *Exchanging the past: a rainforest world of before and after*, University of Chicago Press, Chicago.
Knudsen, A 2009, *Violence and belonging: land, love and lethal conflict in the North-West Frontier Province of Pakistan*, NIAS Press, Copenhagen.
Koch, K-F 1974, *War and peace in Jalémó: the management of conflict in Highland New Guinea*, Harvard University Press, Cambridge, Mass.
Krasner, SD 1995/96, 'Compromising Westphalia', *International Security*, vol. 20, no. 3, pp. 115–151.
Larson, GF 1987, 'The structure and demography of the cycle of warfare among the Ilaga Dani of Irian Jaya', PhD dissertation, University of Michigan, MI.
Lederman, R 1986, *What gifts engender: social relations and politics in Mendi, Highlands Papua New Guinea*, Cambridge University Press, Cambridge.
—— 1991, '"Interests" in exchange: increment, equivalence and the limits of big-manship', in M Godelier & AM Strathern (eds), *Big men and great men: personifications of power in Melanesia*, Cambridge University Press, Cambridge, pp. 215–33.
Lemonnier, P 1990, *Guerres et festins: paix, échanges et compétition dans les Highlands de Nouvelle-Guinée*, with an introduction by M Godelier, Editions de la Maison des Sciences de l'Homme, Paris.
Leopold, M 2005, *Inside West Nile: violence, history and representation on an African frontier*, James Currey, Oxford.
Levine, H 1996, 'Ethnogenesis among urban New Guinea Highlands', in H Levine & A Ploeg (eds), *Work in progress: essays in New Guinea Highlands ethography in honour of Paul Brown*, Peter Lang, New York, pp. 198–211.
McKillop, B 1982, 'Papua besena and Papuan separatism', in RJ May (ed.), *Micronationalist movements in New Guinea*, Political and Social Change Monograph 1, Australian National University, Canberra, pp. 329–58.
Meggitt, MJ 1965, *The lineage system of the Mae Enga of New Guinea*, Oliver and Boyd, Edinburgh.

―― 1974, '"Pigs are our hearts": the Te exchange cycle among the Mae Enga of New Guinea', *Oceania*, vol. 44, no. 3, pp. 165–203.

―― 1977, *Blood is their argument: warfare among the Mae Enga tribesmen of the New Guinea Highlands*, Mayfield Publishing Co., Mountain View, California.

Merlan, F & Rumsey, A 1991, *Ku Waru*, Cambridge University Press, Cambridge.

Middleton, JFM 1960, *Lugbara religion: ritual and authority among an East African people*, Oxford University Press, for the International African Institute, London.

―― & Tait, D (eds) 1958, *Tribes without rulers: studies in African segmentary systems*, Humanities Press, London.

Modell, AH 2006, *Imagination and the meaningful brain*, MIT Press (a Bradford book), Cambridge, Mass.

Modjeska, CN 1977, 'Production among the Duna', PhD thesis, Australian National University, Canberra.

―― 1982, 'Production and inequality: perspectives from Central New Guinea', in A Strathern (ed.), *Inequality in New Guinea Highlands societies*, Cambridge University Press, Cambridge, pp. 50–108.

―― 1991, 'Post-Ipomoean modernism: the Duna example', in M Godelier & AM Strathern (eds), *Big men and great men: personifications of power in Melanesia*, Cambridge University Press, Cambridge, pp. 234–55.

Oliver, DL 1991, *Black islanders: a personal perspective of Bougainville, 1937–1991*, University of Hawai'i Press, Honolulu.

Ploeg, A 1969, *Government in Wanggulam*, Martinus Nijhoff, The Hague.

Rappaport, RA 1967 [1968], *Pigs for the ancestors: ritual in the ecology of a New Guinea people*, Yale University Press, New Haven.

―― 1999, *Religion and ritual in the making of humanity*, Cambridge University Press, Cambridge.

Reay, MO 1959, *The Kuma: freedom and conformity in the New Guinea Highlands*, Melbourne University Press for the Australian National University, Melbourne.

Regan, AJ 2010, *Light intervention: lessons from Bougainville*, United States Institute of Peace Press, Washington, DC.

Riches, D 1986, 'The phenomenon of violence', in D Riches (ed.), *The anthropology of violence*, Basil Blackwell, Oxford, pp. 1–27.

Robarchek, CE 1994, 'Ghosts and witches: the psychocultural dynamics of Semai peacefulness', in LE Sponsel & T Gregor (eds), *The anthropology of peace and nonviolence*, Lynne Rienner Publishers, Boulder and London, pp. 183–96.

Robbins, J, Stewart, PJ & Strathern, A (eds) 2001, 'Pentecostal and charismatic Christianity in Oceania', Special Issue of *Journal of Ritual Studies*, vol. 15, no. 2.

Rumsey, A 2009, 'War and peace in Highland Papua New Guinea: some recent developments in the Nebilyer Valley, Western Highlands Province', Discussion Paper 2009/7, Research School of Pacific and Asian Studies, Australian National University, Canberra.

Ryan, D'AJ 1959, 'Clan formation in the Mendi valley', *Oceania*, vol. 29, no. 4, pp. 257–89.

―― 1961, 'Gift exchange in the Mendi Valley', PhD thesis, University of Sydney, Sydney.

Scaglion, R (ed.) 1981, *Homicide compensation in Papua New Guinea: problems and prospects*, Monograph no. 1, Law Reform Commission, Port Moresby.

Scheffler, HW 1964, 'The genesis and repression of conflict: Choiseul Island', *American Anthropologist*, vol. 60, no. 4, part 1, pp. 789–804.

—— 1965, *Choiseul Island social structure*, University of California Press, Berkeley and Los Angeles.

—— 2001, *Filiation and affiliation*, Westview Press, Boulder, CO.

Schlee, G 2008 (pbk 2010), *How enemies are made: towards a theory of ethnic and religious conflicts*, Berghahn Books, New York and Oxford.

—— & Watson, EE (eds) 2009, *Changing identifications and alliances in north-east Africa vol. 2: Sudan, Uganda and the Ethiopia–Sudan borderlands*, Berghahn, New York and Oxford.

Sillitoe, P 1978, 'Big men and war in New Guinea', *Man*, vol. 13, no. 2, pp. 252–72.

—— 1979, *Give and take: exchange in Wola society*, Australian National University Press, Canberra.

—— 1981, 'Some more on war: a Wola perspective', in R Scaglion (ed.), *Homicide compensation in Papua New Guinea: problems and prospects*, Monograph no. 1, Law Reform Commission, Port Moresby, pp. 70–81.

—— & Sillitoe, J 2010, *Grass-clearing man: a factional ethnography of life in the New Guinea Highlands*, Waveland Press, Long Grove, IL.

Sinclair, JP 1966, *Behind the ranges: patrolling in New Guinea*, Melbourne University Press, Melbourne.

Standish, WA 1992, 'Simbu paths to power: political change and cultural continuity in the Papua New Guinea Highlands', PhD thesis, Australian National University, Canberra.

Steinbauer, F (ed.) 1974, *Shaping the future: Papua New Guinea personalities*, Kristen Press, Madang.

Stewart, PJ 1998, 'Ritual trackways and sacred paths of fertility', in J Miedema, C Ode & RAC Dam (eds), *Perspectives on the bird's head of Irian Jaya*, Rodopi, Amsterdam, pp. 275–90.

—— & Strathern, AJ 1998a, 'Money, politics, and persons in Papua New Guinea', *Social Analysis*, vol. 42, no. 2, pp. 132–49.

—— & Strathern, A 1998b, 'End time frustrations in Hagen: the death of Moka and polygamy. Is there a better world?', Okari Research Group Prepublication Working Paper No. 6, for the session 'Humiliation and transformation: emotion, subjectivity, and modernity in Melanesia' at the 1998 American Anthropological Association conference, Philadelphia, pp. 1–11.

—— & Strathern, A 1999, 'Feasting on my enemy: images of violence and change in the New Guinea Highlands of Papua New Guinea', *Ethnohistory*, vol. 46, no. 4, pp. 645–69.

—— & Strathern, A (eds) 2000, 'Millennial countdown in New Guinea', *Ethnohistory*, Special Issue vol. 47, no. 1.

—— & Strathern, A 2000a, 'Introduction: latencies and realizations in millennial practices', in PJ Stewart and A Strathern (eds), 'Millennial countdown in New Guinea', *Ethnohistory*, Special Issue vol. 47, no. 1, pp. 3–27.

—— & Strathern, A 2000b, *Speaking for life and death: warfare and compensation among the Duna of Papua New Guinea*, Senri Ethnological Reports 13, National Museum of Ethnology, Osaka.

—— & Strathern, A 2000c, 'Introduction: narratives speak', in PJ Stewart & A Strathern (eds), *Identity work*, University of Pittsburgh Press, Pittsburgh, pp. 1–26.

—— & Strathern, A 2001a, 'The great exchange: Moka with God', in J Robbins, PJ Stewart & A Strathern (eds), 'Pentecostal and charismatic Christianity in Oceania', *Journal of Ritual Studies*, Special Issue vol. 15, no. 2, pp. 91–104.

—— & Strathern, A 2001b, *Humors and substances: ideas of the body in New Guinea*, Bergin and Garvey (Greenwood Publications), Westport, CT.

—— & Strathern, A 2001c, '*Timbu Wara*: figures from Pangia, Papua New Guinea', *Records of the South Australia Museum*, vol. 34, no. 2, pp. 65–77.

—— & Strathern, A 2002a, *Violence: theory and ethnography*, Continuum Publishing, London and New York.

—— & Strathern, A 2002b, *Remaking the world: myth, mining, and ritual change among the Duna of Papua New Guinea*, Smithsonian Institution Press, Washington and London.

—— & Strathern, A 2002c, *Gender, song, and sensibility: folktales and folksongs in the Highlands of New Guinea*, Praeger, Westport, CT.

—— & Strathern, A 2002d, 'Transformations of monetary symbols in the Highlands of Papua New Guinea', *L'Homme*, vol. 162, pp. 137–56.

—— & Strathern, A 2004, *Witchcraft, sorcery, rumors, and gossip*, New Departures in Anthropology Series, Cambridge University Press, Cambridge.

—— & Strathern, A (eds) 2005a, *Expressive genres and historical change: Indonesia, Papua New Guinea, and Taiwan*, Ashgate Publishing Company, Farnham, UK.

—— & Strathern, A 2005b, 'The death of Moka in post-colonial Mount Hagen, Papua New Guinea', in J Robbins & H Wardlow (eds), *The making of global and local modernities in Melanesia*, Ashgate Publishing Co., Farnham, UK, pp. 125–34.

—— & Strathern, A (eds) 2008, *Exchange and sacrifice*, Carolina Academic Press, Durham, NC.

—— & Strathern, A (eds) 2009, *Religious and ritual change: cosmologies and histories*, Carolina Academic Press, Durham, NC.

—— & Strathern, A (eds) 2010a, *Landscape, heritage, and conservation: farming issues in the European Union*, European Anthropology Series, Carolina Academic Press, Durham, NC.

—— & Strathern, A (eds) 2010b, *Ritual*, The International Library of Essays in Anthropology, Ashgate Publishing Co., Farnham, UK.

Strathern, A 1968, 'Sickness and frustration: variations in two New Guinea Highlands societies', *Mankind*, vol. 6, no. 1, pp. 545–51.

—— 1969, 'Finance and production: two strategies in New Guinea Highlands exchange systems', *Oceania*, vol. 40, no. 1, pp. 42–67.

—— 1970a, 'The female and male spirit cults in Mount Hagen', *Man*, vol. 5, no. 4, pp. 571–85.

—— 1970b, 'To choose a strong man: the House of Assembly elections in Mul–Dei 1968', *Oceania*, vol. 41, no. 2, pp. 136–47.

—— 1971 [2007], *The rope of Moka*, reissued with new preface by A Strathern & PJ Stewart, Cambridge University Press, Cambridge.

—— 1972a, 'The Supreme Court: a matter of prestige and power', *The Melanesian Law Journal*, vol. 2, pp. 23–28.

—— 1972b, *One father, one blood: descent and group structure among the Melpa people*,

Australian National University Press, Canberra.

—— 1974, 'When dispute procedures fail', in AL Epstein (ed.), *Contention and dispute*, Australian National University Press, Canberra, pp. 240–70.

—— 1976, 'Seven good men: the Dei Open Electorate', in D Stone (ed.), *Prelude of Self-Government*, University of Papua New Guinea, Port Moresby, pp. 265–87.

—— 1977, 'Contemporary warfare in the New Guinea Highlands: revival or breakdown?', *Yagl-Ambu*, vol. 4, pp. 135–46.

—— 1978, '"Finance and production" revisited: in pursuit of a comparison', *Research in Economic Anthropology*, G Dalton (ed.), vol. 1, pp. 73–104.

—— 1979, 'Gender, ideology, and money in Mount Hagen', *Man*, n.s. 14, pp. 530–48.

—— 1981, 'Compensation: should there be a new law?', in R Scaglion (ed.), *Homicide compensation in Papua New Guinea*, Law Reform Commission, published by the Office of Information, Port Moresby, pp. 5–24.

—— 1982a, 'The scraping gift: alcohol consumption in Mount Hagen', in M Marshall (ed.), *Through a glass darkly: beer and modernization in Papua New Guinea*, Monograph 18, IASER, Boroko, pp. 139–53.

—— 1982b, 'The division of labor and processes of change in Mount Hagen', *American Ethnologist*, vol. 92, pp. 307–19.

—— 1984, *A line of power*, Tavistock, London.

—— 1992, 'Let the bow go down', in RB Ferguson & NL Whitehead (eds), *War in the tribal zone*, School of American Research Press, Santa Fe, pp. 229–50.

—— 1993a, *Voices of conflict*, Ethnology Monographs no. 14, Department of Anthropology, University of Pittsburgh, Pittsburgh.

—— 1993b, 'Violence and political change in Papua New Guinea', *Pacific Studies*, vol. 16, no. 4, pp. 41–60.

—— 1993c, 'Big man, great man, leader: the link of ritual power', *Journal de la Société des Océanistes*, vol. 2, pp. 145–58.

—— 1993d, 'Compensation: what does it mean?', *Taim Lain: A Journal of Contemporary Melanesian Studies*, vol. 1, no. 1, pp. 57–63.

—— 1995, 'Ritual movements reconsidered: ethnohistory in Aluni', in A Biersack (ed.), *Papuan borderlands*, University of Michigan Press, Ann Arbor, pp. 87–110.

—— 1997, 'Compensation, or moving swiftly over broken ground', in S Toft (ed.), *Compensation for resource development in Papua New Guinea*, Law Reform Commission, Port Moresby, pp. 1–9.

—— 1998, 'Sacrifice and sociality: a Duna ritual track', in LR Goldman & C Ballard (eds), *Fluid ontologies*, Bergin and Garvey, Westport, CT, pp. 31–42.

—— & Stewart, PJ 1997a, 'Introduction: millennial markers in the Pacific', in PJ Stewart & AJ Strathern (eds), *Millennial markers*, Centre for Pacific Studies, James Cook University, Townsville, Qld, pp. 1–17.

—— & Stewart, PJ 1997b, 'The problems of peace-makers in Papua New Guinea: modalities of negotiation and settlement', *The Cornell International Law Journal*, vol. 30, no. 3, pp. 681–99.

—— & Stewart, PJ 1998a, 'Embodiment and communication: two frames for the analysis of ritual', *Social Anthropology*, vol. 6, no. 2, pp. 237–51.

—— & Stewart, PJ 1998b, 'Shifting places, contested spaces: land and identity politics in the Pacific', *The Australian Journal of Anthropology*, vol. 9, no. 2, pp. 209–24.

—— & Stewart, PJ 1998c, 'The embodiment of responsibility: "confession" and "compensation" in Mount Hagen, Papua New Guinea', *Pacific Studies*, vol. 21, nos. 1–2, pp. 43–64.

—— & Stewart, PJ 1999a, 'Objects, relationships, and meanings: historical switches in currencies in Mount Hagen, Papua New Guinea', in D Akin & J Robbins (eds), *Money and modernity*, ASAO Monograph Series No. 17, University of Pittsburgh Press, Pittsburgh, pp. 164–91.

—— & Stewart, PJ 1999b, *Collaborations and conflicts: a leader through time*, Harcourt Brace College Publishers, Fort Worth.

—— & Stewart, PJ 1999c, *"The spirit is coming!": a photographic-textual exposition of the female spirit cult performance in Mount Hagen, Papua New Guinea*, Ritual Studies Monograph Series No. 1, Deixis Foundation, Pittsburgh.

—— & Stewart, PJ 1999d, 'Outside and inside meanings: non-verbal and verbal modalities of agonistic communication among the Wiru of Papua New Guinea', *Man and Culture in Oceania*, vol. 15, pp. 1–22.

—— & Stewart, PJ 2000a, *Arrow talk: transaction, transition, and contradiction in New Guinea Highlands history*, Kent State University Press, Kent, Ohio, and London.

—— & Stewart, PJ 2000b, '*Mi les long yupela usim flag bilong mi*: symbols, identity, and desire in Papua New Guinea', *Pacific Studies*, vol. 23, nos. 1–2, pp. 21–49.

—— & Stewart, PJ 2000c, 'Creating difference: a contemporary affiliation drama in the Highlands of New Guinea', *Journal of the Royal Anthropological Institute*, vol. 6, no. 1, pp. 1–15.

—— & Stewart, PJ 2000d, 'Further twists of the rope: Ongka and Ru in a transforming world', in PJ Stewart & A Strathern (eds), *Identity work: constructing Pacific lives*, Association for Social Anthropology in Oceania Monograph Series No. 18, University of Pittsburgh Press, Pittsburgh, pp. 81–98.

—— & Stewart, PJ 2000e, 'Accident, agency, and liability in New Guinea Highlands compensation practices', *Bijdragen*, vol. 156, no. 2, pp. 275–95.

—— & Stewart, PJ 2000f, 'Recent ethnological studies from the Highlands of Papua New Guinea', *Bulletin of the National Museum of Ethnology*, vol. 25, no. 2, pp. 271–85.

—— & Stewart, PJ 2000g, 'Dangerous woods and perilous pearl shells: the fabricated politics of a longhouse in Pangia, Papua New Guinea', *Journal of Material Culture*, vol. 5, no. 1, pp. 69–89.

—— & Stewart, PJ 2001, *Minorities and memories: survivals and extinction in Scotland and Western Europe*, Carolina Academic Press, Durham, NC.

—— & Stewart, PJ 2003, 'Conflicts vs contracts: political flows and blockages in Papua New Guinea', in B Ferguson (ed.), *The state, identity and violence: political disintegration in the post Cold-War world*, Routledge, London and New York, pp. 300–317.

—— & Stewart, PJ 2004a, 'Cults, closures, collaborations', in P Bonnemère (ed.), *Women as unseen characters: male ritual in Papua New Guinea*, University of Pennsylvania Press, Philadelphia, pp. 120–38.

—— & Stewart, PJ 2004b, *Empowering the past, confronting the future: the Duna people of Papua New Guinea*, Palgrave Macmillan, New York.

—— & Stewart, PJ 2005, 'Ceremonial exchange', in JG Carrier (ed.), *A handbook of economic anthropology*, Edward Elgar Publishing, Cheltenham, UK, pp. 230–45.

—— & Stewart, PJ & Whitehead, NL (eds) 2006, *Terror and violence: imagination and the unimaginable*, Pluto Press, London and Ann Arbor.
—— & Stewart, PJ 2006a, 'Introduction: terror, the imagination, and cosmology', in A Strathern, PJ Stewart & NL Whitehead (eds), *Terror and violence: imagination and the unimaginable*, Pluto Press, London and Ann Arbor, pp. 1–39.
—— & Stewart, PJ 2006b, 'Narratives of violence and perils of peace-making in north-south cross-border contexts, Ireland', in A Strathern, PJ Stewart & NL Whitehead (eds), *Terror and violence: imagination and the unimaginable*, Pluto Press, London and Ann Arbor, pp. 142–70.
—— & Stewart, PJ 2010a, *Curing and healing: medical anthropology in global perspective*, 2nd edn, Carolina Academic Press, Durham, NC.
—— & Stewart, PJ 2010b, 'Introduction. Ritual: a perennial topic', in PJ Stewart & AJ Strathern (eds), *Ritual*, The International Library of Essays in Anthropology, Ashgate Publishing Co., Farnham, UK, pp. xv–xxx.
—— & Stewart, PJ 2010c, *Kinship in action: self and group*, Prentice-Hall, Upper Saddle River, NJ.
—— & Stewart, PJ (forthcoming), 'Hagen settlement histories: dispersals and consolidations', in P Swadling, J Golson et al. (eds), *Nine thousand years of gardening: Kuk and the archaeology of agriculture in Papua New Guinea*.
Strauss, H & Tischner, H 1962, *Die Mi-Kultur der Hagenberg Stämme*, Cram, de Gruyter and Co., Hamburg.
Sykes, K 2000, 'Raskolling: Papua New Guinea sociality as contested order', in C Banks (ed.), *Developing cultural criminology*, Monograph Series no. 13, Institute of Criminology, Sydney, pp. 174–94.
Tambiah, SJ 1990, *Magic, science, religion, and the scope of rationality*, Cambridge University Press, Cambridge.
Toft, S (ed.) 1997, *Compensation for resource development in Papua New Guinea*, Monograph no. 6, Law Reform Commission, Port Moresby.
Trompf, GW 1994, *Payback: the logic of retribution in Melanesian religions*, Cambridge University Press, Cambridge.
Turton, D 1994, 'Mursi political identity and warfare: the survival of an idea', in K Fukui & J Markakis (eds), *Ethnicity and conflict in the horn of Africa*, James Currey, London.
Watson, JB 1983, *Tairora culture: contingency and pragmatism*, University of Washington Press, Seattle, WA.
Whitehead, NL 2002, *Dark shamans: kanaimà and the poetics of violent death*, Duke University Press, Durham, NC.
—— 2006, 'The sign of kanaimà, the space of Guayana, and the demonology of development', in A Strathern, PJ Stewart & NL Whitehead (eds), *Terror and violence: imagination and the unimaginable*, Pluto Press, London and Ann Arbor, pp. 171–91.
Wiessner, P & Tumu, A 1998, *Historical vines: Enga networks of exchange, ritual, and warfare in Papua New Guinea*, Smithsonian Institution Press, Washington, DC.
Woolford, D 1976, *Papua New Guinea: initiation and independence*, University of Queensland Press, St Lucia, Qld.
Wormsley, WE & Toke MC, 1985, *Final report: the Enga law and order project*, Enga Provincial Government, Wabag, Papua New Guinea.

Index

Abaijah, Josephine, 152
Abbink, Jon, 198–9, 200
adjudication, 192
adultery, 27, 57, 69
Afghanistan, 1, 206
Africa, 139, 146, 197–201
airport security, 8, 10
alcohol consumption, xi, 125, 131–4, 154, 177, 216, 217
allies, 54–5, 59–60, 133, 179, 240–2
    exchange and compensation, 142–3
    parishes, within, 58
    warfare and intermarriage patterns, 71–2, 133, 181–2
Aluni Valley, 62, 64–8, 173
Ambukla (Ambugga), 86, 92
ambushes, xi, 3, 16, 29, 131, 134, 149, 220, 229
    hijackings, 135
anarchy, 105, 139, 197, 223
ancestral protection, 29, 42, 70
Andakelkam clan, 227, 234
anger (*popokl*), 21, 27, 41, 174–5, 204
apologies, 188
Arapesh people, 5
arbitration, 192–3
'arrow-talk' (*el ik*), 68, 145, 161, 165, 183, 239
assassination, 16, 103, 197
Australian Colonial Administration, xv, 34, 39, 47, 74, 122, 129, 130, 150–1, 212

elections, 75–80, 87–9, 93–4, 98–100, 102–4
Australian explorers, 110, 141, 142
authorised acts, 166
autonomy, xi, 23, 98, 144, 149, 150, 185
autopsy, 31, 34, 217, 234

Baiyer Valley, 32, 77
baler, 113, 114
ballads (*pikono*), 66–7, 174
betrayal, 3
    home-grown terrorist, 9
    secrecy and, 11–12
big-men, 41, 50, 52–3, 73, 75, 79–80, 82, 85, 119–20, 142–3, 145, 180–1, 186, 213, 225, 234, 235–6, 242, 245
    councillors, distinguished, 80–1
    tee exchanges, 53–5
Blair, Tony, 8
blood-feud, 37, 38, 39, 40, 143, 228
Bougainville, 239, 243
Bougainville Freedom Movement (BFM), 150–1, 159
Bougainville Revolutionary Army (BRA), 150–1, 155, 157, 162
Bougainville separatists, 156–8, 163
bribes, 22, 31, 32–3, 36, 43, 125, 216, 225
    election, 218
brideprice, 57, 112, 115, 122, 123, 172, 173
bridewealth, 34, 84, 97, 238
bridges, xviii, 221–4
Brown, Gordon, 8

Index

'business', 111, 119, 121, 136, 160
    elections and, 80–4, 87, 91, 97–8, 100

cash crops, xiv, 48, 74, 109, 123, 160
category names, 68
censussing, 80
ceremonial dress, 36, 51, 183, 184
change
    colonial contexts, 145–7
    continuity versus, 110
    narratives of, 114–18
    political relations, 130–1
    post-colonial contexts, 145–7
    'secular' and 'sacral' dimensions, 112, 128
    valuable, use of, 113–14
Chuave people, 220
Chimbu (Simbu) area, 51, 52, 78, 92, 135, 239
Choiseul, 195–7, 244
Christianity, xv, xvi, 28, 78, 80, 89, 92, 110, 111, 120, 132, 134, 136, 185, 187–8, 219, 220, 242–3
clan-pairs, 30, 43, 44, 46
clans, 27, 30, 31, 32, 33, 37, 38, 88–9, 140, 141, 144, 145, *passim*
    clan and state, 153–8
coercion, 106–7, 129–30, 193
coffee growing, xiv, 18, 78, 80, 88, 117, 119, 130, 131, 136
cognatic ties, 56–7, 62, 196
colonial influences, xiv
colonial narratives, 105
colonial practices, 129, 212
colonial state policy, x
colonial strategies, 106–7
Colson, Elizabeth, 195
commercial interests
    compensation and, 135–6, 221
communication
    ritualised, 145
    talk, metaphors for, 170–1
compensation, xii–xiii, xv, xvi, 16, 35, 46, 49–50, 73, 122, 132, 134, 136, 140, 163–4, 186, 191–2, 217, 220
    abolition of, 109
    ally-compensation, 40
    ceremonies, xvii, 40
    clan and state relations, 153–8
    commercial enterprises, and, 135–6, 221
    Council boundaries, across, 101–4
    customary law, 177–8
    death-compensation, 24, 39–42, 51, 90, 143, 178
    Duna warfare, 61, 65
    electoral violence and, 23
    Huli warfare, 59–60
    ideology, 175
    increases in payments, 213
    medicine, as, 172
    modalities and messages, 159
    moka exchange see moka exchange
    ongoing exchanges, transformation into, 47–8
    payment stages, 182
    peace-making and, 142–3
    physical violence, for, 40–1, 51
    poisoning sorcery, for, 40–1
    political support and, 135
    ritualised processes, 180–1
    rules, 142
    speeches, 67
    urban contexts, 214–18
    wounds, for, 59
competitive exchange, xv, 15, 50, 51, 98, 107, 143, 192, 235
conflict
    causes, intermeshing of, 132–3
    exchange and, 135–6
    fighting *see* fighting
    mediating and settling *see* mediating and settling conflict
    patterns of violence and peace-making, 3, 15
    violent *see* violence
consensus, 85, 96–7, 200
conspiracy theories, 11–12
continuity versus change, 110
cordyline bushes, planting, 168–9, 210; *see rumbim*
corruption, 125, 131, 176, 212

cosmological frameworks, 12
cosmos, 4, 66, 110, 128, 166–8, 180, 201
councillors, 80–1
   authority, 98
Councils, 14, 45, 48, 76, 80, 84, 88, 89, 91, 97–102, 104, 114, 130, 146, 201
   escalation of conflict, 131–2
   establishment, 76–81
counter-poisoning, 25–6, 40
cowrie, 63, 113–16, 210
crime, growth of, 74
cultural values, x
currency 22, 108, 113, 119, 160, 188, 213, 237 *see also* money
customary law, 177–8, 185

damba (blood compensation), 61, 172, 173
death, xi
   causes, 25–9
   celebrating and enemy's, 36
   compensation for *see* compensation
   spirits, by, 26
debt, 54, 57, 119
Dei Council, xv, 42, 45, 47, 76, 96–9, 100, 104, 113–14, 118, 191, 201, 216
   background, 76–81
   cadidates, 93–5
   election results, 95–6
   Mul–Dei opposition, 88–93, 191
democracy, 23, 74, 87–8, 92, 102, 223
Dentan, Robert Knox, 204–5
dependency syndrome, 99, 122
destruction, acts of, 188
diplomacy, 141, 155, 163
disease 126
dispute settlement, 30, 43, 52–3, 132, 170–2, 178, 184, 186, 193, 203, 208, 213–14
   metaphors, 170–5
   modalities of settlement, 141–4
   tribal fighting 178
   Village Courts, 131, 153, 177, 185–6, 214–16
District Commissioners (DCs), 90, 91, 92

districts, 69–70
divination, 34–6, 60, 140, 175, 179, 217
   Halaka, 63
   mi test, 233, 238
Dizi people, 199
dreams, 94–5
Duna, 49, 55–6, 59–69, 170–5, 188, 195
   metaphors, 171, 173
   parishes, 55–6, 60–2, 65–8, 69
   warfare, 60–8
Durkheim, Emile, 168

East Africa, 197–201
Eastern Highlands, 107–8
economic development, x
   clan and state relations, 154–5
Ekit Kuk, 132
el ik ('arrow-talk'), 68, 145, 161, 165, 183
el kwun koklamon ritual, 41–2
el öninga (minor enemies), 39, 42, 43, 46–7, 51
el parka (major enemies), 32, 36, 39, 43, 44, 46–7, 51, 104, 227
elections, x, xiv–xv, 18–23, 74, 100, 223
   background, 75–81
   candidates, 77, 78, 82, 86–7, 93–5, 101–2, 135
   intimidation and, 19–20, 22–3
   national contexts, 218–22
   post-electoral violence, 21–2, 99–100
   pre-electoral violence, 19–20, 90–1, 154
   revenge violence, 21–2, 23
   violent victory celebrations, 20
   voting, 84–7, 96
electorates, xiv, 19, 86, 94, 97, 100, 104, 135
   amalgamation, xv, 76, 130
   divisions within, 88
   establishment, 76, 130
Elti tribe, 35, 159
emotional dispositions, ix
enemies
   friends becoming, 170
   major (*el parka*), 32, 36, 39, 43, 44, 46–7, 51, 104, 227

making, 206–8
minor (*el öninga*), 39, 42, 43, 46–7, 51
unmaking, 206–8
Enga Law and Order Project (1982–1985), 176–7
recommendations, 177
Enga Province, xiv, 49, 51–5, 155, 176, 178–9, 181–5, 187, 190, 197
Engambo clan, 45, 228
environmental issues, 155
epistemologies, 221–2
Erima, 215–16
escalation, xv, xvii, 13, 14, 22, 56, 58, 59, 72, 105–37, 163, 197, 203, 207, 220, 241
elections, and, xiv, 75–104
espionage, 11–12
ethnic conflict, 206
exchange, 108, 116, 141, 161, 180, 190, 235–6
colonial strategies and, 107–8
competitive, xv, 15, 50, 51, 98, 107, 143, 192, 235
conflict and, 135–6
funeral, 194
giving and receiving as ritual, 170
ideologies, 111
institutions of, xv
Jalé, 194
moka see moka exchanges
peace-making and, 143–4
persistence of practices, 111
processes, 54–5, 137, 193
shell, 18, 50, 108–9, 190, 213
violence and, 107
exogamy, 227
expatriates, 73, 78, 81, 82, 88, 89, 91–5, 99, 131, 183, 217

Female Spirit fertility cult, 119, 123
feud, 46
blood-feud, 37–8, 143, 228
definition, 37–8
joint responsibility, 37–40
warfare, distinguished, 38–9

fight initiators (*wei tse*), 57–61, 71–2, 171, 180
fighting *see also* conflict, warfare
causes, 30
contexts, 179
relationships, 45
Filer, Colin, 221–2
fire-thong test, 34–6
force, use of, xi, 2, 21, 23, 40, 53, 73, 102, 105, 107, 136, 144, 150, 162, 187, 200, 215
Fortune, Reo, 5
framing devices, 165, 166
Frazer, Sir James, 169
friendship, 54–5
funeral rituals, 10–11, 126–7, 194, 218

Gebusi people, 202
genocide, ix
ghost-diviner, 27–8
ghosts, 205 *see also* spirits
spells against, 28
gift transactions, 111–12, 120, 123, 175, 181–2, 218
ginger, edible, 25
Glasgow airport crash, 8–9
Glasse, RM, 38–9, 52, 55–65, 72, 197
Gluckman, Max, 132, 196, 203
Goddard, Michael, 214–16, 218
Goldman, Laurence, 62, 171–2, 174, 186, 207
Gordon, Robert, 19, 147, 153, 176, 183–5, 191
gossip, 2, 3, 6, 215, 222
government courts, 153
green snail, 113
grief, 145
aggression and, 36
ritual dramatisations, 180
guns, 3, 18, 21, 107, 129, 131, 134, 154, 198–9, 207–8

Hagen–Kui Council, 98
Hanuabada, 214
Heald, Suzette, 198
health and illness metaphors, 172

262 Index

hegemony, 106–7, 122
heroes, 5
'heroic' qualities, 65–6
Highlands, x, xii, xiv–xvii, 2, 22
historical processes, 110–11, 114, 121–4, 128, 143, 162
historical progress, 116, 137
honorifics, 174
honour, ix, 170, 174, 192, 197
House of Assembly, 76, 79–82, 85–8, 97–100
    Members (MHAs), 82–3, 87, 90–2, 97–9
House of Representatives, 130
Huli, 49, 52, 55–60, 62, 65, 72, 170–5, 188, 194, 197, 207
    metaphors, 171–3, 174–5
    parishes, 55–60
    warfare, 55–60
human rights protection, 161

Ialibu, 69
ideology, ix, x
images and messages, 2
imagination, xii, 14, 167, 214
    positive change and, 13
    ritual and, 167–8, 221
    terror and, xiii, xvii, 1–2, 7–10, 222–4
incarceration, 102, 109, 129, 149, 153, 183–4
indemnities for deaths, 57–61, 172
Independence, xi, 83, 99, 102, 191, 212
inter-group conflict, xiv, xv–xvi, 5, 30, 138, 202
inter-group relations, xii, 139–40
    rules, 141–4
intermarriage, 17, 47, 51, 69–71, 79, 133, 140–1, 156, 161, 195, 196
    patterns, 69–72
intermediate sovereigns (IS), xvi, 138–64, 192
    clan and state relations, 153–5
    conflicts, 144
    dealing with, 158–64
    resistance movements, 150–3

stability, need for, 162
'statist' terminology, use of, 157
international relations, 139–40, 156, 238
intimidation, 7, 15–17
    electoral, 19–20, 22–3
invariance, 166
Iraq, 7–8

Jalé, 192–5
Jimi (Jimmi) Valley, 29, 32, 45, 77, 95
joint responsibility, 37–40, 203

Kabui, Joseph, 157
kaiko, 168, 170, 208, 211
Kambila, 228
kango, 59, 61–2, 173
Kauona, Sam, 162
Kawelka tribe, 31, 32, 35, 45, 47, 70, 77, 83, 96, 113, 115, 117, 118, 126–36, 141, 142, 217–18, 220, 226–9, 238
    Kundmbo clan, 35–6, 118–20, 126, 131–4, 142, 220, 226, 228–9, 238
    Kurupmbo sub-clan, 35–6, 113, 133, 226, 230
Kelly, Raymond, 202–4
Keme tribe, 32
Kendike clan, 39, 44, 229, 230, 233
    Milyembo sub-clan, 230
    Wölyembo sub-clan, 229
Kendipi tribe, 89, 96
kendo, 70
Kengeke clan, 133, 229
Kenya, 198
Kiaps, 73, 82–3, 86, 90, 95, 96–9, 114, 176–7, 183–5
Kiklpuklimbo, 119
killings, xi, xii, 3, 7, 21, 37–8, 49, 51, 53, 57, 73, 107, 109, 129, 131, 134, 143–4, 153–4, 156, 157, 168, 181, 188, 195, 200–1, 207, 208
    compensation for *see* compensation
    revenge *see* revenge
Kilwa, 226
Kiminkae clan, 32
kinship networks, 47, 56, 57, 81, 106, 140, 178, 202, 203, 209

kinship polity, 140, 152, 156, 161
Kira cult, 65
Kitepi clan, 44, 229, 230, 233, 234
Klamakae tribe, 45
    Rokmbo clan, 45
Knoebel, Joseph, 188
Koch, Klaus-Friedrich, 192–5
Koipke (Koibuga), 90, 102
Koliri, 68, 70–1
Kombukla tribe, 42, 44, 45, 47, 133, 134, 226, 229
Kompiam, 49, 52
Konedobu, 214
Kotna Lutheran Mission, 80, 90, 94
Kuk, 126–7, 132
Kuklup, 226
Kulga tribe, 188
Kulir (Ku Waru), 46, 240, 242, 244
kum, 26, 29
Kum (Councillor), 90
Kumndi tribe, 89, 227
Kundmbo clan, 35–6, 118–20, 126, 131–4, 142, 220, 226, 228–9
Kuria people, 198
Kurupmbo sub-clan, 35–6, 113, 133, 226, 230

Lake Kopiago, xiv, 49, 188
Lake Mbuna, 69
land
    arguments over, xi, 2, 18, 52, 65, 194, 245
    competition for, 109
    encroachments, 57
Lap, 228
leadership, 53, 58, 75–6, 79, 82, 127, 162, 184, 220
    big-men *see* big-men
    change, impact of 127
    church, 127–8
    dispute settlement, 58–9
    gender issues, 127
leaks, 13
legends, development of, 14
legislation, use of, 151, 163, 186
Leopold, Mark, 199–201

London Ungerground bombings, 8
long-term trajectories, 112, 123, 125, 127, 132, 218
Lugbara politics, 199
luluai, 80, 93, 142

Mae Enga, 52, 54, 179, 181, 187
Malalaua, 215
Maring people, 168, 179–81, 208–11
marital alliances, 3, 4, 50, 51, 204–5 *see also* intermarriage
    colonial pacification, impact of, 73
    familial loyalties, 33–4
    killings and, 17, 203
    poisoning relationships, 43–6
marriage, arguments over, xi, 2
Mataungan Association, 151, 156
media, role of, 1–2, 7
    rumour and conspiracy, 11–12
mediation, 192
    dispute settlement *see* dispute settlement
medicine metaphors, 172
Meggitt, Mervyn, 19, 52, 53, 147, 153, 176, 178, 179–87, 191, 197
Mel, 229
Melanesia, 139, 156, 159, 186, 189
Melpa, 54–6, 61, 68–72, 180–3, 190–1, 204, 208, 210
    language, xviii, 24, 25, 26, 28, 32, 49, 77, 89, 94, 112, 133, 170–5, 185, 188, 197, 209, 220
    metaphors, 170–5
    warfare, 54–5
Membo–Mandembo pair-clan, 226
men
    big *see* big-men
    low status (*wuö korpa*), 31–2, 78, 225, 227
    ordinary, 78
    senior bachelors (*uruwali*), 62
menstrual blood, 28, 33, 60
metaphors, 170–5
micro-nationalist movements, 138, 150–3
Middle East, 1

Middleton, John, 199–201
migrants, 215
Mile tribe, 89
Milyembo sub-clan, 230
Mimke clan, 45
min (friendship), 175
min (spirit), 218
Minembi tribe, 32, 44, 45, 90, 96, 100, 101, 118, 131, 132–5, 226–8, 238
    Andakelkam clan, 227
    Engambo clan, 45
    Kiminkae clan, 32
    Mimke clan, 45
    Papeke clan, 44, 45, 133, 228
    Yelipi clan, 44, 90, 118, 132, 228
mining, 135, 137, 138, 147, 150–1, 154, 155, 157, 163, 176, 191, 212
modalities and messages, 159
'modernity', 74, 92, 104, 109–10
Moep, 227
moka exchanges, xv, 50–2, 54–5, 112–17, 122–9, 132–3, 136, 142–3, 154, 165, 175, 191, 193–4, 226
    allies and, 54–5
    money, revalorising, 124–5
    shells *see* shells
    tobacco-*moka*, 113, 118–21
money, 18, 20, 81–3, 86, 90, 99, 108–9, 118–21, 184–5 *see also* currency
    local ritual enterprises, 124
    narratives of change 114–15
    revalorising, 124–7
    rituals, 187–8
    sacralisation, 120–2, 128
    shells as *see* shells
    state, xvi, 42, 113, 116–17, 121–4, 128, 190, 213
    tax, 80, 83, 88, 89, 117, 120, 124, 130, 220
    women and, 125
monge (friendship), 54
moots, 145, 186
Motuan people, 214, 215
Mount Hagen, xiv, xv, 16, 17, 24, 46, 49–50, 53, 56, 73, 75, 103, 107, 141, 145, 160–2, 170, 185, 188, 207, 216, 220

    exchange in, 110–14
    Hagen town, 21, 22, 34, 42, 76, 77, 90, 92, 160, 220
Mowa, 229
Mul Council, xv, 76, 96–9, 100, 104, 191, 201
    background, 76–81
    cadidates, 93–5
    election results, 95–6
    Mul–Dei opposition, 88–93, 191
Mundika tribe, 89
mutual respect, 158, 163

Namaliu, Prime Minister, 157
naming lists, 174
Napidakoe Navitu, 150–1
narratives
    change, of, 114–18, 139
    colonial *see* colonial narratives
    historical, dissemination of, 200
    metaphors, 170–5
    nationhood, 219
Nasioi people, 157
nassa shells, 113–15
nation
    creating a, 149–50
    ideas of nationhood, 219
    state, distinguished, 148–50
'nation making', 147
Ndamba, 118–20, 132–4
Ndekane, 226
ndekao, 62–3
Ndikambo clan, 228
Nebilyer tribes, 45, 46, 77
Nebilyer Valley, 34, 42, 45, 46, 77, 160, 188, 242–4
negotiation, 192
    forms of, 144–5
Nengka tribe, 89, 90–1, 100, 102, 227
Ngglammbo sub-clan, 226, 227
Nggolke, 127, 132
Ngonyembo sub-clan, 229
9/11 1
Nipa (Was Valley), 53
non-state collectivities, 146–7
Northern Ireland, 6, 11–12

Nuer people, 146, 198, 199
Nyangatom people, 199

Oklembo clan, 44, 45, 229, 230, 234
old age, 26
Ona, Francis, 162
Ongka, 95–6, 129, 141–3, 145, 211, 217, 227, 242
Ongka-Kaepa, 117, 210
oratory *see* speech-making
'ordered anarchy', 139, 197
origin stories, 68–9

pacification, x–xi, 17–18, 52, 105, 109, 129–30, 196, 199, 212
    colonial narratives, 105
    processes, 212
    warfare and intermarriage patterns, 72–4
pair-clans, 43–7, 78, 133
    poisoning accusations, 228–30
pair-tribes, 45–7, 78, 133, 140
Palke tribe, 32
Pangia, xiv, 49
    warfare, 68–74
Papeke clan, 44, 45, 133, 228
Papua Besena movement, 151–3, 156
Papua New Guinea, x, xii, 2, 14, 152–3, *passim*
    Highlands *see* Highlands
parishes, 173
    Duna, 55–6, 60–2, 65–8, 69
    Huli, 55–60
    inter-parish cooperative rituals, 66
Parliament, xi, 76, 79, 130, 146
    Members of Parliament, 18, 97, 135–6
    parliamentary elections *see* elections
payback, 186–9
peace ceremonies, 39
peace-making, 46, 49–50, 73
    bridges, xviii, 221–4
    compensation and, 142–3, 191
    cycles, 179
    exchange and, 143–4
    Ilaga Dani people, 240–2

    imagination of, xii
    indirect, 193
    multiple wishes, satisfying, 162–3
    processes, 18, 78, 132, 142, 143, 159, 167, 180, 191, 210, 212
    ritual *see* ritual
    rules, 142
    women and, 159–62
peaceful societies, 201–5
pearl shell *see* shells
Penambe tribe, 34, 35, 159–60
'performativity', xvi–xvii
Peri, 68, 70
personal consumption, 126
personal disputes, 57, 60
phratries, 69, 179
physical violence, 15, 26, 29
    elections and, 20
    poisoning *see* poisoning
    revenge, 38
pig-sacrifices, 27–8, 41–2, 128
pig-theft, 2, 30, 57, 69, 132, 195, 233
    women, by, 60
pigs
    compensation payments, as, xvi, 35, 59, 61, 182, 190, 194, 213, 240–1
    disputes over, 2
    exchanges, 4, 18, 109, 112, 124–5
    killing festivals, 52, 70, 168
    metaphors, 172
pikono (ballads), 66–7, 174
place-root-men (*tapinango*), 68
Plateau Tonga people, 195
poisoning, 25, 29, 38, 43, 44, 226–7
    compensation for, 41
    menstrual blood, 28, 33, 60
    relationships, 42–6
poisoning sorcery 26, 41, 226
poisoning/sorcery 26, 29, 38
poisoning-sorcery 43–4, 227
Poka, 226
police, 2, 9, 12, 18–20, 129, 149–50, 153, 163, 176–7, 183, 215–16, 219–20
political parties, 92–3, 130, 219

politics, 18–19, 212
    Africa, 199–200
    clan ideology and, 154
    compensation payments and, 135
    conflict, xv
    development, x–xi
    education, 84–8
    elections *see* elections
    equilibrium, ix
    money and, 124
    new political bodies, creation of, 130
    political change, 81–4
    segmentary systems, 139, 149, 196
    vertical integration, xvi, 18
    women, 109–10
pollution, 155
Poloko, 71
popokl, 21, 27, 41, 174–5, 204
positional connection, 166
positive exchanges, 3
power, perceptions, ix
Poyaka–Paklim pair, 45
praise terms, 174
prescription, 166
prestige, 196–7
Provincial Government, 157, 160, 191
psychology, 110, 205
punan (unhappiness), 204

raiders, 198–9
Ranuguri, 215
rape, 22, 30, 57, 131, 141, 156, 219
Rappaport, Roy, 167–9, 179, 180, 208–9
'raskol' problem, 74, 136, 176, 198
rationality, x
Reipa, 228
religion, ix, x
    Christianity, xv, xvi, 28, 78, 80, 89,
        92, 110, 111, 120, 132, 134, 136,
        187–8, 219, 220, 242–3
    divisions, 127
    leadership and, 127–8
Remndi tribe, 77–8, 104
rent for land, 84
repetition, use of, 173–4
representation and discourse, 14

resistance movements, 150–3, 156–8
respect, 106, 145, 158, 163, 184, 218
revenge, ix, x, xiii, xiv, 10, 13, 14, 24, 38,
    46, 103, 175, 202–3
    counter-poisoning *see*
        counter-poisoning
    deaths, for, 16
    electoral, 21–2, 23
    intimidation and, 16–17
    killings, 32–3, 136, 195, 198
    poisoning, 39–40
Riches, David, 5
ritual, xvi–xvii, 157–8, 164, 192, 198,
    223
    bricolage, 224
    bridges, xviii, 221–4
    Christian 132, 134–5, 188, 242–3
    communication, 145
    conflict, xiii, xvii
    cult areas, 70
    dramatisations of grief, 180
    efficacy, 135
    exchange *see* exchange
    failure of, 169–70
    features of action, 165–7
    funeral, 10–11, 126–7, 194, 218
    government, 184
    imagination and, 167–9
    inter-parish, 66
    messages, 159
    payback, 187
    processes, xiii, 165, 175, 178–83, 186,
        208, 223
    reconciliation, 4
    resetting social relations, 200–1
    stages of, 175
    warfare *see* warfare
    weapons-burning, 188
roads, 19, 76, 78, 80, 82, 83, 89, 94, 100,
    130–1, 155, 177, 184, 216, 219–20
    metaphorical, 31, 33, 40, 43, 175,
        184, 192–3, 208, 210, 224, 233
Robarchek, Clayton, 205
Römndi tribe, 77–8, 104
Rumba, 228
rumbim, 168–9, 210

rumour, xviii, 3, 6, 7, 11, 13, 101, 222–3
Ryan, Dawn, 215

Salmond, Alex, 9
Scheffler, Harold, 196–7
Schlee, Günther, 206
secrecy, 11–12
seduction, 106–7, 129
segmentary political systems, 139, 149, 196
segmentary social systems, 141–3, 147, 150, 159, 179, 191–3, 195, 199
Self-Government, 73–4, 83, 91, 94, 102, 191
    elections *see* elections
    Gazelle Peninsula, 151
self-interest
    elightened, x
    perceptions, ix, x
self-reconceptualisation, 117
Semai people, 203–4
settlements, 39, 46, 49, 56, 138, 157, 158, 163, 170, 170–2, 181, 195
    forms of negotiation, 144–5
    functions, 144
sexual offences, xi, 2
    rape *see* rape
shared values, 159–62
shells, 107, 113
    currency, 114–18, 188
    exchanges, 18, 50, 108–9, 190, 213
    valuables, 112–13
sick and wounded, care for, 64–5
sickness, 26–9
    metaphors, 171–5
Simbu Province, 220
sinangge, 196
singing, 66–7, 181
sister's sons, 38–9, 133, 140, 225, 227, 228
sleep metaphors, 174
sleight of hand, 3
social contract, 219
social engineering, 220
social integration
    Enga areas, 52–3
    moka exchanges *see moka* exchanges

segmentary systems, 141–3, 147, 150, 159, 179, 191–3, 195, 199
social status
    cognatic ties, 56–7
social structure, 55, 68, 78–9, 127–8, 179
Solomon Islands, 157, 158, 192, 196–7
Somalia, 206
sorcery and witchcraft, xiv, 2, 9–11, 14, 46, 59, 215
    accusations, structure of, 42–6, 48
    bribes, and, 32–3, 36
    establishing guilt, 31–7
    ndekao, 62–3
    revenge, 38
    terror, distinguished, 3–4
sorcery/poisoning 41
Southern Highlands, 19, 20, 49, 52, 53, 68, 216, 220
sovereigns, intermediate *see* intermediate sovereigns
sovereignty, 138, 139–40, 144, 154, 159
    contested, 147–50
    definition, 148
speech-making, 2, 50, 75
    compensation, 67, 182
    functions, 176
    funeral, 126–7
    historical, 107–8
    leadership and, 61–2
    repetition, use of, 173–4
    ritualised communication, 145
    women, 160–1
spells, 28, 233
spirits, 26, 123, 175, 218
    Female Spirit fertility cult, 119, 123
    ghosts, 27–8, 41
    Payame Ima, 66–7
    transcendent, 29
    warfare rituals, 62–3
    wild (*tipu römi*), 26, 28
state, xi, xii, xvi–xviii, 11, 18, 23–4, 106, 110, 117, 135, 138, 140, 144, 147, 148–9
    clan and, 153–8, 163, 176
    law and order, 178

state (Cont.)
   locality, enmeshed with, 216
   nation, distinguished, 148–50
state money, xvi, 42, 113, 116–17, 121–4, 128, 190, 213
   substitution, 112, 122, 123, 125, 127–8
Sudan, 146, 198–9
suicide bombers, 13
suicides, xi, 13
Suri people, 198–9
symbolic action, 166
symbolic communication, 145
symbolic violence, 106
symbolism, 59, 109, 113, 143, 147, 155, 156, 158–60, 166–9, 172, 184, 188, 190, 209, 223–4
   gender, 159–62

Taiwan, 6
Takuru, 68, 70–1
talk, metaphors for, 170–1
tamba (compensation), 173
tapinango (place-root-men), 68
Tari Basin, 65
taro test, 34–5
taxation, 80, 83, 88, 89, 117, 120, 124, 130, 220
tea production, xiv, 78, 88
Tee (*Te*) cycles, 52–5, 178, 191
   allies and, 54–5
   big-men, role of, 53
Temboka, 77, 89
Tepi, 229
terror, xii–xiii
   crime, as, 9
   global, 1
   historical approach, 14
   imagination and, xiii, xvii, 1–2, 7–10, 222–4
   instruments of, 2
   intimidation and, 15–17
   processes, 14, 222–3
   processual model, 12–13
   witchcraft and sorcery, distinguished, 3–4
terrorism, defining, 10–11

terrorist
   characterisation, 9
tipu römi, 26, 28
Tipuka tribe, 41–2, 44–5, 47, 77, 83, 96, 101, 115, 133–4, 142, 228–9
   Kendike clan, 39, 229
   Kengeke clan, 133, 229
   Kitepi clan, 44, 229, 230
   Oklembo clan, 44, 45, 229
Toaripi people, 215
Tok Pisin (Pidgin English), 87, 93, 113, 117, 155, 188, 220
Tombema Enga, 52–5, 181
   warfare, 54–5
trade, 78, 114, 122, 123, 129, 140
traditionalism, 166
transactional theory of interactions, 4–5
transcendence, x, xvi, 167–9
transformation, 108, 112, 121, 122, 123, 125, 128, 186, 209, 212
treachery, 36, 69, 229
'triangle of violence' 10
tribe-pairs *see* pair-tribes
Trompf, Garry, 186–9
Trouble Committees, 131, 134, 153, 187, 220
Tsembaga, 168, 170
tultul, 80, 93, 142, 237
Tunda, 68, 70–1
Turton, David, 200

Uganda, 199–200
Ulga tribe, 188
unique function, 166, 167, 173
urban contexts, 214–18
urban–rural relations, 217–18
urbanisation, xv, 74
uruwali (senior bachelors), 62

values, shared, 159–62
Vayda, Andrew, 170
vehicle accidents, xi, xv, 18, 131, 187
   hijackings, 135
Village Courts, 131, 153, 177, 185–6, 214–16

violence, x, 2, 222
  colonial strategies and, 106
  conflict, and, 2, 128–35
  cost of, 182, 197
  exchanges, and, 107
  interpretations, 15–16
  legitimacy, 5
  meanings, 5–6
  opposing views on, ix
  patterns, 15, 24
  processes of, xvi, 1–4, 10, 12–13, 15, 24, 68, 111
  rhetoric of, 9–10
  ritual and imagination, 168–9
  situating, 7
  transcending, 167, 191
voting, 84–7, 96

Wabag, 52, 78, 86, 92
Wahgi Valley, 51, 52, 76, 77, 131
wai emene (minor war), 58
wai timbuni (major war), 58
Wanyembo clan, 228
war cries, 2
war-gardens, 61
warfare, xiv, 46, 143
  cycles, 179
  Duna, 60–8
  feud, distinguished, 38–9
  fighting *see* fighting
  Huli, 55–60
  intermarriage and, 71–2
  joint responsibility, 37–40
  kin and affines fighting on opposing sides, 58
  lethal acts, interpretation, 5
  Pangia, 68–74
  provocation, 134
  radial patterns, 71–2
  ritual, 62–3
  segmentary patterns, 71–2
warless societies, 201–5
wealth
  exchange of, 53–5, 130, 190, 203

  leadership and, 61–2
weapons, 21–2, 30, 32, 38, 134, 145, 226, 228–9
  axes, 129, 229
  guns, 3, 18, 21, 107, 129, 131, 134, 154, 198–9, 207–8
weapons-burning ritual, 188
Weber, Max, x
wei tse (fight initiators), 61, 171
wergild (payments to enemies), 59–60, 65, 194
Western Highlands, 16
  Mount Hagen *see* Mount Hagen
Westphalian principle, 149
Wiru, 49, 68–70
  language, 68
witchcraft *see* sorcery and witchcraft
witness perspectives, 10–11, 13
Wola people, 52, 235
Wölyembo sub-clan, 229
Wölyi tribe, 44
women
  clubs (*amb klap*), 160
  Duna warfare, 63–4, 65
  gender symbolism, 159–62
  Huli warfare, 60
  intermarriage *see* intermarriage
  menstrual blood, 28, 33, 60
  money, and, 125
  peace-making processes and, 159–62
  pig-theft, 60
  poisoners, 33–4
  politics, 109–10
  sorcery guilt, establishing, 31, 33–4
  speeches, making, 160–1
  tobacco *moka*, 118–19
  violation of, 17, 21, 30, 57, 131, 141, 156, 176, 219
wuö korpa, 31–2, 225, 227

Yelipi clan, 44, 90, 118, 132, 228
youth alienation, 74